FROMELLES

Rue Petillon Cemetery, the final resting place of Chaplain Spencer Maxted, who helped 150 or more wounded after Fromelles, and of the champion Carlton footballer, George Challis. (PATRICK LINDSAY PHOTO)

FROMELLES

AUSTRALIA'S DARKEST DAY AND THE DRAMATIC DISCOVERY OF OUR FALLEN WORLD WAR ONE DIGGERS

PATRICK LINDSAY

Hardie Grant Books

Published in 2008
Hardie Grant Books
85 High Street
Prahran, Victoria 3181, Australia
www.hardiegrant.com.au

Cataloguing-in-Publication data is available
from the National Library of Australia

ISBN 978 1 74066 6848

Edited by Carl Harrison-Ford
Cover and text design by Nada Backovic Design
Cover photography Getty Images and Patrick Lindsay
Typesetting by Bookhouse, Sydney
Printed and bound in Australia by Griffin Press

10 9 8 7 6 5 4 3 2 1

To
Lisa, Nathan, Kate and Sarah, as always

For
The missing men of Fromelles and their families ...
may they, at last, find eternal peace

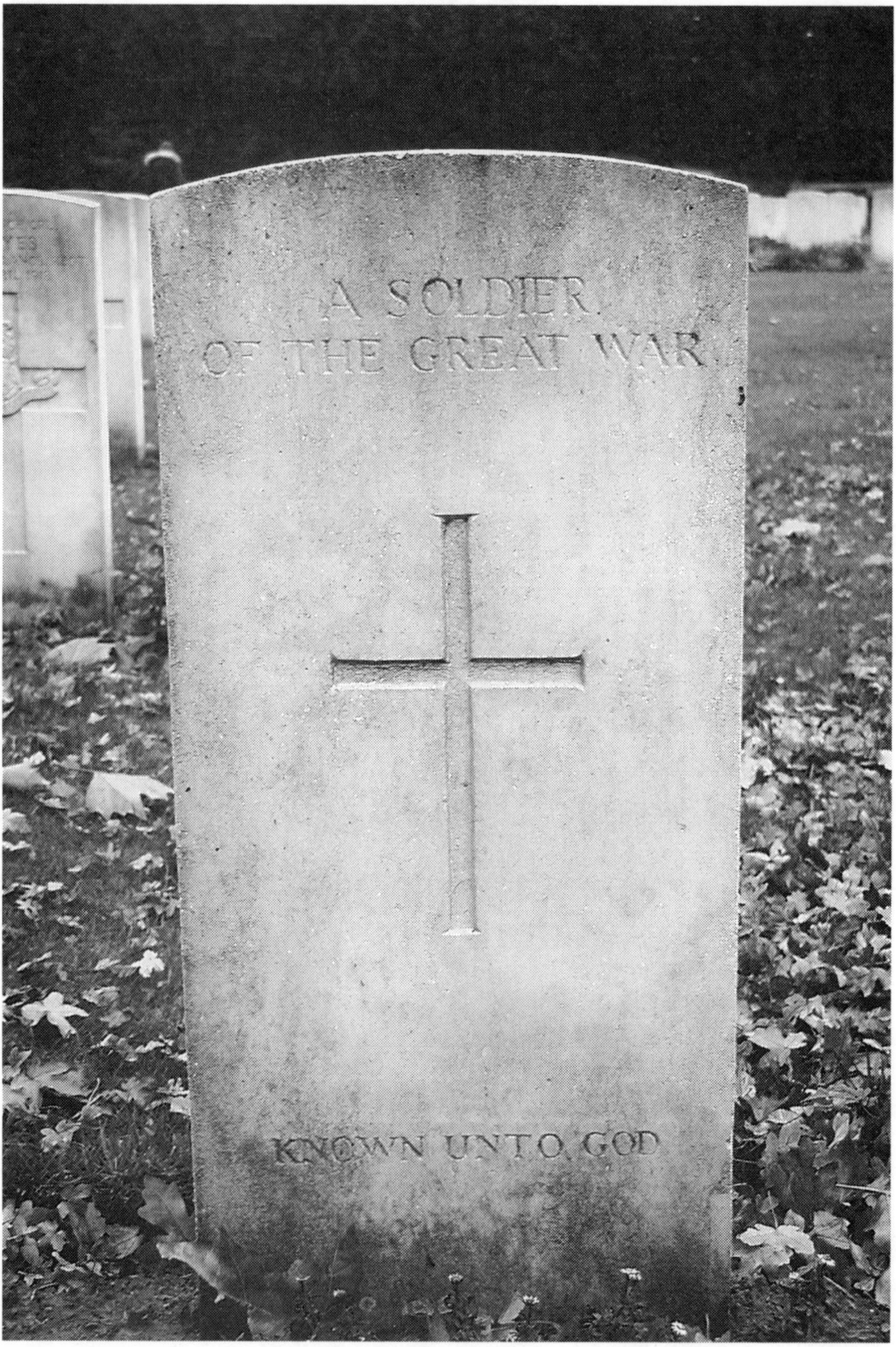
A SOLDIER
OF THE GREAT WAR
KNOWN UNTO GOD

CONTENTS

BRAVE BLOOD

*Never let me hear that brave blood has been shed in vain; it sends
an imperious challenge down through all the generations.*

Sir Walter Scott

It is a land sown with sadness and suffering and sacrifice. Although
almost 100 years have passed since the horrors, the memories and the
spirits linger here.

The day is dull and grey and the cold hangs like a melancholy
mantle over the flat, freshly ploughed fields. A bitter wind swirls and
spits the rain into my face. But the scene is mesmerising and soon the
cold and the rain seem to recede and another picture emerges like a
slow dissolve in a movie.

I am standing on the battlefield at Fromelles in French Flanders.
It has long been restored to farmlands. The bomb craters and the death
and destruction have been ploughed over. The homes and the church
and the buildings have been rebuilt. But the memories remain.

The longer I look out over the fields, the clearer the picture becomes. In July 1916 – the European summer – this was part of the line gouged across Europe where two armies faced each other locked in a death struggle. I am standing in the Australian lines. We are hunkered down behind our two-metre high parapet of sandbags in a trench full of young men, brimming with promise and potential. They show no outward fear but their eyes betray them. All around the air is foul with cordite and death and menace. The noise is so pervasive you can feel it in your bones and the concussive force of the massive artillery shells raining down from both sides reinforces the ever-present risk of random death or mutilation. Yet the men wait for their moment of truth with a pent-up kinetic energy, straining like dogs on the lead as they count down the minutes until the order to go over the top. For many this is their first taste of battle. For all, it is the first time they have seen action in France, or have taken part in what has already become known as 'trench warfare'. They are scared but each is cocooned in the invincibility of youth and is keen to prove his manhood in front of his mates.

Before us no-man's land stretches as much as 300 metres across the flat Flanders clay. On the other side of this killing field, the enemy waits. He knows we are coming. He holds the high ground and he has seen us prepare for this attack. He has held this position for almost two years now and his defences are intricate and almost impregnable – concrete bunkers and machine-gun nests, protected by thick skeins of barbed wire and massive waves of sandbags. Beyond the ridge behind him, his artillery lurks ready to unleash a hell of lethal metal against the fragile humanity facing it.

The Diggers will have to cross no-man's land, running the gauntlet of the machine guns and the artillery before they can come to grips with the Germans manning the trenches opposite them. There is no cover there, only the scattered shelter of craters torn from the earth

Australian Sculptor Peter Corlett's wonderful Cobbers statue, at the Australian Memorial Park at Fromelles, depicts the heroic rescues carried out by Sergeant Simon Fraser of the 57th Battalion. The statue looks across from the German front line toward the Australian front line over the deadly open ground of no-man's land. (PATRICK LINDSAY PHOTO)

as the projectiles, some as big as car engines, pound into the soil. The Germans have positioned their machine guns with lethal efficiency, especially at the jutting headland known as the Sugar Loaf where they can fire to both sides along the killing field, as well as to the front.

Even before they make their charge, the Australian casualties are mounting. The German artillery gunners have the range of the Australian trenches and here and there men fall, luckless victims of the hail of shrapnel and jagged chunks of high-explosive metal. In places, whole sections of trenches and the men sheltering in them are blown into small pieces and tossed high into the air.

But the Diggers have faith in their leaders. They've been told that their artillery will smash the German defences, tearing open the barbed wire and the bunkers and killing the defenders or sending them fleeing. One of their most trusted chiefs is with them in the front lines and he said: 'Boys, you won't find a German in the trenches when you get there'.

He was wrong. And the Diggers were wrong to place their faith in the men who sent them out on this attack.

As I sit here looking over the killing field, I am struck by an overwhelming feeling of sadness. There can be few more stark examples of the futility of war than the events that took place on this land on one day in the summer of 1916. The tears of sadness soon turn to frustration as I think of the lost potential of the young men destroyed

The cross marking the original grave of Captain Norman Gibbins of the 55th Battalion, killed in action on 20 July 1916 as he returned to the Australian lines after his heroic rearguard action during the Battle of Fromelles. The small plaque hanging from the cross bears a message from his sister Violet: 'With my soul's homage and my heart's utmost love to my beloved and deeply mourned brother. Violet Gibbins.' Captain Gibbins was later reburied in the Anzac Cemetery at Sailly-sur-la-Lys.
(AWM PHOTO P03788.003)

here by the stupidity and the cavalier indifference of the High Command.

For the simple fact is that these Diggers had no chance of success. They died needlessly and futilely in their thousands here because of the ineptitude and the callous glory-seeking of their British commander. His guilt is the greater because, unbelievably, a year earlier he had made the same mistake and sent thousands of his own men to their deaths over the same ground.

Many factors predisposed the attack to calamitous failure: poor reconnaissance; inadequate preparation; flawed execution of the preliminary artillery barrage; the size and lack of cover of no-man's land; the depth and quality of the enemy's defences; and the superior experience of its troops. One factor above all others condemned it to certain disaster: the lack of any proper objective or any plan for either holding the ground won or making a tactical withdrawal.

Around 6 pm on Wednesday, 19 July 1916, in full daylight on a clear sunny day, the 5th Australian Division answered the call to attack and was thrown against the German front line as a diversion to help support the massive British offensive then in the balance at the Somme.

The Australians charged into the teeth of German machine guns, which survived the Allied artillery bombardment in their purpose-built concrete bunkers. Our casualties were devastating – 5533 out of around 7000 attackers, with almost 2000 killed – the greatest loss of life in a night in Australian history. Amazingly, despite these losses and against all the odds, hundreds of attackers managed to break through the German front-line trenches and force the defenders to retire. But without support they were trapped by German counter-attacks and eventually either killed or captured.

The fate of many of those who died behind the German lines has been unknown for more than 90 years. Some bodies were recovered

The wall at VC Corner Cemetery Fromelles which contains the names of 1299 Australians missing after the Battle of Fromelles. The bodies of 410 Diggers found but not identified after the Armistice are buried here in groups of ten in 41 mass graves. This is the only all-Australian cemetery on the Western Front and the only one with no headstones, as none of the dead could be identified. (PATRICK LINDSAY PHOTO)

after the war ended in November 1918 and buried in nearby cemeteries. Many of those who charged that day simply disappeared: 1299 of them are listed as missing on the wall at the VC Corner Cemetery, near the Australian front line on the Fromelles battlefield.

In a war fought by 65 million soldiers over four years, where 37.5 million were killed, wounded, captured or went missing, you might think that thirteen hundred or so missing Diggers are a drop in the ocean.

But that is until you remember that they weren't numbers. They were once sons, brothers, husbands, fathers, mates. They were garbos and teachers, labourers and lawyers, farmers and posties. The dead included 24 sets of brothers and a father and son. They all had hopes of long lives, contented families and quiet retirements.

Many of them had already survived the Gallipoli campaign only to have their lives snuffed out in a single night. As far as their families or the rest of the world knew, on 19 July 1916 they simply disappeared near a small village in north-eastern France called Fromelles.

They remained in the mists of history until a Greek-born Australian art teacher from Melbourne began his quest to find them about five years ago. Lambis Englezos and his team of supporters now believe they know the fate and the final resting place of around 170 of those missing Diggers of Fromelles.

PART ONE

THE WRETCHED, HYBRID SCHEME

... a wretched, hybrid scheme, which might well be termed a tactical abortion.

BRIGADIER GENERAL HAROLD 'POMPEY' ELLIOTT
(ON THE PLAN FOR THE BATTLE OF FROMELLES)

The Cross of Sacrifice at VC Corner Cemetery. The only all-Australian cemetery in France, it is the final resting place of 410 unknown Diggers from Fromelles.
(PATRICK LINDSAY PHOTO)

1

THE BREWING STORM

One thing is clear; we are entering the first act of a
world-wide tragedy.

MAXIM GORKY, 1914

Because of the vast spread of European colonisation, when war flared in
Europe in August 1914 it ignited the first global conflict in history. While
the main theatre remained centred in Europe, the reverberations were
felt from America to the Pacific, from the Middle East to Japan.

In 1870 Germany's 39 separate states had merged to form a united
nation. She had much ground to make up against the existing dominant
colonial nations like France and Britain. Knowing that 'the sun never
set on the British Empire' prompted Germany to seek its own place
in the sun by embarking on colonial expansion in the final years of
the nineteenth century. It rapidly established African colonies in
Togoland and Namibia, Pacific outposts in New Guinea, Samoa and
Micronesia and a naval base at Tsingtao in China.

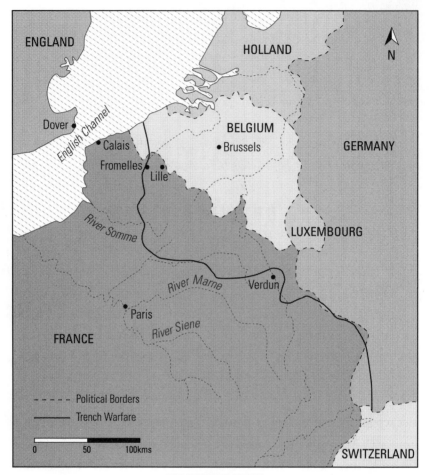

THE WESTERN FRONT

Britain grew increasingly wary of Germany's aggressive growth and soon realised that her own far-flung Empire had become a two-edged sword: it enabled her to influence events around the world but it provided Germany with the means to stretch and divide Britain's forces as she tried to protect her territories.

Germany's expansion soon threatened the world's political status quo. Germany eyed the Panama Canal and even briefly toyed with a hare-brained scheme to attack the east coast of the USA. By 1912, it was evident that Germany was gearing up for a conflict in Europe.

Clearly, the conflict evolved from a complicated cauldron of national and individual imperatives, but perhaps the underlying causes were best summed up by the British philosopher Bertrand Russell:

And all this madness, all this rage, all this flaming death of our civilisation and our hopes, has been brought about because a set of official gentlemen, living luxurious lives, mostly stupid, and all without imagination or heart, have chosen that it should occur rather than that any one of them should suffer some infinitesimal rebuff to his country's pride.

It was a bizarre situation in which Germany's Kaiser Wilhelm, oldest grandson of Britain's Queen Victoria, took up arms against his first cousins, King George V of Britain and Tsar Nicholas II of Russia. Wilhelm, who still ruled Germany as an autocrat, said: 'The sword must now decide'.

In the summer of 1914 Germany's 3.8 million troops lined up against a similar number of French soldiers to its west and around 3 million Russians on its eastern border. Germany moved swiftly and invaded Belgium in early August, sweeping aside the mismatched

German troops in high spirits as they head off to battle early in the war. The initial, mobile stage of the fighting quickly deteriorated into static trench warfare.

Belgian forces and using systematic terror to subdue the civilian population. The invaders used Belgian civilians as human shields, took hostages and torched towns and cities. On 4 August, Britain declared war on Germany. More than 6000 French and Belgian non-combatants, including women and children, were killed in the first month of hostilities. Around 180,000 Belgians fled across the Channel to Britain. Reports of the vicious German behaviour spread around the world, giving the Allies a powerful propaganda weapon to inflame anti-German sentiment and promote enlistment.

The original Anzacs head off in convoy from Albany, Western Australia, on 1 November 1914. The New Zealand Expeditionary Force, the largest body of men to ever leave New Zealand, had rendezvoused with the Australian Imperial Force in Albany before heading off to Egypt and then Gallipoli. (AWM PHOTO P00252.002)

The opening days triggered a flurry of minor conflicts around the world as Britain's allies moved against nearby German territories. On 19 August, Colonel William Holmes led the newly formed Australian Naval and Military Expedition Force (AN&MF) to Palm Island, off the Queensland coast, where it trained for three weeks. On 11 September, the force sailed to Rabaul, the capital of German New Guinea, where it captured the radio station two days later and subdued the colony. Elsewhere in the Pacific, New Zealand occupied Samoa on 30 August. By December, all the German outposts in the region had been occupied or subdued.

On 1 November 1914, a convoy of 38 ships sailed from Western Australia taking the 1st Australian Division and a Light Horse Brigade of the Australian Imperial Force (the AIF), together with a New Zealand infantry brigade and mounted rifle brigade. After some indecision about its final destination, it landed at Alexandria in Egypt on 3 December, where the Australians met their new British commander, Lieutenant General William Birdwood. Birdwood combined the force with subsequent arrivals from Australia and New Zealand to create an Army Corps, comprising two infantry divisions and one mounted division. It would go on to win fame under the acronym, ANZAC (the Australian and New Zealand Army Corps).

At about this time the German fleet was trapped at Tsingtao after Japan agreed to Britain's request to capture the port in what would prove a turning point for Japan's international aspirations and a harbinger of Pearl Harbor 27 years later. Although a combined force of 60,000 Japanese and 2000 British troops overcame the 4500-strong German garrison at Tsingtao, the German fleet escaped and scattered. Its massive battle cruisers roamed the world's sea lanes causing havoc and threatening Britain's supply lines until the *Emden* met its fate at the hands of the HMAS *Sydney*, which had broken off from the Anzac convoy, off the Cocos Islands on 9 November. The German

Admiral Graf von Spee went down with his flagship and five others near the Falkland Islands.

In Europe, meanwhile, the 100,000-strong British Expeditionary Force landed in France, and by 21 August it had moved alongside the French 5th Army to defend the Belgian city of Mons, near the French border. Three days later, 280,000 Germans launched themselves against 70,000 British. Overwhelmed, the British and French defenders were forced to retreat in a nightmare march back to the Channel.

In this early, mobile, period of the war the Germans made good progress and by the beginning of September they were just 45 kilometres from Paris. The French government abandoned its capital and moved to Bordeaux and a million Parisians fled westward. However, the German High Command realised that its advance was outstripping its supply lines.

This was particularly difficult to remedy when its main form of transport was horse-drawn vehicles. Indeed, this period saw the start of the transition from ancient to modern forms of warfare: cavalry with lances was still a major player; many troops still wore gaudy parade-ground uniforms into battle making them stand-out targets; and tin helmets hadn't been introduced. At the same time, artillery was being developed at an astonishing pace and some guns were already able to fire massive projectiles. Aerial observation was expanding, with balloons and slow-moving bi-planes acting as reconnaissance sources and, increasingly, as deliverers of bombs.

The first of many massive set-piece battles began on 5 September 1914. The Battle of the Marne was the start of years of incessant bombardment and trench warfare. In retrospect, it was probably Germany's one genuine chance to inflict a crushing defeat on the French. But a combination of German indecisiveness and resolute French defence resulted in what the French called 'the miracle on the Marne'. In three days of devastating fighting, the Germans and the

French each suffered a quarter of a million casualties – the highest average daily casualty rate throughout the entire war.

The Germans were forced to break off and retrace their steps through the French villages they had earlier vanquished. Although they never conceded the point, it was the Germans' first defeat in the field and many experts believe their chance of an ultimate victory went with it. It saw more than 30 German generals surreptitiously sacked and General Erich von Falkenhayn brought in as Chief of Staff, replacing General Helmuth von Moltke who had held that position since 1906.

Falkenhayn tried to outflank the French and British armies in a series of engagements in Belgium and north-eastern France that became known as the Race to the Sea. Having failed there, in November he ordered his armies to fall back to higher ground and dig in. It was to be the start of four years of relentless, murderous trench warfare. The French and their Allies mirrored the German defences and soon both front lines were a series of trenches, separated by no-man's land, which formed an ugly scar that ran 760 kilometres across Europe from the North Sea to the Swiss Alps.

The problem facing the commanders from both sides was simple and apparently insoluble: because of the mirror-image front lines that stretched across the continent, there were no flanks. If you can't outflank your enemy, you must attack them head on. In that case, the conflict becomes a grim test of strength, a war of attrition, where men and machinery are thrown against each other in continually growing numbers. The tactics wound the clock back to mediaeval times, to the days of siege warfare.

As each side learned from its errors, the fighting developed into a pattern. Because the Germans had adopted a defensive posture, it was normally the Allies who attacked. Ever-increasing artillery bombardments presaged an infantry attack. The bombardments were designed to

Germans prepare to attack at the Battle of the Marne in September 1914. It signalled the start of four years of trench warfare and was probably Germany's one real chance at a conclusive victory over France. But German indecisiveness and heroic French defence ended in 'the miracle on the Marne'. In just three days, the Germans and the French each suffered a quarter of a million casualties.

General Erich von Falkenhayn took over from von Moltke as German Chief of Staff after the Battle of the Marne. He unsuccessfully tried to outflank the French and British armies in what became known as the Race to the Sea, then ordered his armies to dig in, creating a trench line that soon stretched from the North Sea to the Swiss Alps.

destroy the opposing front-line trenches and to force the defenders to withdraw or to take shelter in their bunkers. The infantry would then attack on foot across no-man's land, hopefully before the enemy could reset its defensive position. Usually, despite terrible casualties, the attackers were able to break into the opposing front line. Often they broke through into the second line of defensive trenches. But both sides soon developed a very effective response – counter-attacks by troops held aside from the front lines who cut off the attacking troops, encircled them and killed them or took them prisoner.

So while small gains, usually measured in metres, were made, the attacks invariably petered out as the counter-attacks recaptured the positions. The over-arching problem facing the commanders from both sides was how could they break through all three lines of the defences and continue the momentum so that they could achieve a strategic victory.

2

AT THE CROSSROADS OF HISTORY

Stay then, village, for round you spins
On a slow axis a world as vast
And meaningful as any posed
By great Plato's solitary mind

R.S. THOMAS, 'THE VILLAGE ANALYSIS', 1955

Behind the German lines, 11 million Belgian and French civilians found themselves under occupation in what was soon run as a military state. Clocks were set to German time, whole towns and cities were dragooned into labour forces, with daily dawn parades and German identification passes. Thousands of teenagers, male and female, were rounded up and sent to industrial centres as forced labour. Resistance was swiftly and violently crushed – hostages were taken and armed resisters executed. In a frightening preview of the horrors of a future war, 3000 French civilians and almost 60,000 Belgians were packed in cattle trucks and taken to concentration camps.

The Germans scoured their newly won territory for raw materials and systematically transported them back to Germany to replace the materials denied its war machine by the blockades imposed by its enemies. The invaders also took full advantage of their conquests, which already included some of the powerhouses of French industry, using forced local labour to turn their capacity to support their war effort. Lille, in French Flanders, was an excellent example. It remained in German hands for the entire war, providing substantial industrial muscle to Germany, and was a constant Allied target.

Situated around 11 kilometres from the French–Belgian border Fromelles, was one of the tiny villages nestled in the gentle western slopes of the Aubers Ridge on Lille's outskirts. It would become the site of Australia's first battle on the Western Front and the central focus of this book.

When Falkenhayn's order to fall back to the higher ground came, the German forces around Lille took up positions along Aubers Ridge. Using the proven system of 'defence in depth', they extended their forward defences in front of the high ground along a line that ran about a kilometre west of Fromelles. The British forces opposing them dug in on the flat ground facing the German trenches with a no-man's land between the two front lines that varied from about 100 metres to 400 metres.

Civilians flee the German advance in 1914. The invaders used systematic terror tactics against civilians to subdue Belgium. More than 6000 French and Belgian non-combatants were killed in the first month of hostilities and 180,000 fled across the Channel to Britain.

The flat Flanders farmlands on which the Battle of Fromelles was fought. This is one of a series of photos taken from near Fleurbaix in 1915 and covering the area from Bois-Grenier to Fromelles. (AWM PHOTO H15912J)

Although the ridge only rose to a maximum of 36 metres above sea level it was the highest ground in the area and the Germans clearly held the superior position. They could observe any movement on the British side without the need for aerial observation. This was to prove a telling advantage in the battles to come.

Fromelles occupied ancient land that had seen conflicts for thousands of years, from Roman times through the Normans to the Hundred Years' War which started in 1337. The Battle of Agincourt, where England's Henry V defeated the French army in 1415, was fought only 60 kilometres from Fromelles. Later that century the region was controlled, first by the Holy Roman Empire, then by Spain. By 1618, it was embroiled in the Thirty Years' War which involved most of

Europe's major powers. Twenty years after that conflict ended, in 1667, Louis XIV waged war against the Spanish Netherlands and besieged Lille, just 16 kilometres east of Fromelles. With Louis' victory, the region became French. Fromelles enjoyed its longest period without conflict after Napoleon was defeated in 1815 at the Battle of Waterloo, about 120 kilometres away.

By the outbreak of World War I, Fromelles was a rural township of around 1000 people in a little over 200 houses. The railway had arrived in 1902 and the rich, well-irrigated soil of the surrounding 60 farms supplied the town with meat, vegetables and grains like wheat and maize. Just before war broke out in 1914, electricity reached the town's main street and a weaving mill was opened to join the brewery, distillery, laundry, taverns, butchery, bakery, school, the tailors, the doctor, the tobacconist, the blacksmith, the grocer and a dozen other shops. The Fromelles church and its tower dominated the skyline, just as it had done from the late fourteenth century.

The overwhelming impression of Fromelles and the surrounding countryside is its flatness. At its highest, Fromelles is just 25 metres above sea level. The village of Aubers, about 3 kilometres south-west, is only 11 metres higher. Yet such is the bowling-green terrain of the region that these meagre vantage points became vital strategic positions.

The Germans regarded Lille, an industrial centre with almost a million inhabitants, as a crucial asset from the beginning. That made the surrounding countryside strategically important territory because, in order to attack Lille, the Allies would need to win the high ground at Aubers Ridge and Fromelles. The Germans supported their front lines with a covering network of artillery placed well behind the high ground and with reserves housed in underground bunkers.

In the early stages of the war, some positions changed hands a number of times as the two sides sparred to establish their dominance

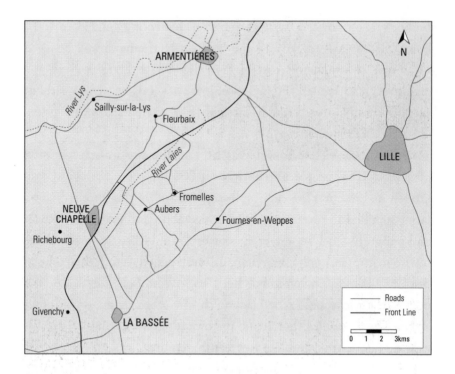

and to lay claim to positions of strategic value. Neuve Chapelle was one of them. A small town on an important crossroads, a few kilometres south-west of Fromelles, between La Bassée and Béthune and the road to the city of Armentières, it was taken by the Germans in early October 1914, won back by the British on 16 October and then reclaimed by the Germans on 27 October.

By March 1915, British plans were well advanced to retake Neuve Chapelle and then advance on Lille. Two British and two Indian divisions would attack Lille through Neuve Chapelle while another British force would recapture the town of La Bassée.

In what would be a preview of the disastrous Battle of Fromelles a year later, the attack was a deadly amalgam of miscalculations, mismanagement and mistakes. Poor coordination of the infantry charge

Germans bury their dead somewhere on the Western Front. Germany mobilised 11 million men during World War I. Of these, 7 million, or 65 per cent, were either killed, wounded, missing or taken prisoner.

The chief members of the Armistice Commission which sat in Spa, Belgium, in November 1918. The first three members in uniform are: General R.C.B. Haking (British), General Nudan (French) and General Dellobe (Belgian). (AWM PHOTO H09449)

and its artillery support saw the attackers charging into their own bombardment. In some areas, communication breakdowns saw them being thrown against undamaged defences instead of being sent to the battered parts of the enemy's front line. At one stage the commanders believed that the Middlesex Regiment had broken through successfully, 'for not a man came back to report otherwise'. Later they found out none came back because they were all dead.

Despite all these difficulties, the British troops burst through the German defences and took Neuve Chapelle on 10 March. But their observers did not see the German support lines on the higher ground behind the town and, while the British High Command dithered over the next step, the Germans rushed in reinforcements and then began a massive artillery barrage from behind Aubers Ridge which shattered the British lines. The first German counter-attack was beaten back on the outskirts of Neuve Chapelle. Then the British Commander Sir Douglas Haig tried to gain the upper hand by attacking Aubers Ridge with an infantry charge. By the time he called off the assault, he had lost almost 13,000 men against the German machine guns and artillery for no territorial gain.

Despite these shattering losses, less than two months later the British tried to storm Aubers Ridge again. The attack ran along a 15 kilometre front from Bois-Grenier, just south of Armentières, to Festubert, south-east of Neuve Chapelle, with the main thrust at Rouges Bancs, on the flat in front of Fromelles.

After the first attack, the Germans had worked overtime to repair and then greatly improve their defences, building thicker concrete bunkers and emplacements and adding shrapnel-resistant, heavy-gauge barbed-wire entanglements protected by earthworks. These were covered by a patchwork of machine-gun emplacements that could direct withering fire at troops held up by the entanglements.

The British attack was once again a costly failure. Around Aubers Ridge when the offensive was called off after less than 24 hours, 10,000 British and Indian casualties had fallen victim to the German machine guns and artillery. Among the thousands who perished around Neuve

Chapelle was 31-year-old New Zealand-born Anthony Wilding, one of the finest tennis players of his generation, who had won Wimbledon from 1910 to 1913 and who was beaten in the final in 1914 by Australia's Norman Brookes. To the south-east at Festubert, the fighting continued for two weeks before the British High Command ordered the troops there to dig in and hold the line. Another failure, another 17,000 British casualties.

It was symptomatic of the system and the times that neither of the key British commanders of these total failures was held accountable. In fact, both Haig and the Corps Commander, General Sir Richard Haking, emerged with their reputations unsullied. Haking was to play a seminal role in the Battle of Fromelles, but before that he would reprise his failure at Aubers Ridge in late September 1915 at Loos, about 15 kilometres to the south.

At Loos, for the first time, Haking commanded the British XI Corps – two divisions totalling perhaps 40,000 troops. As always, Haking brimmed with confidence before the battle, as author Lyn MacDonald wrote in *1915: The Death of Innocence*:

> *He compared the German line to a crust of pie – one thrust and it would be broken and behind it he expected there would be so little resistance that they would have no trouble in carving a way through.*

The now recurrent Haking characteristics were again present: poor intelligence and reconnaissance; lack of surprise; insufficient preliminary bombardment; chaotic behind-the-lines organisation of reinforcements and casualty evacuation; flawed and insufficient training and acclimatisation; and, bizarrely, the removal of cooking facilities so that many men went into battle hungry.

Nevertheless, Haking threw his troops against the German 'pie crust' with abandon, only to see two of his divisions destroyed and then replaced by another two which he fed into the meat grinder. Apparently, neither he nor Haig considered the impossible odds facing their men as they poured them into the killing zone. Alan Clark, in *The Donkeys*, writes that Haking's men were

> *expected to cross No-Man's Land in broad daylight with no gas or smoke cloud to cover them, with no artillery support below divisional level, and attack a position as strongly manned as had been the front defences and protected by a formidable and intact barbed wire entanglement.*

The slaughter was so terrible that even the Germans were moved and they didn't fire a single shot at the British for the rest of the day. In three and a half hours, the British had lost more than 8000 men. The Germans did not lose a single man. Author Robin Corfield notes in *Don't Forget Me, Cobber!* that of 59,247 total British losses in the battle, Haking's command contributed 16,830. In six months, he had racked up more than 20,000 casualties.

Such was the man and the situation awaiting the Australians.

The Germans defending the high ground around Aubers Ridge learned their lessons well from their shock loss of Neuve Chapelle. They increased their troops from two divisions to three in the front line and redoubled their efforts at improving their defences. The new troops in the German line, the 6th Bavarian Reserve Division, took over the sector in front of Fromelles. They had been rushed across from Lille during the early stages of the Neuve Chapelle attacks. Official Australian World War I historian, C.E.W. Bean described the unit as having been *raised immediately after the outbreak of war from untrained men under or over military age, with a proportion of fully trained but elderly reservists.*

While they may have been inexperienced 'trench' troops rather than crack infantrymen, the Bavarians soon adapted superbly to defensive trench warfare. They built an extensive network of interlinked breastworks, incorporating reinforced machine-gun pits, introduced pumps to drain their positions and created massive blockhouses and concealed concrete-reinforced strong-points in farms, churches and other buildings. Their defences extended kilometres back from the front lines. The second line of troops held the strong-points and blockhouses perhaps a kilometre behind the front line and a third line looked down from the Aubers ridgeline. Some of their massive concrete strongholds even had electricity for their pumps and lighting. Reserve units were sprinkled around the surrounding villages, ready for deployment to plug any holes and to counter-attack. It was an imposing and cleverly interwoven defensive system giving maximum protection to its troops and allowing lethal firepower to be brought to bear on attackers.

3

THE ANZACS' JOURNEY

I don't care for war, there's far too much luck in it for my liking.

NAPOLEON III, 1859

In November 1914 Ottoman Turkey had thrown its hand in with Germany on the side known as the Central Powers (Germany, Austria-Hungary, the Ottoman Empire and Bulgaria – so named because they fell between Russia on the east and France and Britain to the west). The Allies (or the Entente Powers) were France, Britain and her Dominions, Belgium and Russia. Many other nations, including Italy, Japan and the United States, joined the Allied side as the war progressed.

Turkey's entry into the war changed the initial equation. As early as 2 August 1914, the Young Turks, led by Enver Pasha and bypassing their Cabinet, had concluded a secret alliance with Germany. Enver saw the possibility of a new Turkic Empire and succumbed to Germany's bribes and the pretence of the sale of two German warships. He declared a *jihad* against Russia and the Allies and called on his countrymen to join the battle for 'victory, martyrdom and paradise'.

Responding to German requests to distract the Russians, the Turkish fleet harried the Russian Black Sea ports and Enver personally led an attack against the Russians at Sarikamis, an Anatolian town the Turks had lost to the Russians in 1878. Enver set out in December 1914 but he and his troops were trapped as winter intervened and more than 25,000 froze to death before they even made contact with the Russians. Although the Turks made some inroads with their remaining troops, the Russians counter-attacked and drove them back through Armenia. Enver and the Turks blamed Armenians serving with the Russians for the defeat. They enforced a mass deportation of Armenians in a deadly exodus to Syria (then Turkish territory) which saw some 800,000 die.

Australians from all walks of life joined the growing number of recruitment marches from inland towns to join up. After Gallipoli, the average monthly enlistments jumped from around 6000 to 36,000. (KNYVETT PHOTO)

The Russians called on their Allies to relieve the pressure on them by launching an offensive against Turkey. The response would be the genesis of the Gallipoli campaign.

Meanwhile, the Russians were locked in an increasingly costly campaign against the Germans and the Austro-Hungarians on the Eastern Front, a logistic nightmare that ran from the Urals to the Alps.

At the outbreak of war, the Allies had known that the Russians would take much longer than Britain or France to mobilise their massive forces. Things started off well as the Russians initially invaded Germany and forced the German Army back 160 kilometres. But the Germans rallied and halted the Russian advance at the Battle of Tannenberg where about 150,000 German troops completely demolished

Diggers preparing to move up into the line on the southern side of Lone Pine, Gallipoli, in August 1915. In four days of uncompromising conflict more than 4000 Turks and 2200 Anzacs died. The battle saw seven Australians win the Victoria Cross. (AWM PHOTO A00847)

the Russian Second Army of about 190,000 men. The Germans killed or wounded around 30,000 and captured almost 100,000. The Russian commander, General Alexander Samsonov, shot himself rather than report the disaster to the Tsar.

Despite the massive setback at Tannenberg, the Russian numbers began to take a toll on the Austro-Hungarian troops facing them, forcing the Germans to step in. By winter of 1915, the Germans had moved eight divisions from the Western Front to the East. Their plan was to attack Russia with the aim of forcing the Russians to make a separate peace with them, thus neutralising the Eastern Front and leaving them free to concentrate on the Western Front. The German offensive began well and the Russians fell back in disarray as the Germans claimed Poland, Lithuania, and parts of Belarus and Ukraine – the most successful German territorial gains of the whole war.

On the sidelines, Italy, Greece, Bulgaria and Romania waited, weighing up which side they would support. As the conflict drew on, Romania, Italy and Greece joined the Allies while Bulgaria chose the Central Powers after being promised a share of a defeated Serbia's territory following Germany's attack on Serbia in the winter of 1915.

The Serbian Army and many of its people retreated on foot, heading for the Mediterranean and hoping to sail to safety. Someone called it the 'funeral procession of the Serbian State'. By the time they reached sanctuary on the island of Corfu, more than half of the Serbian Army – 200,000 troops – had died on the march.

By this time, Australian and New Zealand troops had travelled halfway around the world and had landed on Turkish soil on the Gallipoli Peninsula on 25 April 1915. Against the odds, and despite the ultimate failure of the campaign, the Anzacs acquitted themselves with great distinction against the Turks and looked forward to making a contribution to the main theatre on the Western Front.

After their brilliantly executed evacuation from Gallipoli on 20 December the Australians were in high spirits as they sailed, first to Lemnos for a few days, and then to Alexandria. They made their camp at Tel-el-Kebir, near Cairo, where they were reshuffled into new units by integrating the Gallipoli veterans with the influx of new reinforcements who joined them from Australia. This was part of an overarching plan to reorganise the AIF in preparation for its service in Europe on the Western Front, giving it something of a self-contained Australian command structure.

The force was split into two army Corps. General William Riddell Birdwood commanded I Anzac Corps, comprising the 1st and 2nd Australian Divisions together with the New Zealand Division, and General Alexander Godley, another British officer, was in command of II Anzac Corps, made up of the newly raised 4th and 5th Australian Divisions.

Lieutenant General Sir William Birdwood, who had led the Anzacs at Gallipoli, was the commander of the 1 Anzac Corps, 1st, 2nd and 4th Australian Divisions. (AWM PHOTO P03717.009)

The AIF's wonderful achievements in the Gallipoli campaign, combined with the realisation that the war in Europe was going poorly, prompted a surge in recruitment back home. The numbers jumped from just on 6000 in April 1915 to more than 36,000 in July (perhaps also kicked along by a reduction in the height restriction from 5 foot 6 inches to 5 foot 2 inches and the news that a German submarine had infamously sunk the British passenger liner the *Lusitania* on 7 May). The situation was subsequently energised by Australia's new prime minister, William Morris Hughes, who took office in October and immediately offered to increase the monthly quota of 9500 reinforcements being sent to the war zone. Hughes carried out an audit of the available pool of eligible men in Australia. It revealed 215,000 potential recruits within the military age group. Hughes offered the British War Office an additional 50,000 troops. Not surprisingly, they jumped at the offer.

The newly created Australian divisions would soon be sent to France and one, the 5th Division AIF, became the first Division of the AIF to see action there. The 5th Division comprised three brigades of infantry – the 8th, 14th and 15th – each, in turn, made up of four battalions and support troops. The 8th Brigade (drawn from South Australia, Western Australia, Queensland, New South Wales and Victoria) comprised the 29th, 30th, 31st and 32nd Battalions; the 14th Brigade (from New South Wales) the 53rd, 54th, 55th and 56th Battalions; and the 15th Brigade (from Victoria) the 57th, 58th, 59th and 60th Battalions.

The integration of the reinforcements with the veterans required a massive readjustment. It also opened up many opportunities for promotion. Gallipoli veteran, Captain Roy Harrison, was promoted to major and given temporary command of the 54th Battalion. He was charged with forming the battalion and training it while his commanding officer, Lieutenant Colonel Walter Cass, recuperated in hospital. As revealed in Neville Kidd's well-researched self-published biography of

Harrison, *An Impression Which Will Never Fade*, Harrison wrote to his cousin Emily on 17 February 1916:

> *I have been promoted to Major in the 2nd Battalion and have since then been transferred as second in command, with 13 other officers and 400 men to form the 54th Battalion, which I am forming and command temporarily. Lt Col Cass has been appointed commanding officer, but as he is away in hospital, the job has fallen to me to organise the battalion. We have received a draft of 500 men yesterday, and we have now nearly 1000 men, but of course have to organise our signallers, machine gunners, transport, stretcher bearers, band, etc. Naturally we are all kept pretty busy.*

The new units struggled initially with their esprit de corps in the face of their dilution by the new recruits, as Harrison noted on 20 February:

> *I told you I was temporarily commanding the 54th Battalion which was formed a week ago, by transferring 14 officers and 442 men from the 2nd Battalion and then filling us up to war strength by sending a large draft of reinforcements. We were all very sorry to leave the old battalion, but as it is all for the good of the force, we are making the best of it. I am now bucking in to make the 54th the equal of the 2nd and I must say the new men are trying hard.*

The new units trained hard in Egypt, driven by a combination of their desire to reach battle-readiness and the prevailing threat of an attack on the Suez Canal by the Turks, now untrammelled by their defensive commitments to the Gallipoli campaign. The reports of Turkish reinforcements at Beersheba prompted plans for two of the Australian divisions to cover the central section of the Canal defences, a line of around 40 kilometres, from Ferry Post to Serapeum.

Meanwhile, the first Australians bound for France, I Anzac Corps, left on 13 March 1916. While welcomed by the remaining Australian units of II Anzac Corps, the move created some unexpected difficulties for those left behind. The 4th and 5th Divisions had been assigned to take over the defence of the Suez Canal, but because of the massive rail transport needed to move I Anzac Corps to France they were forced to embark on a three-day route march from their camp to the Canal – across 65 kilometres of desert in blazing 40 degree heat.

The commander of the 5th Division, Major-General Sir James McCay (rhymes with sky), decided to make this a training exercise and ordered his men to march in full battle kit, including ammunition, a total load of more than 40 kilograms per man. An appalling lack of planning and supply combined with the terrible desert heat to almost turn the march into a disaster.

The 15th Brigade moved mainly in the afternoon and arrived at the camp at Ferry Post largely intact. The 14th Brigade marched through the heat of the day and was decimated, as Roy Harrison wrote in his diary:

28.3.16 Tuesday. Reveille 5 am, on the march 0700. Lunch 1120. Resumed march 1240. Struck soft sand 1250. Heat awful in the hollows between the sand ridges, old soldiers say they have not had such a terrible march in all their experiences in India or elsewhere. 1500 Heat intense. Men collapsing in dozens. Medical officers busy. Water all done. Men becoming exhausted from their loads and from heat. Reached Moascar 1600 but a remnant of the brigade only. Today's march 19 miles [30 km] through the sand under a blazing sun. Hell on earth – an Egyptian desert during the midday heat with an empty water bottle.
1820 Ambulance wagons, camels with water, and the New Zealand infantry have just gone out to succour the men left in the desert.

The Commander of the Australian 5th Division, General Sir James Whiteside McCay. He was 51 at the time of the Battle of Fromelles and, while undoubtedly a brave soldier, he led by fear and bluster rather than by inspiration. Before the war, McCay was a politician, elected to the Victorian and, later, Federal parliament, where he served briefly as the Minister for Defence. The *Bulletin* wrote in his obituary in 1930 that while he was a 'bold soldier and a brave man', he was 'about the most detested officer in the AIF at an early stage of the war and remained so to the end'. (AWM PHOTO H01890)

1900. Men still coming in. Worst cases going straight to hospital. Thirteen men still unaccounted for in the battalion.

McCay was unrepentant and was scathing in his criticism of his officers, NCOs and troops. In short, in a master-stroke of thoughtless leadership, he earned their lasting enmity. He concluded his tirade:

I am compelled to say plainly that today's failure in soldierliness of the 14th Brigade after crossing the Suez Canal has been a great disappointment to me and that the blame rests largely with regimental officers as well as NCOs and the men themselves. The Brigade must pull itself together and every man must remember he is part of a regiment and not merely an individual, if I am to hope to take it into battle ... until a great improvement takes place I shall not be able to report the 14th Brigade as fit for active service.

The rebuilding of the fitness and the spirit of the men began as soon as they recovered from their march. Their duties guarding the Canal allowed them to rotate the battalions on duty, freeing the others for training. They went hard at it but it was a huge task, made even more difficult by the loss of the division's field guns and the bulk of its artillerymen to the departed I Anzac Corps. The 5th Division should have operated with about 3000 gunners. It had about 500. The rest were hastily recruited from its infantry and light horse troops and trained in relays using the few artillery pieces left. They would soon pay an intolerable price for this lack of foresight.

The climate and the tedium of the training soon took their toll on the men, as Roy Harrison wrote:

Everyone is heartily sick of Egypt, and praying to get away to France. Of course, those of us who have been under artillery fire know it won't be all beer and skittles but knowing all we do it is impossible to keep from turning our faces to France as the Promised Land. When we get there, we shall all be wishing we were somewhere else, but that is the unrest bred of soldiering. The continual uncertainty of everything – even of life – adds to the charm.

4

TO THE 'NURSERY'

Black dresses are greatly in evidence.

Major Roy Harrison, France, 1916

By the time the first Australian troops from I Anzac Corps reached France from Egypt, on 19 March 1916, the war on the Western Front had already degenerated into a muddy, bloody stalemate. The dramatic sweeping movements of the early weeks of the war had long since disappeared. Things first slowed down, then bogged down irretrievably as both sides searched for opportunities and places to break the deadlock.

A month earlier, the Germans thought they had found a chink in the Allied line at Verdun on the Meuse River in north-east France, about 200 kilometres south-east of Lille.

Toward the end of 1915, General von Falkenhayn had told his Kaiser he believed that Russia was effectively paralysed and France almost exhausted and that the war was only continuing because of

Britain's underlying support and influence over her allies. The logical next step was for Germany to knock Britain out of the war, but Falkenhayn conceded that this was too difficult because of Britain's superiority at sea and his forces' inability to deliver a knockout blow to the British front in Flanders. The next best approach, he told the Kaiser, was a full-out attack against France aimed at 'knocking England's best sword out of her hand'.

The Germans decided to centre their attack on the French stronghold at Verdun. Reasoning that French honour would demand that her troops fight to the last man for their sacred soil, Falkenhayn's strategy was to lure France into an apocalyptic battle where it would 'bleed to death'.

Allied aerial observers failed to see their preparations and 100,000 German troops launched a surprise attack on 21 February 1916. That day the German artillery fired a million shells and they unleashed their 'storm troopers' – small groups of soldiers attacking on their own initiative across no-man's land. In the initial stages the Germans outnumbered the French defenders by five to one. But the French threw everything into the defence of the city. General Robert Niville summed up the French resolve when he famously said 'Ils ne passeront pas' ('They shall not pass'). The battle for Verdun would rage for the rest of 1916 as the French rotated three-quarters of its entire army, led by Philippe Pétain, through Verdun to defend it.

The initial German successes in the attacks on Verdun seemed to prove Falkenhayn correct. The massed German artillery caused grievous French casualties and forced the Allies to make major changes to their overall strategy.

Originally, that Allied strategy was to attack Germany simultaneously on three fronts – the British and the French from the Western Front, the Russians on the Eastern Front and the Italians in the Alps. The aim was to stretch and divide Germany and ultimately to wear her down. But the German attack on Verdun altered both the Allies' approach and the burden of its implementation. When the three-front strategy had been agreed, France was to play the leading role in the Western Front offensive. Verdun changed that and the British took on the main thrust. It also meant that the purpose of the Somme offensive would change in character from an attempt to inflict a decisive blow against Germany to a method of relieving pressure on the French who were desperately holding on at Verdun.

The battle for Verdun was raging by the time the second wave of Australians from II Anzac Corps travelled north by train through France, preparing to enter the Western Front battlefields for the first time and bound for the flat farmlands of the Armentières sector, to

Diggers of the Australian 6th Brigade, newly arrived in Flanders from Egypt in 1916, show their spirit. They are holding up their recently acquired steel helmets. (AWM PHOTO EZ0003)

the west of Lille. It was generally regarded as a quiet backwater in the overall turmoil of the conflict. Indeed, the British called it a 'nursery', where they could blood newcomers.

The French welcomed the Australians with open arms, as Lieutenant Hugh Knyvett later wrote:

> They pelted us with flowers and sweets and, while no one objected to the embraces of the girls, we thought it a bit too much when the men as well threw their arms around us and kissed us on both cheeks.
>
> I received no less than six crucifixes that I was assured by the charming donors would protect me from all danger, as they had been blessed by certain archbishops, the favourite being the Archbishop of Amiens. I was mean enough to remark to one of them that it was a wonder any of the Frenchmen ever were killed.

Lieutenant Bob Chapman, a 29-year-old leader in the 55th Battalion, later wrote in his diary:

> Some miles from the firing line it is hard to realise that war is in existence. Crops are growing in the fields – children laugh and run about the streets. There are very few menfolk about though. France is just one great garden. We came through from Marseilles by train and I have never seen a more beautiful place.

Roy Harrison was also caught up in the excitement of the new country and its people:

> France is beautiful beyond description and no words can convey anything which would give you an idea of it all. The Valley of the Rhône is indescribably beautiful and the Saône, just north of Dijon is something out of the bag.

Everywhere, only old men, women, boys and children are to be seen. The women work in the fields, and carry on the farms without aid other than the above. Black dresses are greatly in evidence. The old grandmother at the farm where I am is 80 years old but she makes dresses from morning till night, and they are all black.

By the time the Australians of I Anzac Corps had taken up their positions in the line near Fromelles in April 1916, the sector was quiet again. The earlier disastrous battles for Aubers Ridge were just vague rumours amongst the remaining British troops.

From 20 May, the men of I Anzac Corps held the line for 14.5 kilometres, running northwards from the Sugar Loaf in front of Fromelles to the south bank of the River Lys, just to the east of Armentières. The Sugar Loaf (a salient, or protrusion, roughly in the shape of a popular local loaf of bread) jutted out of the German line, about a kilometre west of Fromelles township and directly opposite the point where the Australian line linked with the British. The Sugar Loaf bristled with German machine-gun emplacements. Because it protruded into no-man's land, it allowed the German gunners to direct fire down the no-man's-land channel on either side. In military terms this is known as enfilade fire. It meant that troops trying to charge across no-man's land there would be caught in a lethal cross-fire from both front and side.

The commanders on both sides were wary of the dangers of the inaction in the sector. Previous experience in the trench warfare deadlock had shown them that an attitude of 'live and let live' developed when the level of fighting dropped away. The leaders believed that this had deleterious effects on morale and dampened the troops' fighting spirit. Their antidote was small-party raids on the enemy's lines.

As soon as the men of I Anzac Corps began raiding they realised the effectiveness and resolution of the troops facing them. The Diggers suffered considerable casualties: 118 in the last week of April, rising to 773 in the first week of July.

These raids were often vicious affairs, man against man in a fight to the death. The preparation and training involved required an uncompromising approach. The instructions set out in the British Army's manual for fighting with the bayonet – 'Guiding Rule Number 8 for weapons training' – were chillingly eloquent:

> If possible, the point of the bayonet should be directed against the opponent's throat, as the point will enter easily and make a fatal wound on entering a few inches, and, being near the eyes, makes the opponent flinch. Other vulnerable and usually exposed parts are the face, chest, lower abdomen and thighs, and the region of the kidneys when the back is turned. Four to six inches penetration is sufficient to incapacitate and allow for a quick withdrawal, whereas if a bayonet is driven home too far it is often impossible to withdraw it. In such cases a round should be fired to break up the obstruction.

By this stage, the second wave of II Anzac Corps (4th and 5th Australian Divisions) was moving up through France from their arrival port of Marseilles. Hugh Knyvett was with them as they completed the final stage of their journey to the front line:

> The brigade did not go by train any of the distance, but marched the whole way to the trenches, taking two days. This part of the country was just on the edge of the Hun advance and, being only visited by some scouting parties of Uhlans [German Cavalry] had escaped most of war's ravages. We marched through beautiful woods, passed peaceful villages and crossed over sleepy canals that we saw not again in France in many long months – most of us, alas, never.

Lieutenant Hugh Knyvett was a scout with the 59th Battalion at Fromelles. He survived the battle but was wounded late in 1916 and invalided out of the army. He travelled to the US and wrote a remarkable account of his experiences, *Over There With the Australians*. Sadly, Knyvett died from complications from his wounds in New York shortly after the book was published in April 1918. (KNYVETT PHOTO)

The troops of II Anzac Corps had done their best while they lagged behind in Egypt to reconstitute their artillery, an enormous task in the limited time available. Charles Bean wrote that the creation of II Anzac Corps' artillery with such speed was 'unparalleled in British experience' and was a classic example of 'the speed with which Australians could be trained'. The new officers were lectured for four hours each day before, in turn, training their men for eight hours.

So the Australians who were about to move into the line near Fromelles did so with distinct disadvantages: they had chronically inexperienced artillery and infantry without experience in trench warfare, both of which were about to operate in unfamiliar territory in a war zone dominated by big guns and endless trench lines.

Waiting for them, on the other side of no-man's land, was a Bavarian division that had been moved into place a year earlier after the Germans strengthened their line following the shock British success in temporarily capturing Neuve Chapelle in March 1915.

The arrival of the 6th Bavarian Reserve Division, comprising the 16th Bavarian Reserve Infantry Regiment (16BRIR), also known as the List Regiment after its first commanding officer, Colonel List, and the 17th, 20th and 21st Bavarian Reserve Infantry Regiments, lifted the number of German Divisions holding the sector from two to three – thus allowing them to reduce the width of their individual regimental front lines.

5

AN AUSTRIAN LANCE-CORPORAL

The young volunteer had become an old soldier.

ADOLF HITLER, MEIN KAMPF, 1925

One of the non-commissioned officers serving with the List Regiment was a nondescript 27-year-old lance-corporal who would change the course of the world two decades later. Adolf Hitler, a pale intense loner, was a despatch runner for the First Company HQ of 16BRIR. In 1925, almost a decade after Fromelles, Hitler would write in his autobiography and political manifesto *Mein Kampf* ('My Struggle') of the overwhelming desire he had to fight for his country when war was declared:

> *For me these hours came as a deliverance from the distress that had weighed on me during the days of my youth. I am not ashamed to acknowledge today that I was carried away by the enthusiasm of the moment and that I sank down upon my knees and thanked Heaven*

*out of the fullness of my heart for the favour of being permitted to
live in such a time …*

*I had no desire to fight for the Hapsburg cause, but I was prepared
to die at any time for my own kinsfolk and the Empire to which they
really belonged.*

There is little doubt that Hitler passionately believed these words.
The famous photograph of the crowd in Munich's city square, the
Odeonplatz, taken on 1 August 1914, shows him clearly in the crowd
– a young man swept up in the moment, perhaps finding a cause giving
meaning to his life for the first time.

Hitler joined up within days. An Austrian, he sought and won
a dispensation to join a Bavarian unit, the 16th Bavarian Reserve
Infantry Regiment. Hitler was given the regimental number 148 and
posted, initially to the 1st Company and later the 3rd Company. In
October 1914, after just a few months training, his regiment was sent
to the front.

Hitler took part in the First Battle of Ypres and the Race to the
Sea when his regiment suffered heavy casualties. He wrote in *Mein
Kampf* of the impact of this introduction to the stark reality of
warfare:

Caught in the crowd in the Odeonplatz
in Munich as war is declared in August
1914 is a 25-year-old Adolf Hitler.
Clearly transfixed, he joined up within
days. Although he was an Austrian, he
sought and gained permission to enlist
in a Bavarian infantry unit.

Adolf Hitler around the time he wrote his manifesto, *Mein Kampf*, aged 36 in 1925. The photo was taken nine years after Fromelles and eight years before Hitler rose to power as Chancellor of Germany.

From right to left: Lance-Corporal Adolf Hitler, aged 27, his friend and later fellow Nazi founder Max Amann and a comrade from the Bavarian List Regiment (16BRIR) at Fromelles in 1916. The dog is Hitler's constant companion Fucshl, who wandered across no-man's land from the British lines.

Boys of seventeen looked now like grown men. The rank and file of the List Regiment had not been trained properly in the art of warfare, but they knew how to die like old soldiers.

That was the beginning. And thus we carried on from year to year. A feeling of horror replaced the romantic fighting spirit. Enthusiasm cooled down gradually and exuberant spirits were quelled by the fear of the ever-present Death ...

Already in the winter of 1915-16 I had come through that inner struggle. The will had asserted its incontestable mastery. Whereas in the early days I went into the fight with a cheer and a laugh, I was now habitually calm and resolute. And that frame of mind endured. Fate might now put me through the final test without my nerves or reason giving way. The young volunteer had become an old soldier.

On 2 December 1914, aged 25, this 'old soldier' won the Iron Cross, Second Class, for bravery under fire at Wytschaete. Hitler was wounded on 7 October 1916 and gassed in 1918. Late in the war, around August 1918, he was awarded the Iron Cross, First Class, although the Official History of the List Regiment has no mention of this feat. (Interestingly, author Robin Corfield reports that in Hitler's later life, the only decoration he wore was his Iron Cross, Second Class.)

Hitler's job as a despatch runner at Fromelles was a very dangerous one with a short life expectancy in the front lines. Indeed, years later, during World War II, he claimed that his experiences in that role enabled him to look at warfare through the eyes of the common soldier and thus to understand their needs and views.

Hitler was with 16RIR when it faced and repulsed Haking's attack at Neuve Chapelle in March 1915. The initial success of the British assault galvanised the regiment into a massive re-think of its defences and attitudes. Sixteen months later, at the height of the Battle of Fromelles, Hitler would find himself under direct fire from the advancing Australians as he carried his despatches back to the reserves. Many a World War I Digger later rued the missed opportunity to change the course of history with a single shot.

Some of Hitler's comrades at the battle rose to play significant roles in the Third Reich. One of his sergeants, Max Amann, shown with Hitler's arm around him in a photo that survived the period, rose to become a founding member of the Nazi Party (member #3) and its business manager. Amann, who formed an arrangement from the start under which he was answerable only to Hitler, became the Party's secretary general and its publisher. He served prison time with Hitler after the 1923 Putsch and, during that time, Hitler dictated part of *Mein Kampf* to Amann. Later, Amann published the book, accounting for all the considerable royalties to Hitler down the years. He eventually became the most powerful publisher in Germany – at one stage controlling more than 80 per cent of its thousand or so newspapers.

Hitler's experiences in the trenches in Flanders formed many of his subsequent views, including an early realisation of the potential of propaganda, as he wrote in *Mein Kampf*:

> *through the medium of the schools, the press and the comic papers, an idea of the Englishman was gradually formed which was bound eventually to lead to the worst kind of self-deception ... the delusion was so profound that the Englishman was looked upon as a shrewd business man, but personally a coward even to an incredible degree ...*
>
> *I can vividly recall to mind the astonished looks of my comrades when they found themselves personally face to face with the Tommies in Flanders. After a few days of fighting the consciousness slowly dawned on our soldiers that those Scotsmen were not like the ones we had seen described and caricatured in the comic papers and mentioned in the communiqués.*
>
> *It was then that I formed my first ideas of the efficiency of various forms of propaganda.*

During much of his time in the Fromelles area, Hitler had a dog called Fuchsl ('Little Fox'), which apparently strayed over no-man's land from the British lines near Neuve Chapelle around January 1915. He patiently taught it tricks and it appears in many photographs with Hitler and his comrades. As he did later in his life, Hitler apparently found it easier to give affection to his dog than to other humans. In Fromelles and during his service elsewhere on the Western Front, Fuchsl rarely left his master's side, sleeping by him at night and sometimes even accompanying him on his rounds delivering despatches. Hitler made sure he took the dog with him whenever he could find the time during the quiet periods to wander off and paint landscapes, some of which survive. They are architecturally accurate but lack warmth or virtuosity.

Hitler's experiences at Fromelles clearly made a deep impression on him. In 1942 he arranged for this memorial plaque to be erected on the wall of his 1916 billet in nearby Fournes. The plaque was smashed after World War II but was restored and is now on display at the l'Association pour le Souvenir de la Bataille de Fromelles museum above the Fromelles Town Hall. (PATRICK LINDSAY PHOTO)

Immediately after his army defeated France on 25 June 1940, Hitler set off on a tour of the Fromelles battlefield with his comrades from the 1916 List Regiment. He also visited the building where he had been billeted in Fournes-en-Weppes, his regimental cemetery and the blockhouse where he had taken refuge from the attacking Australians during the battle.

Fuchsl survived the battles at Fromelles, and later at the Somme and Arras, but Hitler was shattered when the dog was apparently stolen, along with his painting equipment, during a train journey.

The true impact of Fromelles on Hitler was shown when, in 1940, after his army had invaded France and he had signed the surrender documents – in the same train as was used to sign the German surrender in 1918 – he immediately set off on a tour of French Flanders. On 25 June 1940, Hitler, accompanied by his List Regiment comrades, Max Amann and Ernst Schmidt, spent the night near Fromelles quietly celebrating the time the Armistice would officially come into effect, at 1.35 am.

Hitler and his comrades-in-arms toured the old Fromelles battlefield, visited the building in which he was billeted in Fournes-en-Weppes, his regiment's cemetery at Fournes and the blockhouse where he took refuge during the battle. On 20 April 1942 Hitler arranged for a stone plaque to be solemnly affixed to the wall on his former billet. The plaque was smashed after the liberation in 1945 but was later recovered and reconstructed. Today it is on display at the Fromelles Museum, above the town hall. The Hitler blockhouse still stands near the Fromelles football oval behind Rouges Bancs. Another blockhouse on the Aubers Road is often referred to as Hitler's bunker, but the photos taken on his 1940 visit clearly show him at the former bunker.

6

IN THE PRESENCE OF DEATH

We don't want to lose you but we think you ought to go.

PAUL A. RUBENS, 'YOUR KING AND COUNTRY WANT YOU', 1914

As so often happens in war, the Australians were soon swept up in events far removed from them and over which they had no control.

The bitter reality was the war was a learn-as-you-go experience for both sides, but especially the Allies. First the Germans, with their massive artillery pieces, and then the Allies, realised this Great War was a completely different animal from previous conflicts. At the cutting edge, infantrymen still charged against their opposite numbers. But the real killing was done by mighty unseen guns that spewed death and destruction from 10 or 20 kilometres behind the front lines and by the nests of machine guns that sprayed no-man's land with lethal effect. Against these twin agents of death, the resolution of the humble infantryman counted for little.

In short, manpower had given way to firepower. But it took many commanders a long time and countless casualties before they adapted to the new ways of war. They were still in the process of this transition when the Australians arrived.

While the High Command plotted the next major offensives, the Australians were about to settle into their new homes in the rich marshy soil of French Flanders. Because the water table was so high there the trenches were technically breastworks (shallow trenches were dug down a metre or so to the water level with parapets facing the enemy and parados on the trench wall behind them, all built up by sandbags of soil piled two metres or more above ground level). With experience the troops learned to build the parados higher than the parapet to prevent being silhouetted. The walls of these breastworks were five or six metres thick and could withstand all but the heaviest artillery shells. They usually had wooden floors called duckboards (timber walkways) to keep the troops out of the slush. The front-line trenches and the support lines, 200 to 300 metres further back, were linked by

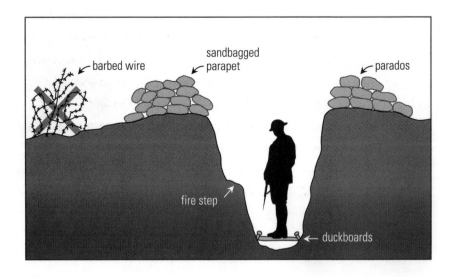

communication trenches that ran back away from the front lines every couple of hundred metres. These communication trenches had walls on both sides to conceal and protect troops moving up to and back from the front lines. The communication trenches had street names: VC Avenue, Bond Street, Brompton Road and Pinney's Avenue.

Originally, the Somme Offensive had been mooted for Flanders. Later, the Allied High Command decided on a major offensive against the German line along a 24-kilometre front just south of the Somme River in Picardy in northern France, where the French and the British Armies' lines joined. This action was to take place about 80 kilometres south of the Australians' position at Fromelles.

Because of the losses sustained by the British Expeditionary Force since the start of the war, its original six divisions of regular army troops had effectively ceased to exist. They were replaced by a combination of the volunteers of the Territorial Force (equivalent to the Australian militia forces) and the units known as Kitchener's New Army (troops who enlisted after the start of the war following a campaign headed by Lord Horatio Kitchener, the British Secretary of State for War). A combined force of 13 British divisions to the north of the Somme River and 11 French divisions to its south would carry out the offensive. They would line up against 11 divisions of the German Second Army under General Fritz von Below. The battle would grow into one of the bloodiest in history, running from 1 July through to 18 November 1916, dragging in 50 divisions from each of the British, French and German armies, and resulting in casualties of more than a million men.

The preliminary bombardment began on 24 June and lasted for five days. Its unprecedented intensity rattled windows in London 260 kilometres away. The British artillery alone fired almost two million shells before the assault began across the entire Somme front at 7.30 am on 1 July, as witnessed by English poet John Masefield:

The price of war! The living mingle with the dead as troops shelter between actions on the Western Front.

all along that old front line of the English came a whistling and a crying. The men of the first wave climbed up the parapets, in tumult, darkness, and the presence of death, and having done with all pleasant things, advanced across no-man's land to begin the Battle of the Somme.

Despite the extraordinary opening barrage, the German front line remained intact in many areas and their machine-gunners took a terrifying toll of the cumbersome British infantry. (It was later ascertained that up to 30 per cent of the British shells had been duds.) Burdened with equipment weighing more than 30 kilograms and organised into slow-moving lines, the British attackers fell like ninepins in the face of the unwavering German artillery, machine-gun and rifle fire.

Thanks to their superior artillery, the French to the south fared much better and in some of their sectors they met all of their first-day objectives. But the first day of the battle was an unmitigated disaster for the British. Communications broke down completely and for some days the British commanders had no accurate idea of progress or the scale of their losses. When the casualty figures eventually came in for that first day they showed the British had lost 19,240 killed, 35,493 wounded, 2152 missing and 585 taken as prisoners, for a total loss of 57,470. By contrast, the German forces against them suffered a total loss of about 8000. That revered and faithful reporter of the facts, *The Times*, reported the opening attack as follows:

EVERYTHING HAS GONE WELL

Our troops have successfully carried out their missions, all counter-attacks have been repulsed and large numbers of prisoners taken.

The reality was summed up by a British captain quoted in Malcolm Brown's *Tommy Goes to War*:

The trench was a horrible sight. The dead were stretched out on one side, one on top of each other six feet high. I thought at the time I should never get the peculiar disgusting smell of the vapour of warm human blood heated by the sun out of my nostrils. I would rather have smelt gas a hundred times. I can never describe that faint sickening, horrible smell which several times nearly knocked me up altogether.

Some of the British units suffered cataclysmic losses. The Newfoundland Regiment was virtually wiped out. This redoubtable band of men from what was then the Dominion of Newfoundland, a vast island in the Gulf of St Lawrence off the Canadian mainland, was the only North American unit to have fought in the Gallipoli campaign and was one of the last to leave as part of the British rearguard in January 1916. During the Somme offensive the regiment went into battle with the British at Beaumont-Hamel, 9 kilometres north of the town of Albert. Unable to reach even its starting point in the forward trenches because of the massive German bombardment, the Newfoundlanders were forced to attack from the reserve lines. The bulk of the regiment was killed before they even reached no-man's land. Of the 801 Newfoundlanders who attacked, only 68 answered the roll call the next day. Over 550 were killed. The unit had a total casualty rate of 91 per cent, and this from a country with a population of around 250,000.

In fact these devastating losses to the island's male gene pool caused lasting social and economic damage and contributed to Newfoundland's decision to become a Canadian province in 1949. To this day, 1 July is a day of solemn remembrance for Newfoundlanders for the sacrifices of their youth on the Somme.

In early July, the Germans fell back in some southern areas of the offensive and opportunities opened to break through their line. But the fleeting chances slipped by, thanks in part to British losses and poor communications, and the Germans rushed reinforcements in from other sectors.

While the British dithered, the French continued to make inroads. They pushed back the German line as much as 10 kilometres in some areas while taking 12,000 prisoners and capturing considerable numbers of armaments. The British tardiness brought conflict between the two allies as the French were forced to halt their advance to avoid opening a gap between their forces and the British.

Despite these setbacks, the offensive on the Somme did bring some benefits to the Allied cause because it forced the Germans to scale down their offensive at Verdun and to rush divisions from other parts of their line to ease the pressure of the British and French along the Somme front. Initially, the Germans moved fourteen divisions into their line against the British on the Somme, along the way to throwing in a total of more than 40 additional divisions. The British response to these German reinforcements had a direct and devastating impact on the Australians just taking their place in the line at Fromelles.

On 5 July, the British on the Somme identified a newly arrived German unit, the 13th Jager Battalion, as one that had been previously defending

The Australian 59th Battalion heading up to the front line at Fromelles in July 1916. Most of these men would have been killed or wounded in the battle. The 59th, which was one of the battalions attacking the Sugar Loaf salient, was devastated by the German machine-gunners there and suffered almost 700 casualties. (KNYVETT PHOTO)

The Diggers of the 59th Battalion calmly await the order to move up into their front-line trenches at Fromelles around 11 July 1916. Within a week, more than 90 per cent of these men would become casualties. (KNYVETT PHOTO)

the area near the Sugar Loaf. A total of nine enemy battalions had been identified as having come to the Somme from the Lille area.

The British Corps Commander, General Godley, issued the following order to II Anzac Corps:

> It is imperative that raids and all possible offensive should be undertaken at once by both divisions of the corps in order to make a certainty of holding on our front such German troops as may be there.
>
> Raids must therefore take place immediately and must be on a larger scale than has hitherto been attempted – about 200 men or a company [around 100 men] ...

At this stage, the Australian 5th Division troops had not yet even reached their lines opposite the Sugar Loaf. But in any event, events elsewhere would change these priorities and the raiding was left to the New Zealand Division. They met with very strong resistance from the German defences which culminated in a bloody rebuff on 13 July when a reinforced company of the 1st Otago Battalion forced its way through the German wires but was thrown back with heavy losses – 52 killed or missing, 123 wounded – only six of the party returning without wounds.

Clearly, far stronger measures were needed to prevent any further German units being moved to the Somme.

The Germans defending the Fromelles area knew they now faced a new combination of British and Anzac units. From right to left across the Allied front line – facing the Germans – the British 61st Division held the position immediately to the right of the Sugar Loaf and then from the left side of the Sugar Loaf the Australian 5th Division lined up as follows: the 15th Brigade, the 14th Brigade and the 8th Brigade. On the far left, the New Zealand Division held the line.

Each of the Australian brigades held back two of its four 1000-man battalions in reserve and moved the other two into its front-line position. The 15th Brigade initially moved the 59th and 60th Battalions into the line. Alongside them, the 14th Brigade moved up the 53rd and 54th Battalions and, next to them, the 8th Brigade brought forward its 31st and 32nd Battalions.

On the morning of 12 July 1916, Brigadier-General Harold 'Pompey' Elliott, the commander of the 15th Brigade, formally took charge of almost 2 kilometres of the front line, starting from the Sugar Loaf salient where his troops butted up against the British 61st Division. Almost immediately, Elliott received bewildering news. The 5th Australian Division was to take part in an urgent full-scale assault along with the British division. The 61st was a Territorial division raised in the South Midlands of England, with no previous operational experience as a unit and which had only sailed from England on 24 May.

The Australians were stunned to be called into action at such short notice, as Hugh Knyvett wrote:

We had not been two days in the trenches before we knew that we were destined for an attack on the trenches opposite and we had not had time even to know the way about our own lines. Few of us had even had a glimpse of no-man's land, or sight of the fellow across the street whom we were to fight.

7

LOOSE THINKING

Take calculated risks. That is quite different to being rash.

General George S. Patton, US soldier

As the Australians checked out the terrain they had inherited, the grim reality of their situation struck home. The flat, featureless no-man's land varied in width from more than 350 metres in front of 15th Brigade on their right to around 100 metres on the Australian left flank in front of the 8th Brigade. Behind them, they were connected to their rear by their five avenues – communication trenches that were the source of their ammunition, supplies and reinforcements. But a number of these were virtually impassable because they were flooded or knee-deep in mud. The 15th Brigade was served by Pinney's Avenue and VC Avenue and both were accessible. The 14th Brigade only had Brompton Road and it was severely hampered by flooding while the 8th had Cellar Farm Avenue, which was clear, and Mine Avenue which was substantially blocked.

On the other side of no-man's land the Diggers could see the foreboding German defensive line – all concrete and bristling barbed wire – and beyond that they looked up at the German high ground along the horizon. The Australians knew that, behind the ridgeline, German artillery nestled out of sight and out of reach and was able to pour its lethal fire into their lines.

What they didn't know at the time was that the Germans could see every movement in the Allied lines opposite them. Pompey Elliott wrote after the war that the Fromelles church had been transformed into a perfect observation post. (In fact he must have been describing another church in the region, perhaps at Aubers, but Elliott's point is still well made):

In the village of Fromelles the church as I saw from personal observation later on, had been turned into a solid cube of concrete, except for a stair so narrow that only with difficulty could a normally-built man ascend it. At its head near the ridge pole it terminated in a loophole for an observer, who, with a telescope could, with perfect safety to himself, count every sentry in our lines. He had also an extensive view across our back areas, and could at once detect any preparation for attack.

Pompey Elliott was one of the dominant characters in the Fromelles tragedy. The others were General Richard Haking, the relentless proponent of the attack, and Major General James McCay, the commanding officer of the Australian 5th Division. The three men were strikingly different characters.

Harold Edward Elliott was known to all as 'Pompey' (a nickname he acquired pre-war after a noted Carlton Australian Rules footballer, Fred 'Pompey' Elliott). He was a genuine eccentric. Widely read, with an acute mind, he was physically imposing and revelled in his rough-

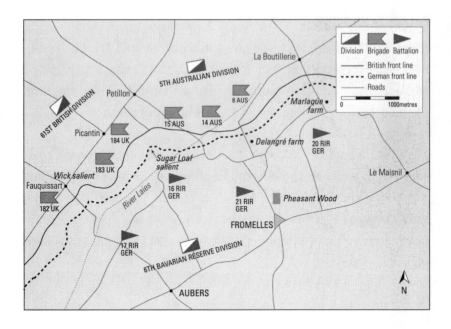

diamond appearance. He was instantly recognised by his men as a soldier's soldier – a man with the ability to lead by example, sometimes a little too instinctively, but at the same time a man with the capacity to speak as an equal to his men. He was one of those rare characters who won and retained his men's affection and loyalty throughout their service.

A fine scholar, Elliott matriculated to university but left after a few weeks to serve with the Victorian Imperial Bushmen in the Boer War from 1899 to 1902. There he won the Distinguished Conduct Medal for 'particularly daring' gallantry and came home as a lieutenant aged 23. He then returned to his arts-law studies at Melbourne University, graduating with a Masters in Law and later forming the law firm, H. E. Elliott and Co. He joined the militia and was a lieutenant colonel when war was declared. He led the 7th Battalion AIF in the landings at Gallipoli, where he was wounded and had to be evacuated. He

Brigadier General Harold Edward 'Pompey' Elliott, commanding officer of the Australian 15th Brigade. A soldier's soldier who led by example, Elliott won a Distinguished Conduct Medal for bravery during the Boer War before leading the 7th Battalion at the Gallipoli landings. His misgivings before the Battle of Fromelles were prescient as his 15th Brigade lost more than 800 men killed in the action. (AWM PHOTO A02607)

rejoined his battalion two months later in time to take part in the heroic struggles at Steele's Post and Lone Pine. Elliott wrote later about it to his wife, Kate:

we had over 3000 Turks against us in those attacks. I never had more than 600 and finished with only about 200, but we held the trenches. Consequently the 7th and your old man would be apt to get swelled heads for all the nice things said about them.

The intensity of the fighting endured by Elliott's battalion is exemplified by the fact that four of his men won the Victoria Cross at Lone Pine and four more won the next best decoration for gallantry, the Distinguished Conduct Medal. Not long afterwards Elliott was struck down with pleurisy and was once again evacuated, this time to England where he recuperated for three months, returning to his battalion on Gallipoli just weeks before the evacuation. As it happened, Elliott badly wrenched his ankle the day before the evacuation and had to leave early. He rejoined his men at their Egyptian base camp at Tel-el-Kebir three weeks later.

Early in 1916, Elliott was promoted to brigadier and given command of the 15th Brigade, under Major General McCay.

James Whiteside McCay was an enigma. In 1916 he was 51, tall, straight-backed, moustachioed, with the bearing of a man used to giving commands. He was undoubtedly a brave soldier. But his manner and his temper often got the better of him. He had landed with the 1st Division at Anzac Cove, Gallipoli and had been appalled by the chaos. He momentarily lost control of himself, waving his pistol and blaming all around him, before regaining his composure when challenged by his divisional commander Major General William Bridges. He managed to take control and despite many close shaves – two bullets passed harmlessly through his cap and another through his tunic – he rallied his men and continued the assault. Unfortunately, by all accounts, he led by bluster and fear rather than by inspiration.

Perhaps the most remarkable thing about McCay being in the front line is that he should have been there at all. Before the war he was a prominent politician, having served in the Victorian parliament before being elected to the new Federal parliament and even briefly serving as the Minister for Defence. It's hard to imagine any modern politician stepping off the gravy train to join his soldiers on active service. McCay was born in Ireland but came with his family to Australia as a baby. An outstanding student, he was dux at Melbourne's Scotch College and then earned masters degrees in arts and law before taking up schoolteaching, even buying his own school, Castlemaine Grammar. He joined the militia and rose to lieutenant colonel before entering politics.

He appears to have been one of those people who manage to tick all the boxes in their career path but who rise to the top with evident personality flaws. The *Bulletin* wrote of McCay in his obituary in 1930 that while he was a 'bold soldier and a brave man', he was 'about the most detested officer in the AIF at an early stage of the war and remained so to the end'.

A more balanced view of McCay reveals that some of the events for which he was despised were beyond his control. For example, on Gallipoli McCay's 2nd Brigade was seconded to help the erratic British General Hunter-Weston in the attack on Krithia. Hunter-Weston ordered McCay to launch an attack without giving him any time for proper reconnaissance or preparation. It was a mad and desperate act and the Australians suffered 1000 casualties, half their number, for no gain. Despite the fact that McCay showed his courage by moving so close to the action that he was shot in the leg, breaking it, his men blamed him for the disaster. In reality, McCay had few options: Hunter-Weston was in command and he issued the order. McCay was sent home to recuperate.

(Incidentally, Sir Aylmer Gould Hunter-Weston, or 'Hunter-Bunter' as he was known, was another politician-soldier and another bizarre eccentric. After being sent home from Gallipoli suffering from 'sunstroke and nervous exhaustion', he was knighted and then elected to the British parliament in October 1916. In between time, he had the dubious honour of leading his corps at the Somme, in July 1916, where it suffered the highest casualties of all the British units and achieved none of its objectives.)

McCay returned to Egypt in March 1916 and was given command of the newly formed 5th Division, largely on the strength of the support of his former political colleague, the then Minister for Defence, Senator George Pearce, who said that the division should be commanded by an Australian – and that McCay was the right man for the job. As we have seen, McCay immediately turned his men against him by ordering them on the crazy forced march through the burning desert to the Suez Canal. His standing had not risen by the time the division took over the trenches in Fromelles.

The architect of the Battle of Fromelles, Sir Richard Cyril Byrne Haking, CBE, KCB, KCMG, was 54 in 1916. He was one of many professional soldiers in the British army who were promoted rapidly because of the massive losses in the war. Many would say he had risen beyond his ability and, worse, he lacked the wit to learn and adapt to the changing face of war. He doggedly held on to his pre-war view that attack was the key to victory under any circumstances and he had even published a number of books on military tactics based on this untenable theory. Haking was one of those peculiar British commanders who believed that individual 'character', or the possession of an unshakeable 'offensive spirit', could overcome physical obstacles such as an enemy with markedly superior numbers, in massive entrenched positions, equipped with overwhelming firepower. He ignored what would become an accepted military reality: that a properly equipped and entrenched defensive force with good morale and command could only be defeated by an attacking force with substantially superior numbers and firepower.

Haking had met and befriended the Commander-in-Chief of the British Expeditionary Force, Sir Douglas Haig, during their time at the British Staff College, where Haking was a lecturer. At the outbreak of war, he was given command of the British 5th Brigade. After recovering from a head wound on the Western Front, he was given command of the 1st Division and then, in December 1915, he was appointed commander of the XI Corps. While Haking won and retained Haig's support, many others saw through him. Lieutenant Colonel Philip Game (later, as NSW Governor, Sir Philip Game, the man who dismissed the Labor Premier Jack Lang in 1932) observed Haking closely as a staff officer. He described Haking as 'really impossible, untruthful and a bully and not to be trusted'.

Haking's proposed assault at Fromelles was his response to the British High Command's calls for diversionary action to make sure no more German forces were transferred to the Somme. But, as Pompey Elliott later explained in 1929, and then in a celebrated lecture he gave to the United Services Institution in Melbourne in October 1930, the planning for the Battle of Fromelles bordered on the absurd:

> The result of the action was to cripple the 5th Division for months to come, and the loss was not in numbers only, for our very finest officers, NCOs and men, many of them Gallipoli veterans, perished there. And what did it accomplish?
>
> In its final form it was intended as a feint to distract the attention of the German staff from Pozières, and inasmuch as German records show that for a few days afterwards the Germans expected a renewal of the attack, the feint cannot with certainty be judged to have been completely ineffective. Yet the value of the result (if any) it can be said with certainty was tragically disproportionate to the cost.

Elliott is crystal clear about the reasons for the failure: 'loose thinking' and 'somewhat reckless' decision-making by the higher (British) staff.

The driving force behind these unformed plans was the same British general who had previously twice tried to take the Aubers Ridge – both at enormous cost and both without success – Haking. Apparently, he had learned nothing from his previous disasters. He maintained his mindless and unjustified belief that an attacking force could overcome even the most entrenched defences provided it had the necessary 'will to succeed'.

If Haking learned nothing, neither did the committee of other commanders who debated, rejected, reconsidered, reconstituted, revamped and finally approved Haking's suggested plan. Charles Bean described the flawed genesis of the battle for Fromelles:

Suggested first by Haking as a feint attack; then by [British General] Plumer as part of a victorious advance; rejected by [British General] Monro in favour of attack elsewhere; put forward again by GHQ as a 'purely artillery' demonstration; ordered as a demonstration, but with an infantry operation added, according to Haking's plan and through his emphatic advocacy; almost cancelled … and finally reinstated by Haig, apparently as an urgent demonstration – such were the changes of form through which the plans of this ill-fated operation had successively passed.

Haking's original plan was for a gas attack followed by an infantry attack to capture the Sugar Loaf. He suggested this while the I Anzac Corps was in the line at Fromelles but it was knocked back. It was revitalised after Haig initially called on the commanders of the 1st and 2nd British Armies, Generals Munro and Plumer, to create an attack that would break through and join up with the Somme offensive – an optimistic concept aimed at crushing the Germans in a pincer movement.

According to Elliott, General Plumer subsequently told Haking to prepare a plan for an attack by Haking's XI Corps, reinforced by a division and artillery from Plumer's Army. Haking came back – yet again – with a wildly ambitious plan to take Aubers Ridge. He was again knocked back. But soon after, when Haig saw progress on the Somme was stalling, he told his staff to look for a diversion to distract the Germans. After reconsidering Haking's plan, Haig's staff decided that a

pretended attack or feint on the Aubers–Fromelles Ridge, undertaken as an artillery demonstration only, might help the Somme operations to some extent by pinning the enemy reserves in this area to their ground.

So, at that stage, the attack was 'an artillery demonstration' possibly combined with a 'few infantry raids' aimed at convincing the enemy that an important offensive was imminent. It was a far cry from Haking's original plan, but somehow Haking was also asked to prepare a plan for an infantry attack on Aubers Ridge in case this 'became advisable at a later stage'.

Elliott believes that it was at a meeting at Haig's General Headquarters on 13 July that the alternative plans were somehow blended into what he called

a wretched, hybrid scheme, which might well be termed a tactical abortion.

The conference decided where the attack should take place: at the junction of the two armies, the British XI Corps and the Australians, around the Sugar Loaf. It appointed Haking to command the attack and it also agreed on another amendment: now 'some infantry' would take part – three divisions, two from the 1st Army and one from the 2nd. Finally, the commanders decided that the attack would be presaged by a three-day artillery bombardment.

The more the plan was changed, the more mistakes were made.

According to the order published by the 1st British Army on 15 July, the aim of the attack was:

To prevent the enemy from moving southward to take part in the main battle. For this purpose the preliminary operations, as far as possible, will give the impression of an impending offensive on a large scale, and the bombardment, which commenced on the morning of the 14th instant, will be continued with increasing intensity up to the moment of the assault.

The Allied Commander in Chief, Field Marshal Sir Douglas Haig, departing after a visit to Canadian Divisional Headquarters on the Western Front in 1916. Born into the Haig whisky family, he became a professional soldier, serving in India, Egypt and the Boer War prior to World War I. Haig directed the Battle of the Somme and approved the disastrous Battle of Fromelles as a feint to hold German defenders away from the Somme front. (AWM PHOTO H06963)

As Elliott pointed out, this was the first – and perhaps the biggest – mistake: the attack surrendered any hope of surprise, 'the supreme element in war'. The bombardment and the preliminary operations giving an 'impression of an impending offensive on a large scale' only made sense if there was no subsequent infantry attack. To attack after advertising it was simply suicidal.

To make matters worse for the Australians, their commanding officer, McCay, had not been consulted on the planning. He had simply been informed on 12 July – before the plan was amended – that his division was to be handed over to Haking's command for an 'immediate infantry attack'.

At a conference at his headquarters at Hinges on the morning of 14 July, Haking gave McCay and his British counterpart, Major General Colin McKenzie, their orders for the forthcoming attack:

Each division will attack with 3 brigades in line, each brigade with 2 assaulting battalions, and each battalion on a front of assault of about 350 yards [320 metres]. The remaining battalions of the division will be kept in reserve and will not be used for assaulting the position without orders from G.O.C. XI Corps [Haking].

That afternoon McCay briefed his brigadiers: Elliott of the 15th, Harold Pope of the 14th, and Edwin Tivey of the 8th. He outlined the plan of the attack. Two assaulting battalions from each brigade would attack in four waves. The first two waves would start from the front trenches and the others would form up behind them in the reserve line of trenches, about 250 metres to the rear. They would go over the top (or 'hop the bags' in Digger slang) about five minutes apart. They were under strict orders not to advance further than the German forward trench system.

To put things in perspective, at this stage only half of the Australian troops had actually seen the front line – and they had only been there for two days!

As well, Haking was, either by misinformation or by self-delusion, completely mistaken about the quality and quantity of the artillery and the ammunition available. He apparently only found out on 14 July that, while he had about the same number of guns in total as he did for his earlier attack in May 1915, instead of 300,000 shells for his field guns and 30,000 for his howitzers, he would only have 200,000 and 15,000 shells respectively. And, in addition, his gunners would not be the artillery from three experienced British divisions but rather the inexperienced gunners from two Australian divisions, the 4th and

5th, who had recently been converted from infantrymen and light-horsemen.

This was just one of the litany of blunders that sealed the fate of the men preparing to charge across no-man's land at Fromelles. The others included: almost certain confusion resulting from an attack centred on the joining of two independent Allied forces at the Sugar Loaf; the woefully inadequate time for preparation; the inaccurate reconnaissance; the lack of a proper reserve to give flexibility to recover from setbacks as the battle progressed; the width of no-man's land that the 15th Brigade in particular had to cross – more than twice the army's recommended maximum; the failure to recognise that the Germans had complete visibility of the Allied lines; and the faulty systems for communication and re-supply for the attackers.

Diggers walk along the path beside the front-line trenches near Fromelles. The photo is an excellent illustration of the parapets which the troops from both sides were forced to use to protect the trenches, which were shallow because of the high water table in the area. (AWM PHOTO P00437.017)

Despite all these clouds hanging over the enterprise, McCay was delighted that his men would have the honour of being the first Australians to take part in a major battle in France. His enthusiasm was not shared by either the commander of I Anzac Corps, Lieutenant General William Birdwood, or his Chief of Staff, Brigadier General Cyril Brudenell White. At Haig's headquarters, they both unsuccessfully tried to put their views that an attack on such a small scale would not deceive the enemy into thinking it was a major offensive and therefore would have no real point. It would sacrifice lives for no justifiable reason.

Pompey Elliott was also racked with doubts. On 14 July, he spotted one of Haig's staff, Major Howard, near his headquarters at Rouge de Bour. Elliott took him aside and explained his concerns. Then he

Brigadier General Harold 'Pompey' Elliott, commander of the 15th Brigade at Fromelles, standing at the door of a captured German divisional headquarters near Harbonnieres in August 1918. (AWM PHOTO E02855)

persuaded Howard to come with him out into no-man's land and gave him a first-hand glimpse at the terrain and the risks facing the attackers. Howard was clearly moved by the 350 metres of totally exposed land that Elliott's men would have to cover before they reached the German lines. Elliott told Howard he did not believe they had 'an earthly chance of success' and called on him to tell him 'as a man' what he thought of it.

His reply was: 'If you put it to me like that, sir, I must answer you in the same way as man to man. It is going to be a holocaust.' Well then, I said, if that is your real opinion, will you promise me that you will go tonight on your return to General Haig, tell him that is your opinion and that it is mine also.

He was much moved by this appeal and promised faithfully to do so. Though I have never spoken to him since or heard from him, I know he faithfully observed his promise.

Haig also paused before he sanctioned the attack with qualifications on 15 July:

Approved, except that infantry must not be sent unless an adequate supply of guns and ammunition for counter battery work is provided.

Haig's Deputy Chief of Staff, General Butler, expanded on this order in a meeting with Generals Plumer and Monro, explaining that Haig did not want the infantry to attack

at all unless the commanders were satisfied that they had sufficient artillery and ammunition not only to capture, but to hold and consolidate the enemy's trenches.

In addition, Butler also confirmed that because headquarters had information about the transfer of enemy reserves to the Somme, the Fromelles attack did not have the same level of expediency and could in any case be delayed, giving time for further preparations. Haking argued strongly that the attack must proceed. The record of the conference states that he

> was most emphatic that he was quite satisfied with the resources at his disposal; he was quite confident in the success of the operation, and considered the ammunition at his disposal was ample to put the infantry in and keep them there.

According to Elliott, Haking also addressed the timing of the attack, scheduled for Monday 17 July:

> The troops are worked up to it, were ready and anxious to do it and he considered that any change of plan would have a bad effect on the troops now.

Elliott believed that Haking was lying, seeking the glory of taking the ridge at Aubers that had eluded him for so long.

> This shows that Haking wished to risk all for a spectacular success that would put himself into the limelight and was not merely anxious to divert the enemy's attention on the Somme.
>
> Haking spoke that which was untrue and unfounded. The infantry in the line were as a fact almost unanimously against the scheme. But they were never consulted, except to the extent that I forced my own opinion upon Major Howard.

In reality, the troops, and the Australians in particular, were almost exhausted by the rushed preparations. They had to shoulder the extra

A remarkable interior shot of the German defences on the Western Front, showing their scale and permanence.

burdens of hauling supplies and ammunition up to the forward position and many had almost no sleep in the days leading up to the attack.

The preliminary seven-hour bombardment was to start at 4 am. However, heavy rain and mist interfered with the artillery's registration (test firing to make sure they had the correct range for their targets) and Haking pushed back the artillery start time, first to 8 am, then to 11 am. But when the mist still shrouded the front at 9 am he wrote to his superiors reluctantly postponing the attack, adding:

> *The infantry and field artillery who are to carry out the attack are not fully trained and GHQ from what was said at your conference yesterday do not appear to be very anxious for the attack to be delivered ...*
>
> *I should be glad to know if you wish me to carry it out tomorrow on the same programme. It is important, with these new troops that this information should be given to me as early as possible so I can issue such instructions as will minimise any loss of moral[e] owing to postponement.*

In making this report to Haig's HQ, Haking failed to mention the shortcomings he had discovered about his artillery support. General Monro was prepared to cancel the attack but he found Haig under growing pressure at the Somme, where a German counter-attack was imminent, and he received a reply from Haig that only compounded the growing confusion:

> The Chief in Chief wishes the operation ... to be carried out as soon as possible, weather permitting, provided always that General Sir Charles Monro is satisfied that the conditions are favourable, and that the resources at his disposal, including ammunition, are adequate both for the preparation and execution of this enterprise.

This response gave Haking considerable leeway in deciding on the next move. As Monro had already indicated he thought the resources were satisfactory, Haking was able to take advantage of Haig's loose language (where he required only 'adequate' resources – a judgment call) to commit his troops to the attack.

8

HOPPING THE BAGS

It is a most pitiful thing to see them all, going about, happy and ignorant of the fact, that a matter of hours will see many of them dead; but as the French say – c'est la guerre.

MAJOR ROY HARRISON, FROMELLES, 1916

Haking issued his orders: a seven-hour bombardment would now start at 11 am on Wednesday 19 July and the infantry would attack at 6 pm. The die was cast and the troops continued their preparations to go into battle.

Hugh Knyvett recalled how the attack was detailed to the men who would make it:

Our company commanders gathered us in small groups and carefully explained the plan of attack. We were to take the three lines of German trenches that were clearly discernable on the aeroplane photograph which was shown us; the first wave was to take the first trench, the second jumping over their heads and attacking the second German line, the third wave going on to the third German line. When all the Germans had been killed in the first trench, those left of the first wave were to follow the third line.

In each battalion the officers inspected their troops to ensure they had field dressings and bottles of iodine to dress wounds, their gas masks, identity discs (in World War I they were made from compressed cardboard) and their pay books. Troops drew their iron rations, two sandbags, 150 rounds of ammunition for their webbing pouches, a further 50 rounds in a bandolier to be worn over the left shoulder and two hand grenades each. They made up their packs, including their rations, their greatcoats and the grenades, but left out all unnecessary gear which they then tied in bundles and labelled. These were collected and put into storage. Officers and non-commissioned officers were issued with periscopes. Stretchers were collected by their bearers and all troops filled their water bottles with boiled or chlorinated water. Every third man was also issued with a shovel. Finally, every man with a luminous compass was instructed to expose it to as much sunlight as possible to make sure it glowed at night as powerfully and as long as possible.

All the while, the engineers were flat out preparing the trenches and defences. Because of the terrain, many of the trenches filled with water, both from the high water table and from rain. Working all through the night of 16 July, the engineers had drained and laid duckboards along the entire length of the flooded Brompton Road communication trench.

Major Roy Harrison knew from his time in Gallipoli the dangers facing him and his men as he wrote to his fiancée Emily on the eve of the battle:

Last night we got sudden orders to move out of our position in the line and in less than two hours were on the way to a new scene of action which we reached at two o'clock this morning. We know why we have been pulled out, for we are going in to capture a German position. By the time this reaches you, the result will be known to you through the paper, so, failing any bad news, you may take it that all is well … it is no use worrying, as I am quite satisfied that what is to be, will be, and nothing can alter it for good or evil.

The men don't know yet what is before them, but some suspect that there is some thing in the wind. It is a most pitiful thing to see them all, going about, happy and ignorant of the fact, that a matter of hours will see many of them dead; but as the French say – c'est la guerre.

The rushed nature of the attack was evident everywhere. Only the first two waves of the Australian attackers had even been issued with steel helmets. The rest were left to combat the coming maelstrom of

An informal portrait of Major Geoffrey McCrae, poet and architect, who was killed as he led the 60th Battalion at Fromelles. He had previously survived the Gallipoli campaign. (AWM PHOTO P02896.001)

lead in their slouch hats, for the first and only time on the Western Front. This, of course, would add immeasurably to their casualties.

From the start, the artillery played catch-up. Some of the Australian batteries had been granted leave, then had their orders cancelled and were rushed back into position. Some hadn't even made it into their positions until after the original start time on 17 July. Yet they were the key weapon on which Haking relied, as he said in his order read out to all troops prior to the attack:

When everything is ready our guns consisting of some 350 pieces of all descriptions, and our trench mortars, will commence an intense bombardment of the enemy's front system of trenches. After about half an hour's bombardment the guns will suddenly lengthen range, our infantry will show their bayonets over the parapet, and the enemy, thinking we are about to assault, will come out of his shelters and man his parapets. The guns will then shorten their range, and drive the enemy back into his shelters again. This will be repeated several times.

Finally, when we have cut all the wire, destroyed all the enemy's machine-gun emplacements, knocked down most of his parapets, killed a large proportion of the enemy, and thoroughly frightened the remainder, our infantry will assault, capture and hold the enemy's support line along the whole front.

The objective will be strictly limited to the enemy's support trenches and no more.

Wednesday 19 July dawned clear, with visibility to the horizon. During the morning, as they tensely counted down the hours, many soldiers wrote a final letter to their loved ones. Major Geoffrey McCrae, a 26-year-old architecture student and poet before being promoted to lead the 60th Battalion, wrote to his family:

Today I lead my battalion in our assault on the German lines and I pray God I may come through alright and bring honour to our name. If not I will at least have laid down my life for you and my country which is the greatest privilege one can ask for. Farewell dear people the hour approacheth.

Pompey Elliott scribbled a note to his wife Kate:

I am writing this in the morning and about 6 o'clock this evening we will start a battle. Nothing like what is going on down on the Somme, but in other wars it would be a very considerable battle indeed. I have taken every precaution I can think of to help my boys along, and am now awaiting the signal which will launch so many of my poor boys to their death. They are all eagerly awaiting the signal, and we hope to pound the enemy's trenches that we won't have much loss at all … I am going to watch the assault from our front line. I cannot stay back here. If mischance comes I can only say God bless and keep you my own dear little true wife and helpmate and our dear little pets comfort you always … my will is in the safe in the office.

Others, like Captain Waldo Zander of 30th Battalion, were naively optimistic at the chance to take part in the attack (or 'a stunt' as they called it):

A stunt! We knew little what it meant, but to us it seemed something wonderfully new and exciting – a chance for a fellow to win his laurels and make good.

In the front line, waiting for the bombardment, Major Roy Harrison, had a clear and perilous role. He had been directed to lead the 54th

Battalion's first wave, taking with him six signallers who would roll out two telephone wires to be used to set up a battalion headquarters. He knew the hardest part would be surviving the opening charge and making it across the vast no-man's land unscathed. Not only would

One of a series of photos taken by a Digger at Fromelles just prior to the start of the battle. At great personal risk, Corporal Charles Lorking took the shot before hopping the bags himself. He survived the battle and the war. (AWM PHOTO A02555)

they have to cross the rough featureless flatlands in front of them, they would also have to clamber across what was euphemistically named the River Laies. In reality the Laies was little more than a drainage canal that ran diagonally across no-man's land from behind the Sugar Loaf to enter the Australian lines between the 15th and 14th Brigades' positions, but in various parts it was a genuine obstacle, about two or three metres wide and too deep to wade through.

Harrison and the others waiting for their moment of truth could only hope that their leaders' optimistic evaluation of the task before them would become a reality and that the enemy would be so damaged and shocked by the planned bombardment that the attackers could cross the no-man's land with minimal casualties.

The preliminary bombardment started on schedule at 11 am and continued with growing intensity through the afternoon. Vast geysers of earth spewed high into the sky as the projectiles bit into the German front. To the Australians, inexperienced in such displays, it seemed the promised damage was being done to the enemy's defences. The German artillery opened up in response, homing in on the front and reserve trenches where its observers had reported that the Allied troops were packed in ready to attack.

Things started to go pear-shaped for the Australians almost from the start. The German observers had clearly seen the massive troop movement in the Allied lines. In the days leading up to the attack, they observed carrying parties ferrying materials and ammunition to the front lines. They had alerted their reserve troops and called for and received additional supplies of ammunition from the rear. Shortly after 7 am on the morning of 19 July, the German reserves were moved forward so they could be deployed as needed to plug any holes that appeared in their defences. By 1 pm all the enemy troops in the front line had been ordered to stand to (the maximum stage of alertness) awaiting the attack.

Diggers from the 2nd Australian Division in their trenches near Bois-Grenier near Fromelles. The soldier in the foreground is looking through a periscope and the man to his left is holding one of the newly acquired Lewis machine guns. (AWM PHOTO EZ0007)

Around 3.15 pm the German observers saw the Australian engineers working to use a 'pipe pusher' – a long cylindrical bomb, which was driven underground by a hydraulic jack out into no-man's land to explode and create a rough trench to provide cover for the advancing troops. The Germans called in their artillery on the engineers and, in doing so, further shelled the Australian front trenches, causing significant casualties. The inaccuracy of the Australian barrage also subjected their own troops to friendly fire as misdirected shots (or 'drop-shorts' as they were called) regularly hit them. When they realised they were being shelled by their own guns, the Diggers reacted sharply, as Hugh Knyvett recalled:

Our first message ... was very polite 'we preferred to be killed by the
Germans, thank you' ... two of our officers being killed, our next message
was worded very differently, and we told them that 'if he fired again we
would turn our machine guns on them'. I was sent back to make sure
that he got the message ... this battery did not belong to our division.

Nerves tingled as the troops in the front trenches waited while the
hours dragged on and shells from both sides continued to pepper them.
The Australians were confronted with their first taste of perhaps the
most horrifying aspect of trench warfare – the almost inexplicable
terrors of a massive artillery bombardment. Some of their Gallipoli
veterans had experienced it in small doses but on the Western Front
they would face it on a scale never before witnessed. One Digger's
experience a few days later at Pozières on the Somme summed it up:

All day long the ground rocked and swayed backwards and forwards
from the concussion ... men were driven stark staring mad and more
than one of them rushed out of the trench over towards the Germans.
[A]ny amount of them could be seen crying and sobbing like children
their nerves completely gone ... we were nearly all in a state of
silliness and half dazed.

Lieutenant John Raws was a journalist from Malvern in South
Australia before joining up. He was 32 years old when he was killed
in action near Pozières on 23 August. He left a wonderfully evocative
series of letters which his family collected and published in a booklet
Records of an Australian Lieutenant – a Story of Bravery, Devotion and
Self-Sacrifice, 1915/1916. He wrote of the pressures:

I have had much luck and kept my nerve so far. The awful difficulty
is to keep it. The bravest of all often lose it – one becomes a gibbering

maniac ... *Only the men you have trusted and believed in proved equal to it. One or two of my friends stood splendidly, like granite rocks round which the seas raged in vain. They were all junior officers; but many other fine men broke to pieces. Everyone called it shell-shock but shell-shock (ie shell concussion) is very rare. What 90% get is justifiable funk due to the collapse of the helm of self-control.*

Another of Corporal Charles Lorking's photos taken from the Australian lines at Fromelles showing the start of the bombardment of the German position just prior to the attack. (AWM PHOTO H02105)

Corporal Charles Lorking's photo across no-man's land immediately before the Fromelles attack on 19 July 1916. It shows the lack of cover ahead of the attackers as they charged across the scrubby killing ground to the German trenches. (AWM PHOTO H02106)

At 3.20 pm in the Australians' front lines, around halfway through the preliminary bombardment, Major Roy Harrison of the 54th Battalion signalled back to his CO, Colonel Cass, a veteran of both the Boer War and Gallipoli, that the six signallers he was to take with him had not yet arrived.

By 5 pm it was evident to Harrison and the others in the front line that the bombardment was not creating anywhere near the promised damage to the enemy front-line defences. Harrison reported back to Cass that the 'enemy parapet opposite ... is not being smashed'. He also added that he couldn't establish telephone contact with Cass yet and that one of his officers 'has just had an arm blown off'. And this was even before the infantry attack had started.

Others had reported back that the German defences around the Sugar Loaf, which was the key to the success of the attack because of the capacity of its machine-gunners to fire down no-man's land on either side, were largely intact. The artillery was directed to concentrate its heavy guns on the stronghold but it was too little and too late.

Behind Harrison and his men, Cass was waiting with the third and fourth waves in the reserve trenches. He could see the damage being done to his men as they hunkered down in the trenches. Just five minutes before the first wave was due to go over, Cass signalled back to his 14th Brigade HQ:

Enemy are enfilading Brompton Road with shrapnel and trench mortars and h[eavy] art[illery]. Communication blocked for the time. More arty support req'd to check enemy arty as most of their guns are playing on parapet and communications.

The casualties in the trenches were so great that, even before the attack, some of the Australian battalions had to combine their third and fourth waves into one. The 32nd Battalion had not even spent a full day in the line, yet before the attack it had already lost three of its four company commanders and all their seconds-in-command.

Nevertheless, many of the Australians believed that judging by the noise, the dust and the smoke, their artillery was causing even more damage to the enemy, softening them up for the attack. Pompey Elliott was one of them. In the front trench with his men, he reassured them: 'Boys, you won't find a German in the trenches when you get there'.

In the front line with bayonets fixed, men of the 53rd Battalion, 5th Division, minutes before the attack at Fromelles. (AWM PHOTO H16396)

Because of the uneven width of no-man's land faced by the various units, the starting times for the attack were staggered so they would all reach the German lines at the same time. Of course, this was based on the assumption that the Allied artillery would do its job of breaking down the German defences, causing heavy casualties and throwing the enemy troops into confusion.

The infantry attack of the Battle of Fromelles began when the first of the British attackers went over at 5.30 pm, at which time, as Bean noted, 'the sun of a bright sunny day was still fairly high'. So the German defenders would have had perfect visibility as, unbelievably, the assault started in broad daylight, with around three more hours before last light. Worse, because of the season, the attackers were effectively charging into the sun while the enemy had perfect vision. Bean continued:

the enemy, observing the movements which were obviously the commencement of the attack, opened heavily upon the front and reserve lines with all available guns.

Those on the extreme right of the Allied attacking line, the British 2/7th Royal Warwickshire Regiment, initially took the German front trenches with relative ease but were then caught by enfilade fire and driven back by a German counter-attack. Other British troops from the 183rd Brigade were heavily shelled and machine-gunned as they tried to attack through sally ports (gaps cut in their parapets) and suffered many casualties. The few who gallantly made it through the firestorm to the German wire were killed there. Elsewhere in the British line, closer to the Sugar Loaf, a combination of accurate artillery bombardment and incessant machine-gun and rifle fire destroyed the attack. The greatest casualties occurred around the Sugar Loaf itself, where accurate enfilade machine-gun fire sweeping down no-man's land cut down the attackers before they could reach the German lines.

Lieutenant Percy Wellesley 'Bob' Chapman, of the 55th Battalion, kept a diary from the time he embarked for Gallipoli in July 1915 until he fell in action on 12 March 1917. His first-hand, contemporaneous description of the battle at Fromelles gives a fascinating insight into the mind and the emotions of the Digger. (JUDITH FITZHENRY PHOTO)

At his headquarters, Haking was receiving garbled reports of the progress of the British assault. Some reports gave rise to misplaced optimism, suggesting that in some areas good progress was being made.

Bean summed up the situation of the Australians waiting for the final minutes until their turn came to go over the top:

For the first time in the war an Australian attacking force was actually meeting the contingency most dreaded by commanders: its intentions had been discovered, and the enemy barrage was crashing upon its assembly position with the object of destroying the attack.

The first wave of the Australians 'hopped the bags' at 5.43 pm. On the Australian right flank, Pompey Elliott's 15th Brigade went over from 5.45 pm in four waves, leaving about five minutes apart. They set off fifteen minutes before their supporting artillery barrage was due to lift and push back into the German support lines. (Just getting over the top of their parapets was a difficult exercise. Because their parapets were up to three metres high, the men built rough timber ladders to allow them to clamber out of their trenches and over the top.)

Lieutenant Percy Wellesley 'Bob' Chapman, of the 55th Battalion, a veteran of Gallipoli, kept a diary from the day he embarked in July 1915 until he fell in France in March 1917. His battalion's initial role was to support the two assaulting battalions in his brigade, the 54th and the 56th. He and his men were assigned the dangerous task of digging the communications trench between the captured German front line and the Australian trenches.

Chapman and his men were under the command of the much-admired Captain Norman Gibbins. Writing in his diary the week after the battle, Bob Chapman noted:

> *We marched along the road in single file keeping to the right under cover of the hedge as much as possible – and about five minute intervals between platoons, till we got to the Communication Gaps leading to the main trench: in these we were slightly congested owing to supplies going forward and wounded coming back.*
>
> *The first wounded man I saw was one lying on the road with a bullet wound through the stomach. The sight seemed to bring to me the first indication that we were actually going into battle – a slight feeling of sickness crept over me and I felt annoyed with myself, but it soon passed.*
>
> *In the gap a shell landed among our front party – but we could not stop, one poor chap was blown to a pulp, bits of legs and arms were scattered about. I trod on his head by mistake as I hurried by and it gave under my foot like a sponge – others were lying about moaning and groaning – but all feeling had left me now. I passed dead men without feeling pity or remorse.*

In the support trench while grenades were distributed to each of Chapman's men. Then, at Gibbins' order, they went over the top. Each man carried fifteen sandbags and most had a pick or shovel. As soon as they made it into no-man's land they started digging.

It did not take us long to settle down to work. But an order came through from the front that they wanted reinforcements so off we went again. Our road was strewn with dead men lying as they had fallen – mostly face downwards and heads towards the enemy – their yellow-white complexions, blue finger nails, and clear staring eyes gazing into vacancy telling that Death had for some time taken his toll.

By the time Chapman and his men had reached the German trench they found that men from the 54th were occupying a small muddy trench in front about a metre deep. They immediately started digging in and built a parapet from sandbags. Chapman ordered fatigue parties to carry sandbags, ammunition and grenades from there and to help dig an emplacement for the machine gunners. He went on to give a wonderful description of what it was like to take part in the battle:

Little incidents fix themselves in one's mind – but the whole seems more or less a blur. During the night reinforcements were called for from the right. Mr Wyllie was sent – but as he got up to go, 'thud' comes something against his side and over he rolled, grasping his side. 'They've got me Chappie – they've got me' he said as I held his head. They carried him to the main German trench and from there to our own trenches. He is in Hospital and doing well now.

Capt Gibbins was the marvel – he kept walking up and down the lines never showing any sign of fear, encouraging people and helping them. Towards dawn our flanks were being attacked by enemy bombers so Capt Gibbins led an attack against them over 'No Man's Land' and drove them back, but back they came and still again. Bombs and bombers were called for and still more bombs but our officers were becoming less. Mendellson was blown up on the right. Jock Mathews was shot. Toliard was wounded. Denoon had been shot through the shoulder.

Elsewhere, the leading men of the 59th Battalion made it halfway across no-man's land without problems, but then they were suddenly caught in an irresistible hail of lead. The Germans had placed observers in the front trenches who had gallantly stayed there even through the worst of the artillery bombardment to warn their comrades of the moment of the anticipated attack. When some of them were killed or wounded, others immediately took their place. As soon as these observers alerted them, the defenders rushed back to their positions to repel the attack. The vast majority of them emerged unharmed from their dugouts to find their positions in the Sugar Loaf surprisingly free from major damage. They quickly manned their machine guns and started sweeping their deadly fire at the advancing Australians.

Because the German machine guns at the Sugar Loaf were able to fire across a clear killing field with no dead ground for cover for the

A typical German heavy machine-gun crew. Teams like this caused devastating casualties as the Australians tried to cross no-man's land at Fromelles.

attackers, the gunners were able to shoot using a method known as 'grazing fire' – sweeping their fusillades at a low angle, not higher than a standing man. This gave them the added effect of cutting men down by, first, hitting them in the legs and then often hitting them again as they fell. They also benefited from ricochets off the ground that caused further injury to those following in the background. Capable of firing 600 rounds a minute – or ten 7.92 mm bullets every second – the heavy machine-guns were fixed on sleds or tripods and set into concreted bunkers which gave their operators maximum protection. Belts fed the ammunition into the weapon and the mechanism was water cooled.

Private Jimmy Downing of the 57th Battalion later recalled what he saw as he waited as part of the 15th Brigade's reserve battalion:

Stammering scores of German machine-guns spluttered violently, drowning the noise of the cannonade. The air was thick with bullets, swishing in a flat, criss-crossed lattice of death ... Hundreds were mown down in the flicker of an eyelid, like great rows of teeth knocked from a comb ... Men were cut in two by streams of bullets [that] swept like whirling knives ... It was the Charge of the Light Brigade once more, but more terrible, more hopeless – magnificent, but not war – a valley of death filled by somebody's blunder.

The blunderer, General Richard Haking, the man they would forever after call 'The Butcher', maintained his mad optimism throughout. Nestled back at his headquarters in a chateau at Sailly-sur-la-Lys, about 8 kilometres north-west of the front lines, Haking and McCay continued to rely on the confused and often inaccurate signals coming back from the battlefield.

Haking's absurd plan for an artillery feint – the lengthening of the range of the bombardment accompanied by the appearance of an attack, followed by a swift renewal of the original bombardment after the defenders had been lured from their cover – was a spectacular failure. Far from drawing the German defenders out into the open, to be caught as the barrage continued, it was ignored by the Germans who easily saw through the ruse, as Hugh Knyvett wrote:

They [the defenders] failed to appear, however, until we actually went over the top, then the machine-guns and rifles swept a hail of bullets in our faces, like a veritable blizzard.

Knyvett was amazed by the courage of his comrades, as they surged from their trenches into the firestorm:

Nothing could exceed the bravery of those boys. The first wave went down like 'wheat before the reaper'. When the time came for the second wave to go over there was not a man standing of the first wave, yet not a lad faltered. Each glanced at his watch and on the arranged tick of the clock leaped over. In many cases they did not get any farther than the first wave. The last wave, though they knew each had to do the work of three, were in their places and started on their forlorn hope at the appointed moment.

While the 15th Brigade's attack foundered on the deadly Sugar Loaf machine guns, the 14th Brigade, to its left, was making good progress. The left-hand flank of the 53rd Battalion and, alongside it, the 54th Battalion swept into the German front-line trenches, captured two machine guns and cleared the position. As per their orders, while this first wave of the attackers then set about clearing the front trench, the following waves leap-frogged them and set about finding the support trenches which they had been told were 100 metres or so deeper into the German territory. When they had cleared the enemy from the

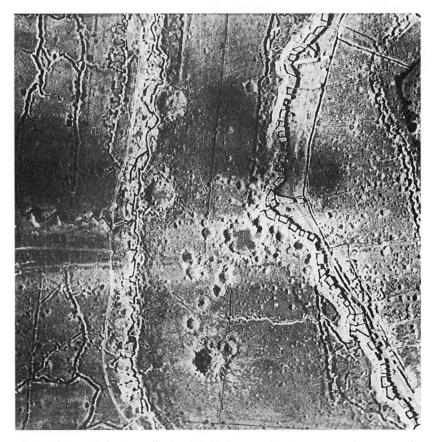

An aerial view of the Fromelles battlefield showing the German trenches captured by the Australians during the battle. Delangré Farm is to the south of the German lines. (AWM PHOTO J03376)

front line, the first wave of attackers moved forward to help their comrades consolidate their defence of the reserve enemy trenches.

The Germans set up a line of riflemen near the area known as Rouges Bancs in front of the 14th Australian Brigade's line. They were tasked with picking off the Australian officers as they led their men across the open ground. The tactic soon began to pay rich dividends. By the time the attackers had made it past the German front line and support works searching for the second line of breastworks, almost all their officers had been killed or wounded. The 53rd Battalion's leadership in the attack by now fell to a 21-year-old Duntroon graduate, Captain Charles Arblaster.

Arblaster and his men expected to see the objective they had been briefed to secure – the second and third German breastworks marked on their briefing maps around 100 metres beyond the front line – but as Bean wrote:

> they found instead, stretching away to the distance, only low open fields covered with coarse grass and traversed here and there by hedges or rows of trees. Away to the left were the broken white walls and tree stumps of Delangré Farm, which according to the original plan was to have been taken by the 8th Brigade; to the right front were one or two similar clusters receding into a distant background of trees and hedgerows.

They pushed forward, looking for their non-existent objective. However, the aerial photographs on which Haking had based his objectives were flawed – or, perhaps more accurately, the interpreters of the photos were deceived by what appeared to be a second line of breastworks. In fact it was first one, then a second, water-logged ditch or drain – at best a long-abandoned shallow trench, probably from the German's defence against Haking's disastrous attacks in the summer of 1915 but abandoned the following autumn when flooded by the River Laies. The attackers continued on still further until they were more than 250 metres past the German front line with still no second or third line of breastworks evident. Then, as Bean notes, they knew they were in a dilemma:

> By this time their leaders realised that the second or third trenches must either have been non-existent in that part of the front or else

were represented by these two ditches. Accordingly, the surviving officers stopped their men at the farther ditch and ordered them to begin rendering it defensible by cleaning it out, filling their sandbags, and placing them along its edge.

By now, the attacking troops had discovered why the Germans were able to withstand the bombardment so successfully. The German front line had comprised 75 shelters dug into the parapet, each protected by 20 centimetres of concrete, and 60 of these 75 shelters were undamaged by the Australian artillery bombardment. The Diggers also found an alleyway ten metres behind the front line that led to a series

Lieutenant Colonel Frederick Toll led the 31st Battalion at Fromelles, breaking through the enemy front lines and taking his men far into German territory in search of the non-existent second and third lines of trenches. He dug in and held on until ordered to withdraw. Toll survived Fromelles, winning the DSO for his leadership. In later fighting he won a bar to his DSO before being badly gassed at Polygon Wood and finishing the war at HQ in London. He was one of the founders of the RSL. (AWM PHOTO E01572)

of dugouts protected by an earth roof about a metre and a half thick. Another ten metres back they found far more substantial shelters. Up to six metres underground and reached by stairways, they contained large comfortable chambers and galleries. Some even had wood panelling and wallpaper, with ammunition supplies and some unexpected comforts like cigars and rations. One, taken over by Colonel Cass of the 54th Battalion as his temporary HQ, had bunks, an armchair, a stove and electric light. (As we see later, the German defensive positions were in reality far more sophisticated than the Australians believed – as revealed by British historian Peter Barton who trawled through the remarkable Munich Archives in late 2007.)

On the far left flank of the Australian attack, the 8th Brigade had made good progress since its first wave went over at 5.53 pm. The vast majority of them were seeing action for the first time and were determined to live up to the expectations of their mates and those from the other units who had already fought at Gallipoli.

Their part of no-man's land was the narrowest along the attacking line – around 100 metres – and while they suffered substantial early casualties the German front line melted away as soon as the first wave of attackers reached it. Thus, the subsequent waves of attackers had an easier time making it through the German front lines and into the meadows behind them. Like the men of the 14th Brigade on their right, the 8th Brigade troops could find no trace of the second and third German lines of breastworks. After checking well forward for the objectives and briefly attacking the German stronghold at Delangré Farm, which they found too well defended, they too fell back to a small hollow just beyond a flooded drainage ditch around 200 metres behind the German front lines. They hastily set about digging in there after being harassed by a hidden machine-gun emplacement in front of them. Their leader, Colonel Toll, then sent a message explaining his actions back to his brigade commander by the fastest way then possible – by carrier pigeon!

Despite the traumas these birds must have endured in battle, they were swift and reliable. Bean reports that they were used on many occasions during the battle, having been brought to the front from the divisional pigeon loft. They took just seventeen minutes to fly from the front lines to the divisional HQ about 8 kilometres away at Sailly-sur-la-Lys.

While his men feverishly dug in, Colonel Toll took his messenger – and the pigeon basket – and reconnoitred his front, moving ahead another 200 metres or so without seeing anything resembling the German secondary defences. When he reached a road that he recognised from the map as being well in front of the phantom objective, he halted. Toll later reported that he saw a German stronghold, which Bean believed to be the one known as Grashof, and saw small parties of the 14th Brigade away to his right but could not make contact with them. When he returned to his men Toll was concerned that the line they were creating was greatly exposed because it was out of touch with the Australian units on either side. Bean set the scene and the choices facing Toll:

The sun was setting, and from Ferme Delangré [Delangré Farm] and the houses of Les Clochers village beyond there came the incessant chatter of machine-guns. The enemy's artillery had found and was effectively shelling the unprotected troops, who were also caught by occasional shells from their own artillery. The men were consequently under no small strain, and German reinforcements could be seen moving from the rear to Delangré Farm. Concluding that the advanced position was unsafe, Toll decided at 7.14 [pm] to make his main position the old German front line, that being the only defensible work he had seen.

9

LOST IN THE FOG OF WAR

The ditch was full of wounded and dying men – like a butcher's
shop – men groaning and crying and shrieking.

DIGGER, FROMELLES, 1916

Already the key factors playing against the Australians' ability to hold
the territory they had captured were evident. First, the massive casualties
they had suffered during the attack meant that they had insufficient
numbers to man the line they held without gaps. Second, Haking's order
that they ignore the German front-line trenches and occupy the deeper
lines was already leading to major confusion and would soon expose
them to German counter-attacks from their rear. Third, they had lost
so many officers that organising the defences and coordinating between
the separate groups was extremely difficult. And fourth, communication
between the attackers and their HQs was virtually non-existent.

To add to the confusion, around 8 pm, heavy smoke started spewing
from the ammunition dumps in the 8th and 14th Brigades' support

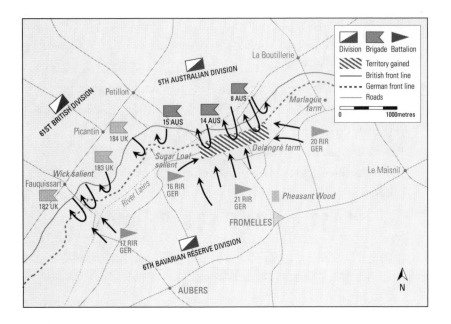

areas in the Australian lines after they were hit by artillery fire. As this smoke billowed across the battlefield it melded into the smoke rising from fires from hits on both Delangré Farm and Les Clochers. This haze combined with the setting sun to exacerbate the poor visibility that was endemic on the battlefield because of the flatness of the terrain. It was almost impossible to distinguish the different features and extremely hard for the various attacking groups to make contact with each other. Finally, it destroyed plans for the Royal Flying Corps to act as spotters for the artillery and to report back on the attackers' progress and the enemy's responses.

Back at his HQ at Sailly Chateau, General Haking had little understanding, either of the true situation on the battlefield or of the massive task facing the attackers as they tried to hold on to their small gains, as Bean wrote:

Whereas, therefore, Haking and his staff assumed that the troops would be transferring the sandbag parapet from one side to the other of an inhabited trench-line, the 8th and 14th Brigades, often knee-deep in water, were endeavouring to fill their few sandbags with mud dug from their grassy ditches. Being short of shovels, the men worked at first with entrenching tools, and so clayey was the soil that it often had to be pulled off the spade with the fingers. To build up in this fashion a defensible breastwork seemed to many of the workers an almost hopeless task.

In the Australian lines, the support troops who were waiting to carry supplies and ammunition across no-man's land to back up the attackers were also stretched to breaking point. The first support troops had followed the fourth wave of attackers across. When the German observers saw this they immediately called their artillery to focus on no-man's land and turned their journey into a deadly lottery. Bean quotes a nameless NCO who was wounded bringing across a machine gun in support:

The moment they cleared the top of the parapet it became hideous with machine-gun fire. There was a slight slope – our line [of men] ran down it, and then went splash into the ditch up to their waists in water. It was slimy, but it gave some protection. The leading Lewis [machine] gunner turned to the right and led the guns along the ditch, and then to the left along a continuation of it, which ran straight towards the German line. It was very good protection for the guns. About 40 yards along it the leader got hit in the neck by a machine-gun bullet. He choked – one of our gunners tied him up, and, with another, they lay there for half an hour or longer. The ditch was full of wounded and dying men – like a butcher's shop – men groaning and crying and shrieking.

Many of these carrying parties were sent straight to the ditches where the attackers were trying to rebuild the defences. They were then often absorbed into the digging teams, with little resistance, as few were keen to make the hazardous journey back to their own lines. Unfortunately, this meant that very few of the carriers came back for a second or subsequent load of the desperately needed supplies.

Added to this was the growing complication caused by the gaps between the four groups trying to build the temporary Australian line in German territory. Colonel Cass (of the 54th Battalion) and Colonel Toll (of the 31st) had set up their defensive positions in the old German front line because they couldn't find anywhere else that was satisfactory. The other two battalions who had made it through had dug in more than 100 metres further into German territory. So, left to right facing the Germans, the 32nd was on the left flank, forward of Toll's 31st. To their right was Cass' 54th and then, further forward, the 53rd. As

Lieutenant Eric Chinner, of the 32nd Battalion, died heroically at Fromelles. He was fighting a desperate rearguard action behind the German lines, holding off the advancing German counter-attack with grenades, when he dropped one in the act of throwing it. He was mortally wounded when he smothered the grenade rather than allow it to harm his men. (AWM PHOTO A02699)

author Les Carlyon vividly put it in his wonderful book, *The Great War*, they were 'four islands in a sea of Germans'. Perhaps even more potentially dangerous was the way the flanks of the attacking line were exposed to German counter-attack.

This danger had been anticipated by the 5th Division's CO, General McCay, at least as it related to the left flank, which he knew would be completely exposed because it was the extent of the original Australian attack. The right flank should have been supported by the 61st British troops who were attacking alongside the Australians. McCay had ordered that the 8th Brigade (making up the left side of the attack) must barricade all trenches on its flank or towards the German rear.

Lieutenant Eric Chinner, the bombing officer of the 32nd Battalion, was assigned to block and hold the old German line on the left flank. A company of the 30th Battalion was to work with the engineers on the Herculean task of digging a trench from the left of the original Australian front trenches, across no-man's land, to form part of the reconstituted front line at the old German front trenches. When the Germans saw what the Australians were trying to do, they rained artillery fire down on them and continually raked the area with machine-gun fire, causing many casualties and making progress extremely difficult. The engineers brilliantly adapted to the danger by pushing out sandbags and creating a screen against the machine-gunners and slowly proceeded with their digging.

On the positive side, on the extreme left of their line, the men of the 32nd Battalion had driven the Germans out of a communications trench they called the Kastenweg (German for 'Chest Way' because it was created by earth-filled ammunition chests). By doing this and securing the adjoining old German front line, they had temporarily secured the Australian's left flank.

But the main problem still remained: the inability of the scattered Australian groups adrift in German territory to link up with each other to protect themselves from the inevitable German counter-attacks. When a party of the 53rd Battalion, to the right of Colonel Cass' 54th Battalion, discovered that the troops occupying the trenches to its right were not Australians but Germans, things started to come unstuck. This party, now reduced to just seven unwounded men, had captured twenty Germans. It had called for reinforcements but with none in prospect, and having thrown all their grenades, they decided to withdraw back to the Australian trenches with their prisoners rather than risk being overrun. Because of the poor communications neither Cass of the 54th, nor even the remaining members of the 53rd, knew they were pulling back. The situation was fast becoming untenable, as Bean noted:

> at the front the shattered waves of the 15th Brigade were pinned down in no-man's land, and on the right flank of the 14th a section of the old German front line, after being temporarily seized, was now lying unoccupied by either side. A hundred yards beyond, in the open fields, Captain Arblaster and the advanced flank of the 53rd, utterly ignorant of the new situation in their rear, but fending off with small bombing parties the Germans whom they knew to be in the old trenches on their right, were busily digging their new front line.

By now, the British attackers were trying to improve their position. Two of their three brigade commanders sought permission from Haking to use some of their reserves and make new attacks. They would try to support their troops on the right which had penetrated the German defences and were then being counter-attacked and to break through elsewhere where they had earlier failed. Brigadier-General Carter, the commander of the 184th Brigade, which was fighting alongside the Australian 15th Brigade at the Sugar Loaf, had earlier arranged with his divisional HQ that they would concentrate their artillery on the Sugar Loaf until 9 pm and then the 184th would try to attack it again.

The ruins of a brick chimney in 1918, all that is left of Delangré Farm on the left flank of the Australian attack at Fromelles two years after the battle. Barbed-wire entanglements can be seen in the foreground. (AWM PHOTO E04044)

This photo, taken after the Armistice in 1918, shows some of the massive German blockhouses near Fromelles against which the Australians launched their attack. These fortresses were originally protected by a network of sandbags and an earthwork parapet. (AWM PHOTO E03970)

At 7.52 pm Elliott received a message from Carter: 'Am attacking at 9pm. Can your battalion co-operate?'

McCay had just given Pompey Elliott permission to use his two reserve companies of the 58th Battalion (about 250 men) to strengthen his greatly depleted attacking force. Pompey now ordered them to prepare to support the British attack on the Sugar Loaf. He moved his remaining reserves, two companies of the 57th Battalion, to move up to the reserve trench line and asked Haking to send reinforcements. Haking declined.

In the meantime, learning of the true position of the British attack, Haking decided to withdraw the whole British line back to its starting point under the cover of darkness with a view to regrouping and renewing the attack the next day. He cancelled the planned 9 pm attack on the Sugar Loaf by the 184th Brigade.

But Haking failed to inform McCay's HQ (or therefore Elliott) that he had cancelled the British attack. Bean suggests that Haking may not have been aware that Elliott had been asked to join it. The first the Australians knew of the changes was when McCay's HQ received this message from the HQ of the British division at 8.35 pm:

Under instructions from corps commander [Haking] am withdrawing from captured enemy line after dark.

The Australian HQ either misunderstood the message or failed to realise the significance of the order to Elliott and did not forward it to him. The first message Elliott received of the changed plans was at 9.25 pm, when McCay forwarded Haking's order:

61st Division not attacking tonight. General Elliott may withdraw 59th Battalion and its reinforcements if he thinks attack is not likely to succeed.

This was all very well, but by then, as Bean describes it, 'one of the bravest and most hopeless assaults ever undertaken by the Australian Imperial Force' was in full swing. Two companies of the 58th Battalion, commanded by 22-year-old Duntroon graduate, Major Arthur Hutchinson, were striding across the 400 metres of no-man's land to their deaths. The son of a Tasmanian clergyman, Hutchinson had been promoted to Major only six weeks earlier. Bean called him 'one of the finest type that his country produces'.

Hutchinson had returned from Gallipoli as a well-respected and battle-hardened captain but it would be the first time in action for the vast majority of his men, as Bean noted:

Before the actual order to advance, the men – as was often the case with Australians, especially when first in action – could be felt straining like greyhounds at the leash, and were not easily restrained from anticipating the word of command. On its being given, they went forward with splendid dash opposite the Sugar Loaf, carrying with them the survivors of the 59th, until, when they were two-thirds of the way across no-man's land, there was opened from the salient a fire of machine-guns so severe that the line was shattered and the men dazed. The survivors obtained slight cover in a ditch. As they lay there, with the terrifying din of the machine-gun bullets cracking overhead, Hutchinson, apparently in an endeavour to lift the wave farther, went on himself alone, and fell riddled by bullets close to the German wire. The two companies of the 58th which made the attack were practically annihilated.

In 1930 Elliott spoke of the event:

A message was sent to me to stop Hutchinson's attack, but this did not reach me till half an hour after he had gone forward with his two companies.

*He himself fell and most of his men were slaughtered. Proper
liaison measures should have prevented this catastrophe.*

The 15th Brigade's attack had failed totally and Elliott advised
McCay accordingly. McCay passed the news on to Haking, then ordered
Elliott to reorganise the defence of his original front line and to start
work on a trench across no-man's land aimed at connecting with the
right flank of the neighbouring 14th Brigade. For the 15th, the attack
had ended and the awful work of bringing in their wounded from no-
man's land now began.

Some time earlier, on the other side of the Australian advanced
line, the Germans had mounted a strong counter-attack against the

German dead in their front-line trenches after the battle at Fromelles. This is one
of a series of photos taken by an unknown German officer and given to an
Australian POW, Captain Charles Mills, by that officer after the Armistice. (AWM
PHOTO A01559)

32nd Battalion. The Australians called for artillery support but the inexperience of their gunners showed and the Australians found themselves peppered by drop-shorts. McCay was forced to order his artillery to lengthen its range, first by 200 yards and then, when the problem persisted, by 500 yards. Forsaken by their artillery, the 32nd called for reinforcements, ammunition, water and 'sandbags in their thousands'. Through a series of outstanding individual acts of bravery and initiative, the Australians held off the first German counter-attack on their left flank. Captain Frank Krinks of the 30th Battalion arrived with a carrying party and, seeing how desperate the situation was, took a group of men to some shell holes near the German position and from there sniped heavily at them, relieving the pressure on the Australian defenders. Another officer from the 30th, Lieutenant Tom Barbour, organised his men to collect ammunition from the dead and wounded to create a much-needed alternative supply.

Some relief came around 9.30 pm when reinforcements from the 55th Battalion arrived to join Colonel Cass. While they bolstered the Australian defence, they still didn't solve the problem of the gaps in their line. Indeed, Cass still wasn't aware that part of the 53rd Battalion had withdrawn, leaving a section of the trench to his right unmanned. Soon German counter-attackers entered this section and moved along it throwing grenades. Australian volunteers from Arblaster's mob forward of the German front line circled behind the trench line and sheltered in bomb craters as they threw grenades at the Germans from their rear, prompting a fierce grenade fight. Eventually, the Australians ran out of grenades and moved back to their trenches.

The Germans had cut into the Australian right flank, although again because of the lack of communications, Cass was not aware of it. Eventually, around 10.10 pm, Lieutenant Colonel David McConaghy, CO of the 55th Battalion, checked out the position and found it in enemy hands. He arranged for his men to pull down sandbags from the parapets to form 'bomb blocks' along the trench and protected them with snipers and bombers – a lesson from Gallipoli that temporarily secured the situation by around 11 pm.

The situation improved in the 14th Brigade's area when their engineers broke through to them with their communications trench. It had been a prodigious feat under the most hazardous conditions and allowed a reasonable flow of supplies in relative safety. But, further to the left, the 8th Brigade's situation was deteriorating. All the carrying parties had remained with the defenders after making the dangerous trip across no-man's land, cutting short the flow of ammunition and supplies. By just after 10 pm, the 30th Battalion's CO, Lieutenant Colonel James Clark, reported that he had sent off the last of his carriers and that none had returned. So, while the 14th's supplies were still trickling through, those to the 8th had virtually dried up.

In addition, the conditions in the trenches began to worsen as the level of water seeping through them rose after the Laies stream became blocked and damaged by the constant shelling. Some later claimed that they believed the Germans were to blame and that they had some special system of damming the water. The mud and the water made life in the trenches miserable and some men who were hit almost drowned as they pitched into the pools of sludge and had to be pulled out by their mates. The conditions also began to affect their weapons. Many began hoarding rifles taken from the dead and wounded in case their own weapons misfired. And as darkness fell the scene took on a ghostly atmosphere as visibility was confined to eerie snapshots provided by shell flashes, incendiary bombs and the occasional flare.

Back at McCay's HQ, confusion reigned as conflicting messages revealed that the artillery had believed that Delangré Farm, a German stronghold on the Australian left, had been captured by the Australians. The artillery had consequently withheld fire from this target. McCay

A 1918 view of no-man's land at Fromelles, from the north-eastern corner of the Sugar Loaf looking towards the line from which the 15th Brigade attacked. The vast field of fire available to the German machine-gunners from the Sugar Loaf is clearly evident. (AWM PHOTO E04030)

immediately ordered them to shell it heavily, which they did but with little success.

By midnight the overall situation along the Australian advanced line was perilous. The two main groups, the 54th Battalion on the right and the 31st and 32nd Battalions on the left, had taken positions in the German support trenches in the area behind the old German front line. The gap between the two groups was where there had been a previous gap in the original German support system.

Haking's order, that the attacking force leap-frog over the old German front line without garrisoning it, was now to prove a fatal mistake. His assumption that the attackers could simply move the sandbags from one side of the German trenches to the other to create

This Digger was killed in the second German line at Fromelles. The photo was taken the morning after the battle by a German officer and given to an Australian POW, Captain Charles Mills, after the Armistice. (AWM PHOTO A01566)

protection was another serious error. When the Diggers tried to move the bags they generally fell apart because they were so rotten with age and water damage. And their attempts to make more sandbags were largely negated by the impossibly glutinous Flanders clay that clung like cement to their shovels. At one point Toll's men resorted to stacking German dead to plug one gap in their defensive wall.

About 11.40 pm, the Germans counter-attacked again, putting extreme pressure on the Australian right flank, which by this time was held by about 200 men. For the first time, Cass discovered that he had no support to his right and was thus completely exposed there. Then the defenders realised that some of them were being shot from behind as the Germans began to encircle them. The enemy was seen

German soldiers reoccupy their second line on the morning of 20 July 1916 after driving out the Australian attackers during the previous night. Another photo later given to Australian POW, Captain Charles Mills. (AWM PHOTO A01562)

moving down its old front-line trenches, between the advanced Australians and their lines.

Arblaster's mob now came under attack and was soon completely cut off. Realising their only chance of salvation was to turn and charge the Germans in their front line, the young leader distributed all the grenades and led his men over the top. As soon as they cleared their cover, they were caught in a terrific hail of machine-gun fire and the gallant Arblaster fell, mortally wounded. The survivors crawled back to their original haven and waited.

Cass now knew the situation was critical, as his message back at 3.45 am indicated:

Position very serious. 53rd now retiring. Enemy behind them and in their old front line ... and within 100 yards of my right.

Indeed, the 53rd was now withdrawing across no-man's land under heavy fire and the communications trench supplying Cass was under immediate threat from the rapidly advancing enemy. An old bushie from Wagga, Sergeant Frank Stringer, rose to the occasion. He jumped up on the parapet and inspired his badly shaken comrades with a withering display of rifle shooting, sending the enemy scattering. Many of his men joined him on the parapet and drove the Germans back hurling their grenades 'like cricketers throwing at a wicket'.

But it was only a temporary reprieve and at 4.20 am the ever-cool Cass despatched the following:

Position almost desperate. Have got 55th and a few of the 54th together and have temporarily checked enemy. But do get our guns to work at once, please. The 53rd have lost confidence temporarily and will not willingly stand their ground. Some appear to be breaking across no-man's land. If they give way to my right rear, I must withdraw or be surrounded.

Luckily, a group then appeared from the Australian lines with a substantial supply of grenades and they attacked the advancing Germans. As Bean wrote:

there followed a Herculean bomb-fight, in which they beat down the Bavarian attack and for the time being thoroughly subdued the enemy in his old front line.

One witness claimed there were up to twelve grenades in the air at any given time during this furious exchange, and Bean reports that one Bavarian bomber later told the Crown Prince of Germany that he had personally thrown more than 500.

Despite this setback the Germans continued to infiltrate behind the Australian advanced line and started firing on them from their largely unprotected rear.

At the other end of the Australian advanced line, the German reserves that had been gathering at Delangré Farm now launched themselves on the Australian left flank. Captain Charles Mills of the 31st Battalion was wounded and taken prisoner when he was suddenly surrounded and Lieutenant Eric Chinner, after some gallant defensive work, was mortally wounded after he heroically smothered a grenade that he dropped when he was hit in the act of throwing it. Under the overwhelming pressure of the encircling counter-attack, the Australians holding the area near the Kastenweg were forced back. This left the neighbouring 32nd Battalion surrounded. Like Arblaster's men on the other flank, the 32nd had no option but to turn and charge through the encirclement. Around 150 of these men tried to break out, through a terrifying cross-fire – from the front, side and rear – across no-man's land aiming for the Australian lines. Only a handful made it to the relative safety of the partly finished communication trench that their engineers had built during the night three-parts of the way to the old German front line.

Many smaller groups of the Australians had not received the order to withdraw and they were quickly overwhelmed and either shot or taken prisoner.

In one remarkable attempt to reach safety, a group of eleven men of the 8th Brigade, under the leadership of Captain Frank Krinks, decided to make a run for it as a group, vowing to stay and help any of their number who found trouble. Having decided to leave their weapons and rely on a surprise dash to safety, they struck trouble in the second German trench when two of them were captured. But, as they had promised, the others turned on the captors and frightened the stunned

Germans into releasing them. They then bolted into no-man's land. Krinks and three companions eventually reached safety in the front of the British trenches. But, as Bean noted, there was a tragic sequel:

> *The 30th Battalion was immediately after the fight sent to reserve, but Krinks and his three companions returned to the trenches as soon as it was dusk, and, taking a stretcher, went out into no-man's land to find their [wounded] comrades. In this they succeeded, and were bringing in Wells on a stretcher when a sentry of their own brigade, catching sight of their figures, fired, killing Wishart and Watts with a single shot.*

Elsewhere, pockets of Diggers on the Australian advanced left flank continued fighting for some hours until, one by one, they were captured or killed. The gallant Cass and his band were still holding on by their fingernails on the right flank when Haking finally decided to abandon the attack completely. By the time the order to withdraw reached Cass about 6.30 am, his men had already told him that the 8th Brigade had gone. Bean captured the mood:

> *The retirement of the 8th Brigade, however, had been seen from parts of the line, and had cast a marked shadow over the spirits of the remaining troops. Probably failure had really been inevitable ever since the repulse at the Sugar Loaf, but it was not until this moment that, for most of those engaged, the operation took on a hopeless aspect.*

Cass knew his position was untenable even though his men had just managed to withstand yet another surging counter-attack. He was not surprised to receive this order from his brigade commander, Colonel Harold Pope:

One of the heroes of the Fromelles battle, Lieutenant Colonel Walter Cass (right), at Gallipoli with Padre Dexter of the 1st Division AIF. Cass led the 54th Battalion at Fromelles with distinction, setting up a field HQ behind the German lines and achieving his pre-battle objective. One of the last to leave, he made it back safely to his lines but never fully recovered from the ordeal. Cass was invalided back to England and never saw action again. (AWM PHOTO J02530)

Be prepared to withdraw on the order being given. The old German line will be held to the end. Make arrangements to dribble men in very small parties back through sap [a communication trench] across no-man's land to our front line. Make no move until I send the word 'withdraw'.

Colonel Cass ordered his machine-gunners back one at a time and assigned the courageous Captain Norm Gibbins and 55 men to act as a rearguard to try to protect their withdrawal. Sadly, as so often happens in the confusion of battle, communications broke down. Cass did not receive the order to withdraw until 7.50 am, although it had reached 14th Brigade HQ by 6.30 am and the forward report-centre by 7.30 am, well after the covering artillery barrage started at 5.40 am. This unaccounted delay contributed greatly to the massive casualties suffered by Cass' men when they eventually tried to fight their way back to their own lines.

By that stage, Bob Chapman and Norman Gibbins were the only officers left of B Company of the 55th Battalion. Chapman later wrote in his diary:

coming through the dusk on our left we saw Germans. Our machine guns opened fire. But word came from the right that they were our men. During the night some of our own men had been found stripped of their clothing and apparently spies were sending false messages. However, although we accounted for a good many, the enemy got in on our left. Then came the sound of bombing. We were being driven in on either flank … As they came our artillery put a couple of shots over, and the 31st Battalion, thinking our own artillery was shelling them, in a body left the trench and retired to our own lines. I got to the tail end just in time to get them back again but the majority left.

Capt Gibbins came along then and we both went round the trench and found it all clear. The men were then extended on the left again – but still the bombers came.

'Get as many bombs as you can – and come with me' said Gib. So I got all the bombs I could – called to some men to follow. Gib led the way on the outside of the parapet. We shifted those bombers – but poor old Gib got a wound in the head and had to retire. Robinson turned back to our own trench to get reinforcements – but they would not come. I took charge of the bombing party and as the Boche had dropped bombs for the present and taken to rifle fire we had to take shelter in the trench. We waited there for perhaps a quarter of an hour ready to bomb Fritz should he come again. But the order came to retire ...

I borrowed a rifle from one of the troops passing and sniped at Fritz till he got up to me with his bombs. It was then time to go so I had to. My return is a bit blurred. I remember picking my way through barbed wire with rifles cracking around me. At one place the grass in front of me was shaking and quivering. I looked at it for a second and realised that a machine gun was playing through there – so I jumped and hurried on. I got in all right and as the trench was becoming too crowded I sent what 55th men I could back into the support. As soon as the enemy saw our men making use of the gap they opened fire with high explosives. 'Crack-crack' came whistling over our heads but we leaned against the parapet and were comparatively safe.

Chapman, Gibbins and the survivors tried to cross no-man's land in small parties, through the crowded communication trench, by crawling from one shell hole to the next or by making a dash for it. Some men's luck ran out tantalisingly close to safety. One badly wounded man crawled across no-man's land and was within metres of rescue when he was hit in the back and killed by a dud artillery shell.

All the while, the rearguard led by Gibbins gave covering fire and attacked with grenades. Cass was among the last to leave and get clear. Gibbins was the last to leave his trench and followed at the tail of his men as they made their way along the communications trench. They had almost reached the Australian lines when they came across a mass of injured Diggers who blocked the exit from the communications trench to the Australian front line. Gibbins tried to by-pass the blockage by hopping over the parapet. Tragically, as he made his final step to safety, he was struck by a bullet to the head and killed instantly.

Chapman concluded his diary note on the battle by writing of Gibbins:

> I have never known a braver man than he. If ever a man died bravely doing his duty old Gib did. Well, so ends the first fight. I am the only officer left in B Company. About 25% of the Battalion are either killed or wounded – but our losses were light in comparison to some. The 60th Btn. have only 61 men and one officer left.

Bob Chapman was awarded the Military Cross for his bravery during the battle. He was wounded in November 1916 and sent to hospital in England to recover. He returned to France, now promoted to captain and given command of B Company of the 55th Battalion. Sadly, at 30 years of age, he was killed in action on 12 March 1917 near Bernafay Wood. His grave is in the Bernafay British Cemetery, Montauban.

10

DON'T FORGET ME, COBBER!

I've been talking to dead men for days. There was two men came up to speak to me who carried their heads under their arms.

Captain R. Hugh Knyvett, *Over There with the Australians*, 1917

So the attack on Fromelles had ended in complete failure. And worse was to come. Some small groups had not received the order to withdraw and fought to the last. Others refused to retreat and fought on until they were killed or ran out of ammunition and were overwhelmed and captured. Some, defenceless because they had run out of ammunition and grenades, surrendered in the face of certain death. Still others, like Lieutenant Robert Burns of the 14th Machine-Gun Company, heir to the Burns Philp shipping fortune, refused to surrender. He smashed his gun and, with a few of his surviving men, tried to make his way back. He was killed and his body never found.

An immediate post-war view of the German concrete blockhouses along the Aubers ridgeline, towards which the Australians attacked on 19 July 1916. (AWM PHOTO E03969)

From the Australian lines, the Diggers saw some isolated defenders vainly signalling for reinforcements for some hours. But at 9.20 am, the Bavarians reported to their HQ:

The last of the Englishmen who were defending themselves have been captured.

In fact it's interesting to view the proceedings through German eyes. Major-General Julius Ritter von Braun compiled the history of the 21BRIR from its war diaries. It provides a snapshot from the enemy's perspective, on 19 July 1916:

7 pm. Several enemy divisions are attacking the three left units of the division. In the third unit the attack is being completely repulsed; in the fourth unit, it is only temporarily successful. On the other hand, the enemy is managing to penetrate the second unit [RIR21], initially near C [11th Company], where their artillery and heavy mortars have swept away the barriers, levelled the defence installations and destroyed most of the garrison. From here the enemy is spreading southwards to sub-unit D, where the 12th Company is blocking its continued advance in a heroic battle, and northwards towards unit 2B. There they are gradually pushing 10th Company, which they are simultaneously attacking on the front in fresh waves, back over the front end of the Kastenweg. Only here are the remaining forces of 10th and 9th Company, which will soon receive backup from the left flank company of Reserve Infantry Regiment 20, able to seal off the position. The enemy is also making deep advances in Kastenweg as far as Toten Sau Heights and to the south-west as far as the vicinity of Hofgarten, Grashof and even as far as 200 m from Brandhof. But then all attempts to secure further territory are being frustrated by our artillery fire and the accurate and superior fire of our infantrymen and the machine gunners from Toten Sau, Schmitzhofe, the left flank of the Türkenecke base and from Brandhof. Unfortunately, the Grashof base is still not ready and therefore unoccupied.

The article goes on to report that reserves were deployed in a counter-attack, which although initially unsuccessful, tried again.

The difficulty of communicating in pitch blackness, made all the more uncertain by the smoke from exploding shells, as well as the heavy deployment of hand grenades, is initially delaying progress. Only after the pioneers move in new munitions does the attack proceed, slowly at first, then more fiercely despite all the resistance of the enemy who have entrenched themselves and are bringing in fresh forces.

The German report notes that by around 7 am the following morning they controlled the position once again. It also reported that the dense ground fog, which greeted the next day

prevented a large section of the enemy forces from surveying the situation. Having left it too late to retreat, they are now finding their retreat path blocked.

Three Australian dead in the German lines after the battle at Fromelles, taken on the morning of 20 July 1916, perhaps at the site of a temporary aid post, as indicated by the bandages and the fact that some of the Diggers' boots have been removed. (AWM PHOTO A01565)

The firing began to ease around midday as both sides began to take stock, doing what they could to rescue their wounded and taking prisoners back behind the front lines. The German positions were substantially damaged as their war diaries noted:

Our own position and the Kastenweg look very bad, as well as the railway track running behind our position. It requires extensive improvements, including re-railing to a large degree. The paradoses have been extensively damaged by our own mortars and batteries during the counter-attack. New work is in progress.

On the other side, the Australian front line was a scene straight from Hades. Hugh Knyvett was there:

The sight of our trenches that next morning is burned into my brain. Here and there a man could stand upright, but in most places if you did not wish to be exposed to a sniper's bullet you had to progress on your hands and knees. If you had gathered the stock of a thousand butcher-shops, cut it into small pieces and strewn it about, it would give you a faint conception of the shambles these trenches were.

One did not ask the whereabouts of brother or chum. If we did not see him, then it were best to hope that he were of the dead.

One of the beloved figures in the 14th Brigade, the Reverend Spencer Maxted, Chaplain of the 54th Battalion, was killed as he worked tirelessly comforting the wounded. He had refused to stay in the safety of the rear echelons and went out with the first stretcher-bearers into no-man's land.

The Division's medical staff had established twelve regimental aid posts (RAPs), six of which were moved forward with the assault battalions and operated from about 500 metres behind the Australian front line. They handled the casualties from no-man's land, those brought back from behind the enemy lines and those wounded by shelling behind the Australian lines.

The RAPs provided rudimentary treatment: morphia for pain, temporary control of bleeding, dressing open wounds, treating shell-shock and splinting broken limbs. They then sorted the wounded into 'walking' or 'stretcher' cases. The walking wounded were sent on to an aid post further to the rear while the stretcher cases were loaded on to horse-drawn or motor wagons and either taken to advanced dressing stations some kilometres to the rear or sent further back to main dressing stations, out of range of the enemy's artillery. The frantic work of the medical staff is evident from the final tallies which show they handled, on average, one casualty every minute, non-stop for 56 hours! A total of 3277 wounded passed through the main dressing stations from noon on 19 July to 8 pm on 21 July.

The reality was that, from midnight on the day of the battle, the flow of casualties had swamped the capacity of the medical staff and the stretcher-bearers and the front-line trenches were chock full of the wounded and dying. Even there they were still in a perilous position until they could be recovered, as the enemy shelling continued randomly. While the front lines were a confusion of wounded and dying, many more still lay exposed in no-man's land. The communications trenches in front of each brigade's lines were full of them. Bean, who had rushed to Fromelles from the Somme when he heard about the battle, was greatly moved:

> *Especially in front of the 15th Brigade, around the Laies, the wounded could be seen raising their limbs in pain or turning hopelessly, hour after hour, from one side to the other ...*
>
> *There followed a stillness never again experienced by the 5th Division in the front trenches. The sight of the wounded lying*

tortured and helpless in no-man's land, within a stone's throw of
safety but apparently without hope of it, made so strong an appeal
that more than one Australian, taking his life in his hands, went
out to tend them.

The Diggers organised rescue parties, and once darkness fell they crept out on their hands and knees and scoured no-man's land to try to find and bring back those who were still alive. The sheer numbers of the wounded meant that they quickly ran out of stretchers and were forced to carry the rescued on their backs. Hugh Knyvett was one of them.

One lad, who looked about fifteen, called to me: 'Don't leave me
sir.' I said: 'I will come back for you sonny', as I had a man on
my back at the time. In that waste of dead one wounded man was
like a gem in sawdust – just as hard to find.

Four trips I made before I found him, then it was as if I had
found my young brother. Both of his legs had been broken, and he
was only a schoolboy, one of those overgrown lads who had added
a couple of years in declaring his age to get into the army. But the
circumstances brought out his youth, and he clung to me as though I
were his father. Nothing I have ever done has given me the joy that
the rescuing of that lad did, and I do not even know his name.

At one stage Knyvett heard a groan. Unbelievably, he claimed this was a rarity. For, despite their terrible injuries, the wounded tried everything they could not to cry out.

Why. Some had gritted teeth on bayonets, others had stuffed their
tunics in their mouths, lest they should groan. Someone had written
of the Australian soldier, in the early part of the war, that 'they

never groan' and these men who had read that would rather die than not live up to the reputation that some newspaper correspondent had given them.

Knyvett witnessed one extraordinary act of bravery during the rescue. He describes an unnamed sergeant (most likely Alexander Gordon Ross of the 57th Battalion, a former horse tamer from Geelong) who was with him when they found a badly wounded man on the German barbed wire:

when we tried to pick him up, one by the shoulders and the other by the feet, it almost seemed that we would pull him apart. The blood was gushing from his mouth, where he had bitten through lips and tongue, so that he might not jeopardise, by groaning, the chances of some other man who was less badly wounded than he.

He begged us to put him out of his misery, but we were determined we would give him his chance, though we did not expect him to live.

But the sergeant threw himself down on the ground and made of his body a human sledge. Some others joined us and we put the wounded man on his back and dragged them thus across no-man's land, through the broken barbed wire and shell-torn ground, where every few inches there was a piece of jagged shell, and in and out of the shell holes.

So anxious were we to get to safety that we did not notice the condition of the man underneath until we got to our trenches; then it was hard to see which was the worse wounded of the two. The sergeant had his hands, face and body torn to ribbons, and we had never guessed it, for never once did he ask us to 'go slow' or 'wait a bit'. Such is the stuff that men are made of.

Sergeant Ross won the Distinguished Service Medal for his gallantry in the rescue. His recommendation read:

During a raid made by a party from the 57th Battalion on the enemy's trenches near PETILLON on the night of the 19th of August 1916, Sergt. Ross displayed great gallantry in reconnaissance work before the trenches were entered. Whilst in the trenches he set an example of absolute fearlessness in leading his party. During the retirement of the party when heavy casualties were suffered crossing 'NO MAN'S LAND' and whilst his enemy's barrage was at its height, Sergt Ross went backwards and forwards repeatedly whilst assisting in the return of the party and the rescue of the wounded men. In addition, this N.C.O. has on many occasions during the three months, July–September at PETILLON, conducted most daring reconnaissance as a patrol leader along the enemy's wire and has repeatedly gained valuable information.

He served from beginning to end of the GALLIPOLI Campaign and did good service throughout.

The recommendation was signed by Pompey Elliott and the award was signed by McCay.

On another occasion Hugh Knyvett found himself in a shell hole with a wounded man who was trapped waist-deep in the mud. Seeing his rescuer, he cried out:

It's so good matey to see a real live man again. I've been talking to dead men for days. There was two men came up to speak to me who carried their heads under their arms.

Unfortunately, the delighted man's booming voice attracted the attention of the German machine-gunners, who peppered the edge of the hole as Knyvett held his man down. No matter how hard Knyvett tried to quieten him, the man yabbered on, even as they dug him out and slipped into a neighbouring shell hole during a lull in the firing. When they had him at last in a stretcher and were trying to silently edge their way back to their lines, the man found his full voice again:

> To cap it all, our passenger broke into song, and we just dropped in time as the bullets pinged over us. These did not worry our friend on the stretcher, nor did the bump hurt him, for he cheerfully shouted 'Down go my horses!'

During this rescue period, an event took place in front of the 8th Brigade's lines where the line was held by the 29th Battalion that could have saved countless further loss of life and suffering. There are a number of variations of the story but Bean's account is that one of the 29th's privates, Billy Miles, a 36-year-old sailor who had fought in the Boer War, was searching for one of his officers, Captain Ken Mortimer, in no-man's land near the German front line when he heard a voice from the enemy lines call out to him in English. The speaker was a Saxon officer who spoke English fluently and asked Miles what he was supposed to be doing. He was tending his wounded, Miles answered, giving them water and making them comfortable until they could be brought back in.

Miles had taken the precaution of wearing a Red Cross arm badge and when the German queried him as to whether he was laying wires, he replied that the Red Cross was always allowed to go about its work unmolested. The German made him stand with his hands in the air while he spoke on a field telephone to his headquarters. Then he asked Miles his rank. Learning he was 'just a private sir', he told him to return to his own lines and bring back an officer.

We will have a parlementaire and see if we can arrange about collecting the wounded.

Promising he would return, Miles hurried back to the Australian lines where he found Captain John McArthur and explained what had happened. McArthur called for a ceasefire along his line and arranged for a rough Red Cross (made from red paper on a board covered with newspaper) to be hoisted above the parapet.

Billy Miles was joined by his company commander, Major Alexander Murdoch, on the journey back to the German wire. On the way out through no-man's land both men distributed as many water bottles as they could carry to their wounded. Soldiers from both front lines watched in silence as they reached the German line. Murdoch asked if they could arrange an informal truce. The Bavarian officer politely replied that he didn't have the authority but would phone through a request to his superiors. The answer came back swiftly. The Germans agreed on the basis that each side's stretcher-bearers would work in their half of no-man's land. Murdoch was to seek his superiors' permission, and if it was granted to return blindfolded to be held as a hostage until the operation was completed in good faith.

Murdoch and Miles returned and telephoned the proposal through to McCay's HQ. While they waited for the response, an informal truce had organically spread along the line. The Australians started leaving their trenches and bringing in wounded close-by and the Germans followed suit. But McCay ordered that the truce be refused. He would later claim he had no option under the 'definiteness of the G.H.Q. orders' to the effect that 'no negotiations of any kind, and on any subject, were to be had with the enemy'. He also claimed that he mentioned his actions subsequently to Generals Haking and Monro and they both supported his action. Bean took a sanguine view:

Lt Simon Fraser of the 57th Battalion, who, as a sergeant, helped rescue hundreds of wounded Diggers from no-man's-land after the battle at Fromelles. He is immortalised by Peter Corlett's evocative Cobbers statue that stands in the grounds of the Australian Memorial Park outside Fromelles. (AWM PHOTO 05926)

In any case, even if he disagreed with the settled policy of his chiefs, he could not disobey their orders or even temporise, unless he was prepared to go back to his country and – at the risk of raising internal dissention in a perilous time – justify his action before his people.

In his inimitable fashion, Bean added:

The horror of knowing that a mate – his living body the prey of flies and ants – is being slowly done to death within two minutes of the succour, to which, without military disadvantage, he could be brought, is less present to distant staffs than to officers and men in the line, and was estimated (though doubtless only after severe internal conflict) as a trifle when balanced against the mighty issues at stake; yet the memory of such horrors lingering in millions of minds unquestionably

leads sometimes, in the long run, to results beside which even the
great war-time issues may seem unimportant.

Whatever his rationale, whatever his constraints, McCay earned
the life-long enmity of his men for refusing the chance to rescue the
wounded. As a result, not only did many of the wounded suffer
unnecessarily agonising deaths, a great many of their mates were killed
and wounded over the following days as they exposed themselves to
try to reach them.

For days after the battle, Diggers heard their mates calling plaintively
from no-man's land. Single men and small groups sneaked out each
night trying to find them and bring them back. On the night of
20 July alone, more than 300 wounded from the 15th Brigade were
brought in by organised parties of stretcher-bearers. Bean highlights the
work of one of these rescuers, 40-year-old Victorian farmer, Sergeant
Simon Fraser of the 57th Battalion, and quotes from a letter Fraser
later wrote him:

It was no light work getting in with a heavy weight on your back,
especially if he had a broken leg or arm and no stretcher bearer was
handy. You had to lie down and get him on your back; then rise and
duck for your life with the chance of getting a bullet in you before
you were safe.

Fraser recalled finding a group of wounded near the German line
and, after bringing them in safely, hearing another call for help. He
went out again and eventually found this man too. He was a big
strapping man wounded in the thigh – too heavy for Fraser to carry
on his back – so he helped him into a sheltering shell hole and
promised to return with a stretcher. As he moved off, he heard another

wounded Digger nearby call: 'Don't forget me, cobber!'. Fraser was able to return with stretchers and bring them both in safely.

The cry, 'don't forget me, cobber!' has come to symbolise the selfless devotion of those who risked, and often lost, their lives to bring in their wounded mates. It is the title of Robin Corfield's prodigious work of research on the Battle of Fromelles and it prompted the wonderful sculpture by Peter Corlett that today stands in the Australian Memorial Park at Fromelles. This statue immortalises Simon Fraser's heroism and stands as a superb symbol of the sacrifice and devotion that characterised the battle and its aftermath. Fraser survived Fromelles and was promoted to lieutenant in April 1917. Sadly, he fell at the battle of Bullecourt and, ironically, his body was never found.

11

COUNTING THE COST

*Each grave will be marked by a piece of wood or anything suitable
and on this will be written the Chaplain's initials and a number.
He will thus have a tally.*

OFFICIAL INSTRUCTION FROM ADJUTANT-GENERAL TO
CHAPLAINS, 1916

On the afternoon of 20 July, the battalions which had attacked the
previous evening gathered near their divisional headquarters and their
losses were chillingly clear. Each of the three Australian brigades lost
more than 1700 men, either killed, wounded, missing or captured. In
one terrifying night the Australians suffered a total of 5533 casualties
– 178 officers and 5355 men. This was more than the combined total
of all Australian losses in the Boer, Korean and Vietnam Wars. The
British lost 1547 killed or wounded while the German casualties totalled
less than 1500.

That toughest of campaigners, Pompey Elliott, could not contain his grief and tears poured down his cheeks as he shook hands with the shattered survivors of his 15th Brigade. His 60th Battalion had gone into the battle with 887 men. One officer and 106 Diggers emerged unscathed to answer the roll call.

The other brigades suffered similarly. The 32nd Battalion, from the 8th Brigade, also lost around 90% of its fighting strength – 701 Diggers and 17 officers. In addition, each of the 31st, 53rd, 54th, and 59th Battalions lost more than 500 Diggers and around 20 of their officers.

While the Australians faced continual fire over the following days as they tried to rescue their wounded from no-man's land, the Germans facing the British to the right of the Australian line allowed them to bring theirs in unhindered in some parts of their line. The 2/5th Gloucesters worked at it for four days, even in broad daylight, and their stretcher-bearers were not fired on.

Remarkably, even after the Australians had stopped sending out recovery parties, having found no further wounded alive, stragglers continued to come in many days, even weeks, later. Some of these survived by dipping their tunics in puddles and sucking in the moisture, crawling a few metres at a time from one shell hole to the next. Some made it to the Australian lines with maggots crawling in their wounds.

In his biography of Roy Harrison, Neville Kidd quotes from a letter of 7 July 1930 from the Regimental Medical Officer of the 57th Battalion, Dr Hugh Rayson of Manilla, NSW, that he wrote to the Official Medical Historian, Colonel A.G. Butler:

During the next week wounded continued to come down as a result of the battle of the 19th; these men had been rescued from No Man's Land. As far as I can remember the last man recovered alive reached

*my post 9 or 10 days after the battle. He had been wounded in both
legs and one arm. He told me that he had managed to drag himself
to a shell hole in which there was a little water. He had not been
able to reach the water himself but had been able to keep his thirst
down by sucking a strip of tunic which he had soaked in the shell-hole
water; by sucking very nearly continuously he had been able to get
just sufficient water to keep him alive ...*

*An outstanding feature of my experience during this operation
was the truly marvellous fortitude of the men who were wounded.
I can hardly remember one man complaining even though in great
pain. I found one man in the front line about two days after the
battle who had the lower part of his face shot away; the lower and
upper jaws, nose and, I think, one eye had been destroyed. By signs
he made me understand that he wanted a drink. It was literally
impossible to decide where to put the water bottle. And yet he was
on his feet attempting to seek help.*

Some of the greatest heroics of the entire battle were displayed by
those rescuing the wounded. Many of the chaplains of the battalions
of the 5th Division distinguished themselves during the rescues. Indeed,
the padre of the 53rd Battalion, Father John Kennedy, was awarded
the DSO and the padres of the 60th and the 54th Battalions, Father
John Gilbert and the Reverend Spencer Maxted, each won the MC
for their actions. (Another, Father Gerard Tucker, went on to be one
of the founders of the Church of England's esteemed charity, The
Brotherhood of St Laurence, during the Great Depression.) The
chaplains at Fromelles worked faithfully in the most dangerous
conditions, in the front lines, helping to recover wounded from no-
man's land, often as stretcher-bearers, tending the wounded and burying
the dead. This melancholy duty was outlined in an official instruction
from the Adjutant-General to the chaplains:

Headstones at Rue Petillon Military Cemetery, showing some of the many nationalities who fell on the Western Front. Major Royal Harrison is one of 291 Australians who rest here. (PATRICK LINDSAY PHOTO)

Bodies will be collected by the burying parties, the identification discs will be removed after all the particulars have been noted on a label supplied for the purpose and this label will be securely attached to the body. The chaplains or other conducting the funeral services will make a careful note of the names of those whom they bury in communal graves. Each grave will be marked by a piece of wood or anything suitable and on this will be written the Chaplain's initials and a number. He will thus have a tally. Details would then be passed to Graves Registration Unit No. 1 Bailleul with a list of the men buried in the said grave.

Sadly, the Reverend Maxted lost his life when hit by a stray shell after he had fallen asleep exhausted in the front line.

The remarkable courage shown by so many of those who attacked on 19 July 1916 and those who helped to rescue the wounded in the following days was recognised by the number of bravery awards made to them. More than 200 men won medals. The Australian 5th Division won 11 Distinguished Service Orders, 46 Military Crosses, 35 Distinguished Conduct Medals, 50 Military Medals, 36 Mentions-in-Despatches and 15 foreign awards.

Major Arthur Hutchinson, the young Duntroon graduate who had led his men of the 58th Battalion on their tragically futile charge against the Sugar Loaf after the main attack, was recommended by Pompey Elliott for a posthumous Victoria Cross:

> At Petillon on the night 19th/20th July 1916, Major Hutchinson displayed conspicuous and gallant leadership. On the evening of the 19th/20th July 1916, a message came from the 5th Division that the 61st Division on our right would renew the attack at 9 pm on the Sugar Loaf salient and notwithstanding that the previous attack by a battalion had manifestly failed, Major Hutchinson led the two companies of the 58th Battalion under his command in the most gallant manner under an appalling fire until he fell riddled with machine-gun bullets close to the German parapet. His life and the lives of his men were gallantly given in the hope of aiding the attack of the 61st Division, which unfortunately was not made.

McCay supported the award but inexplicably the file is marked 'no trace of award'. Some experts have suggested the slight that Pompey's recommendation contained against the men of the British 61st Division may have led to the recommendation being buried in the higher echelons of power.

Of the 496 Australians captured by the Germans during the Battle of Fromelles, 38 died of their wounds. The rest were marched back through Fromelles along the Aubers Ridge, first to Fournes and then on to Lille, where they were paraded before the townspeople as an exercise in propaganda. The prisoners were photographed by an officer of the Bavarian 16RIR, shortly after the battle and during the parade through Lille and its suburbs. The officer later gave the photos to an Australian POW, Captain Charles Mills of the 31st Battalion, who he had befriended when Mills acted as liaison between the POWs and their captives. Mills was released to Switzerland in late 1917 and returned with the Red Cross to Germany after the war trying to trace missing Australian POWs. He gave the photos to the Australian War Memorial.

Australian prisoners, captured behind the German lines at Fromelles, waiting at a collecting station before being paraded through Lille and taken to captivity in Germany. (AWM PHOTO A01547)

Disillusioned and bewildered Australian POWs march into a holding station on the morning after the Battle of Fromelles on their way to two years of captivity in Germany. (AWM PHOTO A01552)

Australian POWs captured at Fromelles being paraded through the streets of Lille for propaganda purposes in the days after the battle. (AWM PHOTO C03112)

The Fromelles POWs were transported to some of the 165 POW camps the Germans had created for their British captives. The Germans used many of their prisoners as forced labour in factories, in mines or on farms. During the war they captured around 2.5 million Allied servicemen and by 1917 they made up about 20 per cent of Germany's adult male labour force. Most of the POWs from Fromelles were held in a range of camps, from Gutesloh, to Minden, to Dulmen and Sennelager.

Many of the Diggers taken prisoner later reported that they were beaten in the early stages of their captivity, and some reported seeing comrades killed in the act of surrender. Most said that they found the German medical staff to be well-meaning and efficient and that their subsequent treatment was generally reasonable. The Red Cross maintained good relations with the Germans throughout the war and kept up a flow of food parcels to most prisoners, along with a postcard mail delivery.

Later in the war, the Germans relieved themselves of the growing burden of caring for badly wounded POWs by establishing a system under which they transferred some to Switzerland. They were then repatriated to Britain.

12

THE COVER-UP

*I think the attack, although it failed, has done both divisions a
great deal of good ...*

GENERAL SIR RICHARD HAKING, AFTER FROMELLES, 1916

The official communiqué after the attack, released by the British
authorities, unbelievably, read:

> *Yesterday evening, south of Armentières, we carried out some
> important raids on a front of two miles in which Australian troops
> took part. About 140 German prisoners were captured.*

The Australian newspapers duly reported the lie. The *Sydney Morning
Herald* ran a story, datelined 20 July and by-lined 'From Captain
C.E.W. Bean, Official Australian Press Representative, British
Headquarters, France'. It serves as an excellent example of how Bean
had to interweave facts with the 'official' line:

Australian war correspondent and official historian, Charles Bean, in 1919. On 19 July 1916 Bean had been covering the Somme offensive when he heard about the disastrous Australian attack at Fromelles. He rushed there the day after the battle to report on the action. (AWM PHOTO P04340.004S)

AUSTRALIANS ATTACK TRENCHES ...
TEMPORARY SUCCESS ...
TAKE 200 PRISONERS

Yesterday evening, after a bombardment, an Australian force attacked the German trenches south of Armentières.

The Australians on the left seized the German front lines, and passed beyond it to the further trenches on the first system. In the centre the Australians carried the whole of the German first system, and reached more or less open country. On the right, the troops had to cross a much wider stretch between the trenches, where the Germans held a very strongly held salient.

The Germans were ready for the attack and had managed to save a number of machine guns from the bombardment. In spite of very brave efforts, the troops on this flank were unable to cross the ground between the trenches and only managed to reach the German trenches in isolated points. From these they were driven out.

This enabled the Germans to concentrate the fire of all sorts of artillery on the portion of the trenches captured. The Germans battered down their own trenches where they were occupied by our men. They also turned water from a channel down the trench on the left flank, and the Australians there, after reaching the trenches, found themselves standing in water which was rapidly rising and waist high. They endured a tremendous bombardment until early the following morning, when, after eleven hours in the captured position, such Australians as retained the small remaining portion of the German line were ordered to retire.

By dint of brave work, the engineers and infantry in the working parties had managed to get communication trenches completely through to the German trenches. These trenches were dug under very heavy shell fire. This work enabled the troops to carry out their retirement with a loss which is slight when the extraordinary difficulty of the operation is considered.

Among the last who returned to our trenches were eight men who said they got lost behind the German trenches and had been wandering about till daylight in the country in the rear of the front line.

Our troops, in this attack, had to face shell fire which was heavier and more continuous than was even known in Gallipoli. Many of them had never previously been tried. The manner in which they carried the operation through seems to have been worthy of all the traditions of Anzac. At least 200 prisoners were captured and several machine guns. Many Germans were killed. The losses amongst our troops engaged were severe.

Bean was apparently pleased to have got this report through the censor in Amiens. He wrote in his diary that he was happy to get away with calling the action an 'attack' and to have reported that our

AT GERMAN THIRD LINE

Kaiser's Troops Strongly Defending Points Now Attacked.

COSTLY BRITISH REPULSE

Berlin Says More Than 2,000 Were Killed in Raid on German Defenses at Fromelles.

ADMITS GAIN BY FRENCH

Lull During the Day in the Main British and French Theatres —Great Aerial Activity.

While the official British communiqué after the Battle of Fromelles lied about the action and its terrible casualties, calling it a 'some important raids in which Australian troops took part', the Germans, not surprisingly, were unabashed and reported the true position as picked up by the *New York Times*, which ran the story on its front page on 21 July 1916.

losses were 'severe'. He made no mention of why he categorised the losses during the withdrawal as 'slight'! But he noted that the censor would not let him refer to the bombardment as 'intense' because the British 1st Army objected to that description. In his notes he referred to the official communiqué which called the attack 'an important series of trench raids' and added:

> *What is the use of deliberate lying like that? The Germans know it was an attack – they have numbers of our wounded as prisoners.*

The authorities added to the confusion and aided the cover-up by referring to the location of the action as variously 'Fleurbaix' (a neighbouring village where some of the Australian units were billeted), or 'south of Armentières', 'Bois-Grenier' or even 'Laventie' or 'Petillon' (also nearby villages). The Germans had no such reticence and always referred to it as Fromelles. The German communiqué after the battle was clear and accurate:

> *The English attack in the region of Fromelles on Wednesday was carried out, as we have ascertained, by two strong divisions. The brave Bavarian Division against whose front the attack was made, counted on the ground in front of them more than 2,000 enemy corpses. We have brought in so far 481 prisoners, together with 16 machine guns.*

Haking's message to McCay for distribution to the 5th Division after the battle is breathtaking in its arrogance, self-delusion and callousness:

> *I should be glad if you would convey to all ranks of the Division under your command my deep appreciation of the gallant and*

successful manner in which they carried the attack on the enemy's lines yesterday afternoon.

Officers and men displayed a fine spirit throughout the attack and drove back the enemy with true British vigour. The Commanders and Staff Officers also worked with untiring energy and great skill in a difficult attack, and I am proud to have such a fine division as yours under my command on such an important occasion.

Although the division was unable to hold the position gained for a long time, the attack must have made a great impression on the enemy and fulfilled its main purpose which was to assist our Comrades who are fighting in the South and prevent the enemy from moving reserves away from our front in that direction. I wish you all a still more complete victory in your next attack and I hope that I shall be somewhere near it when it takes place.

The following day, Haig added his congratulations:

Please convey to the troops engaged last night my appreciation of their gallant effort and of the careful and thorough preparations made for it. I wish them to realise that their enterprise has not been by any means in vain and that the gallantry with which they carried out the attack is fully recognised.

Haking then devoted his energies to finding excuses for the disaster. While Bean attributed it (diplomatically) to 'loose thinking and somewhat reckless decision on the part of the higher staff', Haking, of course, had other ideas. Taking any responsibility for his mistakes was out of the question so he focussed his main blame on what he called the 'newness of the infantry'. In his official report on the attack, he started with some outright lies:

The artillery preparation was adequate. There were sufficient guns and sufficient ammunition. The wire was properly cut, and the assaulting battalions had a clear run into the enemy's trenches.

Then he pointed the finger at the poor men he sent to their deaths, firstly the Australians whom he damned with faint praise:

The Australian infantry attacked in the most gallant manner and gained the enemy's position, but they were not sufficiently trained to consolidate the ground gained. They were eventually compelled to withdraw and lost heavily in doing so.

After which he turned on his own men:

The 61st Division were not sufficiently imbued with the offensive spirit to go in like one man at the appointed time. Some parts of the attack were late in deploying ...

With two trained divisions the position would have been a gift after the artillery bombardment ...

But perhaps Haking's most outrageous statement came next:

I think the attack, although it failed, has done both divisions a great deal of good, and I am quite sure as a result of the attack that the Germans are not likely to move troops away from the front for some time.

As with most of his assessments, Haking was wrong in his view that the Germans would be deterred from moving any forces away from the Fromelles area. The Germans had discovered a copy of Haking's battle orders on one of the captured Australian officers. The limited objectives set out in those orders confirmed what the Germans already believed: that the attack was a feint and the Allies had no intention of renewing it. They therefore released the reserves that they had held near Lille and sent them south to fight on the Somme.

As to the absurd notion that the divisions would benefit from the disaster, Pompey Elliott wrote a few days after the battle:

> one of the best of my commanding officers was killed and practically all my best officers, the Anzac men who helped to build up my Brigade, are dead. I presume there was some plan at the back of the attack but it is difficult to know what it was. I can only say – it was an Order. I trust those who gave the order may be made to realise their responsibility.

After the brief and often inaccurate reports which appeared in the Australian press in the days after the battle, Fromelles quietly disappeared from the Australian consciousness, swamped by the massive losses suffered by the 1st, 2nd and 4th Australian Divisions in the Battle of Pozières on the Somme, which began four days later. The three Australian Divisions there lost a total of 16,780 killed, wounded, captured or missing in two weeks of vicious fighting before they captured their objective, the village of Pozières. The intensity of the fighting was underlined by the four Victoria Crosses won by Diggers. Bean later wrote that Pozières Ridge was 'more densely sown with Australian sacrifice than any other place on earth'.

The Melbourne newspaper, the *Argus*, revisited the Fromelles story in April 1920. In an article headed 'Fromelles 1916! – A Glorious Failure – What Really Happened', it hinted at the cover-up:

> for a long time the secrecy of war kept a veil drawn over the details of this sad page in the history of the Australian Imperial Force.

Overall, the story added little new information and made some incorrect claims – for example, that some men from the 60th Battalion had broken through the German lines. After its publication, the Battle of Fromelles once again disappeared from public view, aside from the occasional mention in memoirs or privately published pamphlets and, as we have seen earlier, Pompey Elliott's speeches in 1929 and 1930.

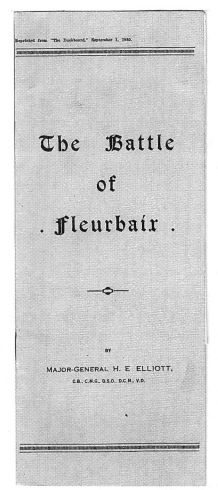

Pompey Elliott caused a stir in Australia and in Britain in 1929 and 1930 when he gave a series of lectures about the Battle of Fromelles (which he still called Fleurbaix). Elliott vehemently criticised the British General Richard Haking's plan, calling it a 'wretched, hybrid scheme, which might well be termed a tactical abortion'.

Perhaps the most disgraceful act of cover-up came from the commander of II Anzac Corps, the British General Sir Alexander Godley. He wrote his autobiography after the war, yet could find neither the time nor the space for a single line about Fromelles. Godley lost 5533 men under his command in that battle but somehow managed to ignore the event completely. Similarly, the commander of I Anzac Corps, another British General, Sir William Birdwood, published a post-war autobiography without a single reference to Fromelles.

Sydney historian Neville Kidd believes the cover-up has continued to the present because the Battle of Fromelles does not appear on our major war memorials. This is a consequence of decisions taken in the 1920s, before most of our major shrines were constructed during the following decade.

Kidd points out that the original decision was taken by the Battles Nomenclature Committee, a British body with an Australian representative, established by the Army Council to King George V in 1922. The Committee classified Fromelles as a 'subsidiary attack' under the heading 'The Battles of the Somme 1916 (1st July – 18th November)'. Kidd adds:

> The evidence before the Nomenclature Committee, sitting so soon after the cessation of hostilities, would almost certainly be received from or based upon information sourced from the British High Command or its bureaucracy. Members of the High Command or their delegates probably sat on the Committee. It is certain in relation to Fromelles that the High Command attitude, the mis-description 'raids' and The Somme connection, would have all come to their notice and been appropriately persuasive.

Kidd also notes that even Pompey Elliott, when he delivered his stinging attacks in 1929 and 1930, titled his speeches 'The Battle of Fleurbaix':

Obviously Elliott even then, felt bound by honour as an Officer and Gentleman, to continue the charade of wartime secrecy.

Neville Kidd has been waging a campaign in Sydney to try to persuade the trustees of the war memorial to honour the sacrifices of the men of Fromelles by including the name among the battles commemorated on the memorial. His efforts have so far been fruitless. The reasons most commonly given by the trustees in the various state war memorials are: that the original memorial was handed to the current trustees in its present form and, as such, has heritage value that would be compromised by change; Fromelles is correctly classified as an 'action' not a 'battle'; in any event, it is sufficiently honoured under the name 'The Somme'; and that recognition of Fromelles would set a precedent leading to a rush of other claims.

Kidd responds that the 'set in stone' argument would condemn the trustees to perpetuating any and all errors they have inherited – surely no legitimate argument if a mistake can be properly demonstrated. He claims that the original decision not to include Fromelles as a battle was tainted by the cover-up then still in existence in official circles.

As to the claims that Fromelles was an 'action', not a 'battle', Kidd points out that Australia's official World War I history, written by Charles Bean, features two chapters, both titled 'The Battle of Fromelles'. He contends that if the heroic Battle of Long Tan in the Vietnam War is classified as a battle, surely so should Fromelles. (At Long Tan one Australian company of about 100 Diggers heroically held off around 2000 Vietnamese troops, losing 18 killed while inflicting around 800 casualties on their enemy.)

Kidd dismisses the claim that Fromelles should be included under the Somme battle honour:

The Somme was about 80 km to the south and had been raging for three weeks when the Diggers attacked at Fromelles. If you take that approach, why wasn't Lone Pine subsumed under the name of Gallipoli in the memorials instead of being rightly accorded its own battle honour?

For Neville Kidd, the men of Fromelles are being treated in disgraceful fashion, similar to the way we initially treated Vietnam veterans, many of whom were refused membership of RSLs because the conflict was considered to be 'a police action' rather than a 'real war':

My hope is that the discovery of the missing of Fromelles will prompt the authorities to reconsider the battle's position on our memorials. It's time to stop the cover-up and honour the Diggers of Fromelles as we have honoured their comrades from other battles down the years.

Memorials in their essence play on the emotions of those who visit them and indeed worship at them. Memorials do nothing for the dead and wounded or the survivors except to honour them. They should not dishonour them by contrived classification and exclusion.

13

WE ARE THE DEAD

We are the dead. Short days ago
We lived, felt dawn, saw sunset glow,
Loved, and were loved, and now we lie
In Flanders fields.

JOHN MCCRAE, 'IN FLANDERS FIELDS', 1915

Jack Bowden and Wally Vaile had been best mates since they were at primary school. After school they joined the State Savings Bank of Victoria together. They joined up together and they hopped the bags shoulder to shoulder at Fromelles and charged into the hail of steel together. Jack was killed outright and Wally was hit in both ankles and badly wounded in his arm. Wally made it back to the Australian lines but he was so badly wounded that he only made it as far as Calais before he succumbed from shock and the massive loss of blood. All he was worried about when they were caring for him was his mate Jack. He wanted Jack's body recovered.

Lifelong mates Jack Bowden and Wally Vaile with Harry Johnston, all of the 59th Battalion. Jack was killed in action at Fromelles and Wally badly wounded. Even as he succumbed to his wounds in Calais, Wally's only concern was that his comrades try to recover Jack's body. (JENNY INGHAM PHOTO)

Remarkably, Jack and Wally's company commander in B Company 59th Battalion was another pre-war manager from the State Savings Bank of Victoria, Captain Keith McDonald. He was wounded in the Fromelles attack and wrote to Wally's sister while he was recuperating at the 3rd General Hospital at Wandsworth, London, on 28 August 1916:

I regret to inform you that (Wally) died of wounds at Calais. I was given this information by Lieutenant Haddon who was in the same hospital as Mr Vaile. Mr Bowden has been recorded as Missing, but Lt Donohoe, who was wounded a couple of days after the charges is now in this hospital, and told me that Mr Bowden was killed in the charge. A man is not officially reported killed unless there is very definite and reliable evidence forthcoming.

Both Mr Vaile and Mr Bowden were officers of my company and they were regarded as two of the 'solidest' officers in the battalion. There were times when changes were being made between companies when I had to fight hard to retain them, as every company commander coveted them.

McDonald explained that his company had formed the first and second waves of the charge and that Jack went over with the first and that he and Wally went with the second wave:

We had about 500 yards to cover over rough country, barbed wire, ditches and the River Laies to cross. Our men were magnificent – they charged in a hail of shrapnel and machine-gun fire and kept going until they were practically wiped out.

I didn't see a great deal unfortunately – I got one in the right arm before we left our trench, but it wasn't too bad, but I got it solid when about 200 yards out through the left shoulder and out of the back. This dropped me like a log. I'm the only officer of the company left – Lieutenants Morrow and Carr killed, Lieutenants Bowden and Howard missing.

Mr Vaile was constantly enquiring for Mr Bowden before he died. The two were like brothers. Mr Bowden was out until 2 am the night before the charge and went all along our front to see if there was sufficient wire cut for us to get through. Thanks to Bowden the preparation in this respect was excellent – we had no trouble in getting through the wire at all.

Bowden and Vaile are men for whom no praise is too great – their men loved them and would have followed them anywhere. I don't think they could have been up against more fearful odds than they were on the 19th, yet they went out to it as one man. I was right through the Gallipoli show yet this was the severest action I've yet been in.

Jack Bowden had almost reached the German wire when he was killed. They never found his body. Perhaps it is fitting that, more than

90 years later, this gallant soldier may well play a key role in unravelling the mystery of the missing Diggers of Fromelles.

After the battle, Bowden was one of 1750 Australians posted as 'missing' – without question the worst classification for their families. The doubts and the fears and the hopes build in the families at home as the days turn into months and then drag on into years without any definite information about their loved ones' fates.

Around the end of August and through to the beginning of September, the lists of those taken prisoner became available and were passed on to their families. For those whose loved ones were not on these lists the long wait then began. They would hold on to any shred of hope: perhaps they are lying wounded but unrecognised in a hospital; maybe there was some confusion with the records and he's been shipped back to hospital in England. Their hopes were often sadly prolonged by letters from well-meaning mates who were convinced they saw them in base camps, or recovering in hospital in London.

Where they had specific knowledge of a man's fate, officers would write to his family and tell them of his last moments and the way he met his death. They usually broke the news as gently as they could and left out the ghastly details. At least these families had some definite knowledge that their man had died and they could begin their grieving.

But, for many, the letters never came. To compound the situation, some wives, in reality already widows, had their pensions suspended or delayed because the bureaucracy could not prove that the soldier had not gone absent without leave.

Given the chaos, the death and destruction at the front and the limited means of communication of the day, it is understandable that the fate of so many individuals remains unknown. In fact, it is remarkable that out of that cauldron so many records have survived. It is a testament to the skill and the determination of the humble clerks and record-keepers who beavered away under constant stress that we have the material through which Lambis Englezos and his ilk can trawl to find the clues that have opened up the quest for the missing so many years later.

That ongoing search is also a testament to the many individual soldiers who committed their experiences to paper both during and after the war. These diaries, memoirs and recollections provide a rich vein of material for the historian and the sleuth. And of course Charles Bean's *Official History* towers above them all. It is surely the most prodigious effort of sustained literary endeavour in Australia's history. When he started writing, Bean hoped to complete the work within five years. It took him 23 years – from 1919 to 1942 – to complete the monumental 12-volume work, of which he wrote the first six, and that's not counting the four years of life-threatening research he did on the ground during the war and in the year after the Armistice when he revisited many of the battlefields. He set himself a lofty goal after he was commissioned to write the work, as he explained in an article in the *Journal of the Royal Australian Historical Society* in 1938:

The first question for my fellow-historians and myself clearly was: how did the Australian people – and the Australian character, if there is one – come through the universally recognised test of this, their first great war? Second was the question: what did the Australian people and their forces achieve in the total effort of their side of the struggle? Third: what was the true nature of that struggle and test so far as Australians took part in it? How well or ill did our constitution and our preparations serve us in it? What were their strengths and weaknesses? And what guidance can our people or others obtain from this experience for future emergencies?

Future generations owe a great debt to Bean. For not only did he complete a monumental work of research, he coincidentally added many other benefits that continue to bear fruit today. He advocated the establishment of the Australian War Records Section which collected, maintained and collated the records he knew he would need in his work. He agitated for the appointment of war artists and photographers to record Australians in action and, perhaps most importantly, he was the driving force behind the creation of the Australian War Memorial, which has earned a world-wide reputation as one of the great repositories of war relics and memorabilia. What is more, the AWM is imbued with Bean's spirit. It is far more than a war museum, it is a shrine that reverently honours those who have made sacrifices for their country and their people.

From the outset, Bean acknowledged that his work would not be definitive or perfect. Indeed, historians have made many revisions and

Dead soldiers, lying where they fell in the German front line, on the morning after the Battle of Fromelles. (AWM PHOTO A01554)

A photo of the battlefield at Fromelles, taken in July 1918, showing the remnants of bullet-torn kits of the Diggers. Two water bottles are visible in the foreground. (AWM PHOTO E04037)

corrections down the years. But what sets Bean's work apart is his relentless attention to detail, his fairness and his understanding of the Digger. While many official histories are written by high-ranking officers, who may or may not have participated in the events, Bean's point of view always includes that of the humble Digger – the man at the sharp end who carries out the orders that the great strategists conceive in their chateaux. In fact Bean was there with the Diggers, in the mud and the blood, whenever he possibly could be, as he observed in the preface to the first volume in 1921:

> *The writer himself, either on the day of battle or soon afterwards, visited as far as it lay in him to do so, every important trench or position mentioned in this and the following five volumes, and of most of them he kept detailed notes. By the kind trust of the authorities and of the men and officers of the A.I.F. he was enabled throughout the four years of the war to make a rule of being present, while the events narrated in these volumes were actually happening, on some part of every battlefield on which Australian infantry fought – the only important exceptions being the battle of Fromelles in 1916 (which he was only able to reach some hours later, when troops were being withdrawn), and the battle of Hermies, which occurred in 1917 while he was for a short time unavoidably absent in England.*

It's interesting that one of only two battles that Bean mentions as being exceptions to his general rule was Fromelles. Yet, even at Fromelles he rushed to the scene from the Somme as soon as he heard about it, arriving in time to see the chaotic withdrawal and the recovery of the wounded.

The impact of Fromelles on Charles Bean is clear when we see that he returned to the battlefield on the very first day he could when the war ended, Armistice Day itself – 11 November 1918. He had realised he had no photograph of the sacred ground there so he took a photographer and he walked in the footsteps of the men who made it into the German lines and he stood at the Sugar Loaf, by then a pile of mangled concrete and metal, and he gazed across no-man's land and he thought of the thousands who died and were maimed there:

> *We found the old no-man's land simply full of our dead. In the narrow sector west of the Laies River and east of the Sugar Loaf*

*Salient, the skulls and bones and torn uniforms were lying around
everywhere. I found a bit of Australian kit lying fifty yards from the
corner of the salient, and the bones of an Australian officer and
several men within 100 yards of it. Farther around, immediately on
their flank, were a few British – you could tell by their leather
equipment. And within 100 yards of the west corner of the Sugar
Loaf Salient there was lying a small party of English too – also with
an officer – you could tell the cloth of his coat.*

Sadly, Bean could only identify two of the remains he found that
day at Fromelles – a microcosm of the problems that would face the
recovery units all over France and beyond.

While Bean's reportage forms the spine of the narrative of the
battles, the recollections of individuals often provide the kind of clues
that sleuths like Lambis Englezos seek to find the fate of individuals
swept up in the maelstrom. The account of Private Bill Barry of the
29th Battalion is an excellent example. He had been in one of the
carrying parties bringing supplies to the 8th Brigade on the left flank
of the Australian attack. He made a couple of successful crossings
before he was badly wounded and captured. Some time in 1917, when
he was recuperating in an English hospital after being repatriated
because he had lost his leg, he wrote a wonderful account of his time
in uniform, now in the archives of the Australian War Memorial.
Writing of the lead-up to his capture, Barry explains how he had just
handed over a load of ammunition to the advanced Australian attackers
in the German trenches when he was trapped in a savage enemy
artillery barrage:

*The German artillery fire was growing fiercer every minute, in fact
it was hellish – the shells were landing with great accuracy and killing
the boys like flies. About ten o'clock I shifted my position and was*

able to get into the German trench and no sooner had I got in when a shell struck the top of the parapet with a terrific explosion. Two lads standing alongside of me started to cry for their Mothers and I told them to stop that but to pray to God to get them out of this. No sooner than the words were out of my mouth than another shell hit the parapet just about my head and that was the end of everything for a while for I was unconscious.

When Bill Barry regained consciousness some considerable time later he felt his legs being pulled roughly. He opened his eyes to find half a dozen Germans surrounding him. He lapsed back into unconsciousness

On the day of the Armistice on 11 November 1918, official historian Charles Bean took a photographer back to the battlefield at Fromelles to record the sacred ground there. This photo shows the old no-man's land and the remains of the River Laies, the German trenches and the ruins of the Sugar Loaf pillboxes to the right of the picture. (AWM PHOTO E04029)

again and woke to find himself among a group of Australians who told him they had been taken prisoner. He came across an English-speaking German officer who first attended to his wounded legs and then turned nasty, apparently ordering some of his men to give Barry a beating. They did such a good job that they knocked him out again. When he came to some hours later, he found he had been robbed of all his belongings. After a number of other beatings, one with a piece of timber, Barry was handed over to the German Red Cross who took him to their dugout and fed him black bread with bully beef and coffee and gave him a greatcoat to keep him warm. Barry said he was beyond caring that the coat was still wet with blood. Shortly after, he was left alone for a couple of hours and he was able to look around outside the shelter:

> to my horror I was in the place where all the dead men were. I was sitting on the edge of a hole about forty feet long, twenty feet wide and fifteen feet deep and into this hole the dead were being thrown without any fuss or respect. It was pitiful to see the different expressions on their faces, some with a peaceful smile while others showed they had passed away in agony.

Shortly afterward the Germans took Barry and some other wounded prisoners to a nearby dressing station and then by a horse ambulance wagon to a hospital to the rear.

Barry's account of the Germans burying the German and Australian dead from the battle provided a powerful corroboration of the subsequent evidence that the Germans had buried many of the missing from Fromelles.

The highest ranking officer among the missing from Fromelles is the CO of the 53rd Battalion, Lieutenant Colonel Ignatius Bertram 'Bert' Norris, who was killed as he led his men into the second line of the German trenches.

In many ways the experience of Bert Norris' loved ones was typical of many of his missing comrades' families. Examining his service file, which runs to 49 pages and is now in the Australian Archives, and his 10-page Australian Red Cross Wounded and Missing Enquiry Bureau file with the Australian War Memorial, gives us a good understanding of, not only what happened to Norris himself, but also how the system operated to inform and compensate his family.

Norris was an experienced militia soldier and an accomplished Sydney barrister who had been a member of the NSW Legislative Council when he joined the AIF. He was the youngest son of Richard Augustine Norris, a well-known Sydney banker and the honorary treasurer of St Mary's Cathedral. Born on 31 July 1880, Bert was educated at St Ignatius College Riverview in Sydney, where he was an outstanding student and sportsman. The college archives show that young Bert almost lost his life at Riverview's very first swimming carnival in 1890. He was just a slip of a boy and he apparently fearlessly, and foolishly, jumped into the pool without having learned how to swim properly. He initially sank without trace but was noticed and saved by a fellow student Charley Lennon and revived by a Jesuit priest, Fr Pigot, who fortuitously had been a doctor before joining the priesthood. The college diarist noted that Bert had been

> preserved for a brilliant and beneficent career, all too brief indeed, and was to meet a nobler end as we shall see anon.

Bert Norris passed his law matriculation in 1896 and took articles of clerkship with a Sydney solicitor while simultaneously reading for the bar. He was called to the NSW Bar in 1908 – apparently the only person to have qualified as a solicitor and a barrister at the same time in NSW. Of slight build – 168 centimetres (5 feet 7 inches) and 63.5 kilograms (10 stone) – he nevertheless represented his state at hockey and was a fine tennis player, cricketer and golfer.

Lientenant Colonel Ignatius Bertram
'Bert' Norris, CO of the 53rd Battalion,
who died leading his men into the
second line of German trenches at
Fromelles. He is the highest-ranking of
the missing Diggers from the battle.
(PHOTO COURTESY ST IGNATIUS COLLEGE
ARCHIVES)

In the militia, Norris quickly rose through the ranks of the NSW
Irish Rifles Regiment, under the future Governor of Papua, Colonel
Hubert Murray. Promoted to captain in 1906, by the time the war
broke out and he joined up Norris was 34, a major in the 34th Regiment
and a prominent barrister with a thriving practice that included service
as Secretary to the Vice-President of the NSW Legislative Council.
Three months earlier, he had married Bessie Lane-Mullens. Norris
sailed for Egypt on the troopship HMAT *Centaur* with the 5th
Reinforcements of the 1st Battalion on 26 June 1915. (Riverview's
Our Alma Mater magazine noted that he was one of four Riverview
barristers who went off to war on the ship that day.) Bessie followed
Bert to Cairo where she gave birth to their son John Richard Bertram
Norris at the end of that year.

In Cairo, Norris started serving with the 6th Infantry Training Battalion but the army quickly drew on his legal skills and he was soon acting as the judge-advocate in courts-martial. Clearly, Norris could have taken the safe staff option and stayed in the rear. He had established a reputation as a leader and planner in Egypt and, at one stage, was appointed acting Brigadier of Anzac Reserve Brigade, commanding about 12,000 men responsible for a large chunk of the Cairo defences. But Norris wanted to get into the fight and he persuaded his superiors to give him command of a battalion. He was promoted to lieutenant colonel and given command, first of the 22nd Battalion and then, during the AIF reorganisation in Egypt, of the newly formed 53rd Battalion in the 14th Brigade of the 5th Division AIF, bound for the Western Front.

When Lieutenant Colonel Norris sailed with the 5th Division for France in late June 1916, Bessie took her infant son to London to be nearer her husband.

During the battle at Fromelles, Norris had led his men across no-man's land and was charging into the German second line when he was cut down. The official report of his death read:

Lt Col Norris was killed shortly after 6 pm on evening 19/20 July '16 while leading men of his battalion in an assault on the 2nd enemy line in front of FROMELLES. He was several times hit by machine-gun fire and death was practically instantaneous. The position was retaken by the enemy next morning and the body was not recovered.

Our Alma Mater reported:

In the action of the 19th July, the Australians were the attacking forces and Lieut-Col Norris led his 53rd over the parapet. The first line of trenches was taken and passed. Lieut-Col Norris kept at the head of his men and encouraged them by calling out, 'Come on lads! Only another trench to take!' About 70 yards beyond the first line he was hit by a machine-gun bullet and died almost on the instant. His last words were, 'Here, I'm done, will somebody take my papers?' The casualties in the fight were very severe, the 53rd Batt alone losing a third of its effectives.

At the time of the battle, Bessie Norris was waiting in London, hoping to see Bert when he was able to travel across the Channel on his first leave. She would likely have heard that her husband had been killed within a week of his death. That she had the financial capacity and the social clout to follow him, first to Cairo where she delivered their son John, and then to London where she stayed with relatives, speaks volumes for Bert Norris' influence and wealth. Bessie would probably have heard through official sources of Norris' fate and later from letters from his comrades, including his battalion padre, Father John Kennedy. Corfield quotes from the letter Kennedy wrote to Bessie:

It is with feelings of the greatest sorrow and deepest sympathy that I write you this letter. I should have written to you some days ago, but I could not brace myself to write.

Your dear husband died a hero's death, leading his battalion in an engagement on the 19th inst. God knows how I pity you – but you have the great consolation of knowing that the Colonel was prepared to die. He was never ashamed of his Holy Faith. Every Sunday he received Holy Communion and often during the week since he was appointed to the Command of this regiment.

On the morning of the battle he knelt down before his men and received Holy Communion from me. He had successfully led his men to the second line of the enemy trenches when a machine gun bullet struck him and killed him instantly. His adjutant Lieut. Moffitt, was killed at the same time.

Oh, Mrs Norris, he died a hero's death, and you will be able to tell your child later how brave his father was, and above all, how noble and conscientious a Catholic.

When a soldier died, the protocol was to gather first-hand reports from those who saw him fall. This was all the more important when his comrades were not able to recover his body, as was the case with Lieutenant Colonel Norris. One of the eye-witnesses' accounts noted in Norris' file was from Private Arthur Rupert Pike who saw him fall:

I saw Col. Norris shot in the abdomen by a bullet and killed instantly.

Pike gave a description of Norris as a 'little man, wore glasses, dark hair, small dark moustache'.

Captain Geoff Street wrote:

I took him orders about the attack which was made. Col. Norris went over in the charge with his battalion and was killed, near the German's second-line trenches. He was at that time, with his Adjutant, who was also killed. I, myself, from my position during the battle, can say that Col. Norris met his death like a solider, and I can say nothing finer than that. All men in his regiment can testify and do testify to his personal courage and leadership, both of which were gallant in the extreme. The fighting was extremely severe.

Another note from the file refers to a request from Private Frank Leslie Croft, a signaller in Norris' Battalion, who wanted an address for Norris' widow Bessie so he could write to her. He had been the last man with him when he died and wanted to tell her of his last moments. Croft was a fine soldier whose claim about being with Norris was corroborated in Croft's belated recommendation for a Distinguished Conduct Medal dated 12 October 1916:

Near Fromelles in the action of 19/20 July 1916, Pte Croft, a signaller, accompanied his C.O. (the late Lieut-Col Norris) into the German trenches and on his C.O. being wounded, Private Croft with others attempted to bring him back to our own lines. A German machine gun was turned on to the party and the C.O. the Adjutant and two others were killed the remainder were ordered to disperse. Private Croft after taking a prisoner went on and reported himself to the O.C. Advanced Company and remained with him maintaining communication with the adjoining battalion and trying to get in touch with our guns. Before leaving he cut all the wires in the German trenches thinking they may lead to a mine. Lieut Myers has brought this man's name to notice as being particularly cool and brave throughout. His clothes and equipment were riddled with bullets. As a signaller, both before and after this action, he very frequently laid and repaired telephone lines under heavy fire and difficult circumstances, and has always been outstandingly cool and brave. The gallantry displayed by Pte Croft has only recently been brought to notice otherwise he would have been recommended at an earlier date for immediate reward.

Another private from the 53rd said of Norris:

He was a man in a million, a gentleman to speak to, and if anyone got into crime street, and came before him, he got sound advice and the minimum penalty. I had a chat with him the morning of the charge, and he might have been a private, so nice and friendly he was to me. He received Holy Communion in his dug-out that morning: Father

Kennedy told me he had done so regularly for some considerable time ... I attended Requiem Mass in the town ... the large church was filled with soldiers of his battalion, and others as well.

As we have seen, despite their best efforts, Frank Croft and his mates had to leave Norris' body behind when they withdrew from the German trenches.

Norris' standing in the community was confirmed when his obituary appeared in the *Sydney Morning Herald* of 1 August. His brother Osborne, a Sydney solicitor, wrote to the army advising that he held Norris' will and that he and Sir Allen Taylor were the executors of

The stained-glass memorial window that stands today in the chancel of the chapel at St Ignatius College, Riverview, in Sydney, honouring Lieutenant Colonel Ignatius Bertram Norris, a former student who died leading his men in the attack at Fromelles. As the inscription at its foot attests, the window was the gift of Norris' son John. It includes the Norris family crest and motto, 'I serve loyally'.
(PATRICK LINDSAY PHOTO)

his estate. Osborne asked the army to send a death certificate when it was available so he could start probate proceedings.

Burdened by the increasing weight of casualties, the official system lagged behind somewhat. In reality, in the light of the massive losses, the system coped remarkably well. The official army notification of Norris' death, the 'Field Service' form, was stamped in Rouen in France on 9 September 1916. Ten days later Bessie was granted a widow's pension of £5 0s. 9d. a fortnight, and their son John a fortnightly pension of £1. Osborne wrote again at the end of that month again seeking the death certificate. It was sent to him on 11 October. That same week, Bessie received Norris' valise and his brown kitbag from the army. The valise contained a copy of the New Testament, a set of dominoes and a dictionary, among his uniform and clothes. The kit bag held his rosary beads, a wallet with photos of Bessie and baby John and a spirit flask among other clothes. A month later Bessie received Norris' black kitbag, again forwarded by Thomas Cook & Sons for the army. It contained his field glasses and a greatcoat.

The following day, on 11 November, Norris' name appeared on the German 'death list', with the notation that he 'fell in the neighbourhood of Fromelles on 19/7/16'. Four months later, the Germans returned Norris' ID Disc via the Red Cross and it was despatched to Bessie at her London address on 21 March, one week after it had been received from Germany.

Like all the other families of soldiers who died, Bessie received her husband's Victory Medal and Memorial Plaque as his next of kin. They arrived early 1923. They were a pathetic compensation for the loss of an outstanding man. It would be the last Bessie or her family heard of Norris or his final resting place until Lambis Englezos began his quest more than 80 years later.

PART TWO
A MAGNIFICENT OBSESSION

Don't bend; don't water it down; don't try to make it logical; don't edit your own soul according to the fashion. Rather, follow your most intense obsessions mercilessly.

FRANZ KAFKA

14

A GROWING PASSION

*It's the soul's duty to be loyal to its own desires. It must abandon
itself to its master passion.*

Rebecca West, Irish journalist and novelist

For the first time since he began his quest five years earlier, Lambis
Englezos was starting to have second thoughts. The constant pressure
was taking its toll. His email box was full and he couldn't work out
how to empty it. He'd taken to hiding the phone bills from his long-
suffering wife, Suzanne, who was starting to look at him strangely. The
pressure was even affecting his bowls: he'd been dropped to the seconds
at his beloved Kew Heights Lawn Bowls Club.

They say you don't choose your obsession, it chooses you. Lambis
Englezos' obsession not only chose him, it crept up on him and then
it subsumed him.

It started innocently enough. He was reading Peter Charlton's
Pozières 1916, about a famous victory by the Australians, when he

185

Lambis Englezos at Fromelles in 2007, doing the numbers in front of the wall commemorating the missing at VC Corner Cemetery. Lambis' quest to find the missing Diggers of Fromelles began with a simple calculation of the number of men missing after the battle compared with the number of unknown dead registered at the cemeteries in the region. (WARD SELBY PHOTO)

came across a reference to an earlier battle at Fromelles – a tiny village in north-eastern France where in July that year Australians were thrown into one of those crazed World War I assaults of man against machine guns with predictable cataclysmic results.

As he read the terrible details, Lambis could not believe that in his extensive Great War reading he had never heard of this mysterious battle where Australia suffered the greatest loss of life in one day in its history – almost 2000 men dead – with another 3500 in casualties. He found himself driven by a nagging desire to find out more about the battle and the men who fought in it. Over time, interest grew into passion and passion into what even Lambis now admits is obsession.

At first glance, it seems a strange obsession for a fifty-something Greek-born art and crafts high-school teacher from Melbourne. But more than half a century of Australian life has imbued Lambis with a deep emotional link to his adopted country and its Anzac heritage and Lambis is now about as Greek as a meat pie.

Lambis Englezos was born in Salonika, Greece's second-largest city. His family originally came from Thrace, a region cramped between Bulgaria, Greece and Turkey. It was an area enmeshed in generations of Ottoman troubles and the Englezos family was one of many chased out in the blood-letting of the early 1920s. They moved to northern Greece where Lambis' father, Evangelos, became a wheat farmer. He served with the Greek Army in World War II but the vicious Greek Civil War, fought from 1946 to 1949, greatly disillusioned him. Evangelos had recently married and he was determined to find a better life for his wife, Sofia, especially after Lambis was born in 1953. The following year, with his mother's distraught curses echoing in his ears, Evangelos emigrated with his family and headed for the biggest Greek city outside of Greece – Melbourne. The journey included a detour via the Nissen huts at the Bonegilla migrant transition camp near Albury-Wodonga in northern Victoria. There, in the Spartan surroundings of Australia's first and longest lasting migrant establishment, the Englezos family became part of the more than 300,000 'New Australians' (as they were called then) to transit through the camp before settling in mainstream Australia.

Like most migrants, Evangelos and Sofia had to take the jobs that many Australians avoided. Evangelos worked in a nickel-plating foundry

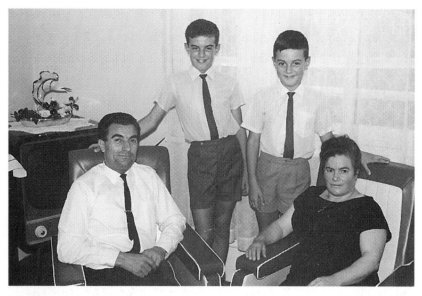

The Englezos family in Victoria in the late 1960s. Left to right: (father) Evangelos, Lambis, (his brother) Costa and (their mother) Sofia. (LAMBIS ENGLEZOS PHOTO)

Lambis' father, Evangelos, as a member of the Greek Army during World War II. He fought against the Germans and was wounded in battle. In the 1950s, disillusioned by the violent political scene in his homeland and seeking new opportunities, he brought his family to Australia. (LAMBIS ENGLEZOS PHOTO)

Some of the survivors of the Battle of Fromelles. (Clockwise from top left) Tom Brain, the last survivor of the 60th Battalion, William 'Bill' Boyce of the 58th Battalion, Charlie Henderson of the 57th Battalion, and Fred Kelly a machine-gunner in the 53rd Battalion who watched the battle from his post. (LAMBIS ENGLEZOS PHOTOS)

while Sofia worked in the Tom Piper canning factory. Lambis and his brother, Costa, born a year after they arrived, were cared for as infants by a kindly Italian lady next door. Lambis' parents each, in turn, travelled back to Greece in the years that followed, and Lambis went over in 1979.

At primary school at Melbourne's Albert Park, Lambis was fascinated by Anzac Day and the stories of the Diggers and he gravitated to the old Diggers who lived near him. They became his quasi-grandfathers and he spent hours sitting with them as they had a quiet beer on the wharf, chatting to the fishermen coming back with their catches. He loved listening to their first-hand tales of the horrors, the humour and the humanity of their war years. He would play out their tales in his vivid imagination as he spent hours walking the Albert Park beach collecting sea shells. Away from his wavy volutes, cowries and conchs, young Lambis also read voraciously – from threepenny war comics and *Parade* magazine to war books like *They Dared Mightily*.

His interest in the Great War stayed with him as he grew up, left school and graduated as an art teacher.

I went back to Greece when I got my first lot of leave in 1979 as a 26-year-old, and saw the fields that would have been mine and the tree my parents sheltered me under. I met my 103-year-old grandmother, who had cursed my dad when he left. She forgave him and then tried to find a good Greek girl for me.

But Lambis returned to Australia and found his own good Australian girl. He and Suzanne raised two children, Anthony and Sophia, as Lambis built his career in Victoria's high-school system. His love of World War I remained a passion and in 1992 he helped to establish The Friends of the 15th Brigade, an association of families and friends dedicated to keeping alive the story of the men of one of Victoria's finest Great War units, the 15th Brigade of the 5th Division of the First AIF, which fought at Gallipoli and later in France, starting with its disastrous introduction to the Western Front at the Battle of Fromelles.

We started the Friends of the 15th Brigade a year after the 75th anniversary of the battle. We started with a handful and now have a mailing list of about 220. We get together for commemorations:

on the anniversary of Pompey Elliott's death on March 23rd; on the 24th of April for the retaking of Villers-Bretonneux; and on the 19th of July for Fromelles. And occasionally we have a social get-together. Now we have The Families and Friends of the First AIF and many other groups. The level of interest is growing each year.

On his regular visits to World War I veterans in their nursing homes, Lambis met the remarkable Roy Kyle on a trip to Geelong. A Gallipoli man of the 24th Battalion, Roy had written a memoir which he entrusted to Lambis with the request that he try to have it published. Lambis was instrumental in doing just that. Edited by Bryce Courtenay, *An Anzac's Story* appeared in 2003 and was an instant best-seller.

Through the 15th Brigade Association, Lambis also met some of the survivors of the Battle of Fromelles. He met Tom Brain, the last of the 60th Battalion to survive the battle and the war, and Bill Boyce of the 58th Battalion. Lambis developed a special friendship with both men and gained a deep insight into them and their mates and the sacrifices they gladly made for their country. The words of another veteran who became his friend, Fred Kelly of the 53rd Battalion – who fought at Fromelles with the 14th Machine Company – have always stayed with him. Lambis asked Fred about Fromelles during an interview in 1998. The images were indelibly etched in the old Digger's memory:

I saw the worst sight I ever saw in my life. Four wounded chaps came back, they walked back. They stopped there for fifteen minutes. This chap's nose and part of his face had been chopped straight off. I put my hand out to touch this chap, he said: 'Don't touch me, my ribs are shattered.' That bloke's face has stopped with me all my life.

Whoever planned the battle of Fromelles was stupid. It was the greatest piece of stupidity since the Charge of the Light Brigade. We were in full view, the Germans chopped the 53rd to pieces ... Haking was a ratbag. It was the worst piece of strategy. It was murder. We had no chance.

Fred Kelly was 101 when he spoke those words. He died on Boxing Day 1998, nine days short of his 102nd birthday.

15

MARTIAL

Hold faithfulness and sincerity as first principles.

CONFUCIUS

Lambis first travelled to Fromelles for the 80th Anniversary of the battle in 1996. He needed to see and smell the ground and to walk in the footsteps of Tom and Bill and their mates who still lie there. He went on a pilgrimage on behalf of these men, especially Bill whose frail health prevented him from travelling.

Like all visitors to Fromelles, Lambis was struck by how clearly defined the battlefield was and how little had changed since the conflict. He found it easy to visualise the front lines of both sides, which remained static for virtually the whole war, and he looked with amazement at the billiard-table flatness of no-man's land, the killing ground between the front lines.

During a subsequent visit in 2002, while he was at VC Corner Cemetery at Fromelles – the only all-Australian Commonwealth War

Passionate believer in the Anzac tradition, Greek-born Australian, Lambis Englezos, the driving force behind the quest to find the missing Diggers of Fromelles. (PATRICK LINDSAY PHOTO)

Graves Cemetery in France – Lambis was struck by the number of names of men missing from the battle that were carved on the stone wall at the rear of the cemetery. His curiosity was piqued also by the other unique aspect of VC Corner: the lack of individual tombstones. The cemetery was built after the Armistice of 11 November 1918, and stands 3 kilometres north-west of Fromelles village. The remains of 410 Diggers found after the ceasefire on the battlefield in 1918 – where they had lain since July 1916 – were buried at VC Corner. Because none of them could be identified, they were buried in mass graves, in 41 groups of ten. They were marked by two stone crosses set flat into the lawn. In front of them, the (then) Imperial War Graves Commission built a beautiful stone wall in which were carved the names of 1299 Australians missing from the battle.

This ghostly group of missing Diggers played on Lambis' mind over the following days as he walked the entire length of the battlefield, guided by his friend, local historian and Commonwealth War Graves Commission officer, Martial Delebarre.

Lambis was astonished to find that almost 90 years after the conflict the ground was still thick with war relics – shell casings, shrapnel, ordnance and personal artefacts like buttons, buckles, spectacles, even false teeth – not to mention the hundreds of massive concrete bunkers that rise from the Flanders clay like carbuncles.

Lambis began to look at the place through different eyes.

During their many walks, Martial Delebarre stirred Lambis' curiosity with his encyclopaedic knowledge of the area and the impact that the war had on it. Few people have a greater knowledge or understanding of this land and the battles which raged over it than Martial, whose family has lived here for 700 years. He roams it constantly and has a deep spiritual link with it. Indeed, when Martial visited Australia in 2006 and learned of our Aborigines' spiritual connection to their land, he declared an immediate affinity with their feelings.

Fromelles, just after the cessation of hostilities (above) and today (below). The village was home to around 1000 people in 200 houses at the outbreak of the war. It was linked to Lille by railway and electricity had reached it just before the war. The church dated from the late fourteenth century. By war's end the village had been reduced to little more than a pile of rubble, surrounded by hundreds of concrete blockhouses and kilometres of trenches. Today Fromelles is again a thriving village with around 1000 inhabitants. (TOP: AWM PHOTO E03723; BOTTOM: PATRICK LINDSAY PHOTO)

Martial was one of the founders and driving forces of the L'Association pour le Souvenir de la Bataille de Fromelles (the Association for the Remembrance of the Battle of Fromelles, or ASBF). Martial and his fellow members of the ASBF have helped to create and maintain an outstanding museum above the Fromelles Town Hall. He and other intrepid ASBF members also regularly go on field trips exploring the hundreds of blockhouses, mines and trenches in the area. They have spent considerable time and effort exploring the Australian tunnels in the area and have unearthed an impressive range of artefacts in surprisingly good condition. These now enhance the ASBF's collection in Fromelles Museum.

Martial regaled Lambis with stories of the battle – some passed down through his family and many learned from his work, his constant study of the land, the published histories, official records and from his contact with veterans' families visiting from all over the world.

Lambis learned that the Germans left Fromelles within a week or so of the Armistice and the townspeople returned to find that their beautiful village had been reduced to heaps of charred rubble and the discarded junk of war. Their homes were completely destroyed, the church was a pile of broken bricks and stone, the roads were broken, and everywhere the land was scarred by flooded trenches and shell craters and littered with unexploded shells and the skeletal remains of Australian, British and German soldiers.

Rebuilding the town must have seemed an impossible task in those early days for the 500 or so villagers who returned (of the 1000 who lived there before the war). But the work slowly began. They cleared the streets and started sorting through the rubble of their homes. They recovered what hadn't been destroyed or stolen and then banded together to build a temporary church. Gradually, as the government and the bureaucracy were re-established, the locals were able to seek compensation for their losses and to join the vast queues of those

Fromelles church today. The original church, dating from the fourteenth century, was destroyed during the war. The first stone of the present church was laid in 1924 and was consecrated three years later. (PATRICK LINDSAY PHOTO)

The war memorial in the grounds of the Fromelles church honouring the 42 soldiers and six civilians from the village 'Morts Pour La France' during World War I. The memorial was opened on 15 July 1923. (PATRICK LINDSAY PHOTO)

trying to rebuild their homes. At first, the most pressing job was clearing the area of the barbed wire, the ammunition and explosives and dismantling the endless fortifications that the Germans had thrown up during the four years of their occupation. The immensity of the reconstruction is shown by the fact that hundreds of concrete blockhouses still remain dotted through the area almost a century later – in fields and backyards and along the roads. Perhaps even more remarkable is that even today, throughout France, farmers working their fields still unearth, and place at their front gates for collection by the army, more than a quarter of a million tonnes of unexploded ammunition every year!

Slowly, the townspeople cleared Fromelles of the piles of rubble and buildings started to rise again. All the while, the memory of those who had never returned lay heavily on the survivors and on 15 July 1923 the town honoured its fallen with a war memorial in the church grounds. It contained the names of the 42 soldiers and six civilians from the village 'Morts Pour La France'.

They laid the first stone for the new church on 2 March 1924 and it was consecrated three years later. During that time, they rebuilt the town hall and the boys' and girls' schools in the main street, Rue de Verdun. Individual families continued to rebuild their homes over the following years, but by the time war revisited the area in 1940 the population was still only around 500.

The Luftwaffe bombed the town on 27 May 1940, destroying some buildings when British ammunition trucks parked there were hit and exploded. The following day the Germans occupied the town once again. Then things went along uneventfully until 25 June, when France surrendered to the Germans. That very day, Chancellor Adolf Hitler, the former humble lance-corporal who had served with the 16th Bavarian Reserve Infantry Regiment at Fromelles, swept back into the village in triumph. With his entourage, including former comrades from 1916, Hitler spent the evening near Fromelles quietly celebrating victory over France at his second attempt. Hitler and his comrades-in-arms then toured the battlefield and were photographed outside the blockhouse where he took refuge during the battle from the advancing Australians, about 800 metres along Rue de la Biette, down the hill from the Fromelles church and behind Rouges Bancs. Hitler then moved off to visit his old billet and his regiment's cemetery in Fournes, never to be seen again in Fromelles.

Throughout the rest of the war the German occupation force behaved reasonably and mainly used the area for training. Except for occasional fly-overs by bombers and the crash of a RAF Spitfire at nearby Fauquissart (behind the old First AIF front lines), World War II largely bypassed the area. The people sullenly endured the occupation until September 1944, when the Germans hurriedly left. Once again, life slowly began to return to normal.

Today, Fromelles has regained its pre-Great War population of around 1000, although most of those who live there now commute to work in Lille or the other surrounding business districts. The village bears its scars proudly and welcomes the growing influx of visitors, many from Australia, who come to see where their forebears fought for the freedom of France. The locals understand the sentiments of the visitors and maintain a deep respect for those who fought for their country's liberty all those years ago. They give special honour to those who gave their lives for the cause and who lie in their sacred soil.

Martial and his workmates from the Commonwealth War Graves Commission ensure that VC Corner Cemetery, the Australian Memorial and the many surrounding war cemeteries are maintained and presented beautifully. The locals try to balance their duty to respect the debts of the past with their natural desire to get on with their lives.

Fromelles has a modern town hall and school and the church and many of the buildings have an understated elegance. The former rural

Le Trou Aid Post Cemetery, which was opened in October 1914, was the site of Pompey Elliott's 15th Brigade HQ during the battle. The cemetery contains 351 graves, including 56 Australians – all probably from the battle at Fromelles. (SARAH LINDSAY PHOTO)

town now has the feeling, and many of the trappings, of a modern suburb, even though farmers still tend the surrounding fields just as their forebears did. But these days the produce is essentially vegetables and cereals, supplemented by the occasional cow.

For Lambis, Fromelles has become a second home. He knows it almost as well as his beloved Northcote in Melbourne and it lingers in his subliminal mind most of his waking hours. During his wanderings around the battlefield in 2002, Lambis became increasingly fixated on the missing and their fate. He knew many of the unknown had been buried at VC Corner. He figured there were others who would have been gathered after the war and interred in other cemeteries.

This led him to conjecture about how many there were who remained unfound and, as he walked, he would imagine where they might be – in non-man's land, in the filled-in communication trenches across it, along the banks of the River Laies, dumped in shell craters and filled in, hidden in long-lost graves in the fields. A growing feeling welled up inside him. These missing Diggers were waiting for him to find them.

16

THE FIRST STEPS

The beginning is the most important part of the work.

PLATO, *THE REPUBLIC*

After he returned home, Lambis Englezos focused his imagination on the fate of the missing Diggers of Fromelles. He studied all the available books, cross-checked the facts and did the basic maths. He confirmed that 410 bodies were gathered up, mainly from no-man's land, after the Armistice in 1918 and buried at VC Corner. The honour roll on the wall there has a total of 1299 names of those missing (actually, it should read 1298 as the body of Major Roy Harrison was discovered in 1927 and identified the following year from an inscription on a silver cigarette case he was carrying. He now rests at the nearby Rue Petillon Cemetery). Lambis concedes his first steps were pretty basic:

> *At the start my research was all fundamental and very amateurish.*
> *I just suspected that the numbers didn't quite add up. I was speculating*

but I had this powerful gut feeling. We were told there were 1299 missing and 5533 casualties. There were lots of cemeteries around with unknown Australians in them and I wondered whether they did add up.

When Lambis did the maths, he realised the numbers clearly didn't tally. But initially he couldn't be sure how far out the numbers were; how many were missing or where they were. He made guesses as to the number – 600, 500, 400. He eventually settled on a preliminary guesstimate of around 250. But where were they? He conceded that some would almost certainly have been blown into unrecognisable pieces by direct artillery hits, but surely this would have been only a relatively small proportion of them. What about the others? He could have accepted a handful who had gone missing through the uncontrollable vagaries of war ... but not hundreds.

Major Roy Harrison's headstone in the Rue Petillon Cemetery. Harrison's remains were found in 1927 and identified by an inscribed cigarette case. He is among 291 Australians, many from the Battle of Fromelles, who rest here. (PATRICK LINDSAY PHOTO)

Lambis wrote, emailed and phoned others with knowledge of Fromelles and a similar interest. His messages travelled all around the world and soon he found himself linked into a vibrant network of people in Australia, Britain and France who shared his passion. He gathered a small close-knit team of like-minded amateur sleuths around him, all dedicated to solving the mystery of the missing Diggers of Fromelles: John Fielding, deputy headmaster of Normanhurst High School in north-western Sydney, a keen military historian and a lieutenant colonel in the Army Reserve; Ward Selby, another military history buff and an executive at BHP-Billiton; and Robin Corfield, author and the definitive expert on the Battle of Fromelles. They pooled their thoughts and attacked the problem. John Fielding was quickly swept up in the odyssey:

I was talking to a friend of mine in the regular army and he said to me: you're really interested in the First World War aren't you? He knew I took school groups over there on tours. He said I've got a mate who's really into it; in fact he's particularly interested in Fromelles. His name's Lambis and he's in Melbourne.

The next minute I get an email from Lambis saying: when's your next trip? I was going in a few weeks' time. He started sending me aerial photographs of Fromelles and he said I have this theory. He captured me straight away. I'm military police in the Army Reserve and I'm very interested in that sort of stuff.

One of Lambis' early clues came from reading Robin Corfield's book *Don't Forget Me, Cobber!*. Corfield quoted from the memoirs of Private Bill Barry of the 29th Battalion. As we've already seen, Barry was captured behind the German lines. He had been caught in an artillery barrage shortly after dropping supplies to the beleaguered men of the 8th Brigade on the left flank near Delangré Farm. Barry recalled being knocked senseless by the bombing and then waking up wounded as a prisoner. Some time later he lapsed into unconsciousness again and when he awoke he was unattended, so he moved out of the bunker in which he'd been held. To his horror, and as recorded earlier, he discovered he was

in the place where all the dead men were. I was sitting on the edge of a hole about forty feet long, twenty feet wide and fifteen feet deep and into this hole the dead were being thrown without any fuss or respect.

Lambis had his first genuine breakthrough: first-hand evidence that the Germans had buried Australians and British dead from the battle in some kind of mass grave. It was a great start, but where was this grave and how many of the missing were buried there?

Lambis had a good idea of how the dead were recovered and taken to the rear of the German lines. He had long ago seen the photograph of the German troops standing beside a small field railway engine, or perhaps more accurately a rough tram, hooked up to a flat-topped, timber-planked tramcar piled with the dead bodies of Australian troops. He knew that the Germans had used this light railway to move supplies behind their lines. It was known to the Germans as the Turkenbahn. It began as the French local rail line in peacetime, Ligne Michon, which originated at Don-Sainghin to the south of Fournes, then ran to Fournes, where the Germans built a rough station near their regimental cemetery. The wartime line then continued through Fromelles and down the hill out of the village towards the front lines, cutting through the south-western corner of a small wood below the church, then heading behind Rouges Bancs to the German front line trench system.

German soldiers transport dead after the battle of Vimy Ridge using light rail similar to that used at Fromelles.

From his readings and his interpretation of the logic of the battlefield, Lambis postulated that this would be the way the Germans collected and transported the Australian dead after the battle in July 1916. He ploughed on, reading every account of the battle that he could get his hands on and speaking to anyone who would listen.

Early in the piece, Lambis had been struck when he read that General Haking and his staff had used aerial photographs of the Fromelles area when they planned the attack. It occurred to him that with so many dead to bury after the battle, any large area of gravesites dug by the Germans should appear on some of the aerials that were taken after the battle by the Royal Flying Corps (the forerunner of the Royal Air Force) and these may be evident if he compared before and after aerials. So he wrote off to the Imperial War Museum in London seeking copies of any photographs of the area behind the German lines taken, either shortly before 19 July or in the days and weeks after.

The Allied map system was based on grids – squares of 6000 by 6000 yards (5.5 × 5.5 kilometres – or 30 square kilometres). Each of these squares was identified by a letter of the alphabet (the map square 'N' covered most of the Fromelles battlefield). These large squares were then subdivided into six rows of six smaller squares – 36 sub-squares each 1000 × 1000 yards (914 × 914 m – about 8 square kilometres). In turn, these sub-squares were split into quarters, noted clockwise as 'a, b, d, and c', and each of these was broken down into tenths by numbering them 1 to 10 along their eastern and northern sides.

Using this system, any individual feature could be identified to within metres by quoting the map letter, the sub-square number, the quarter of that sub-square and then where it intersects on the lines of the tenths of that quarter. For example, the Sugar Loaf would be referred to as N.8.d.7.2. In other words: map square N, sub-square 8, quarter d, 7 tenths along the eastern side and 2 tenths along the northern side. Lambis therefore knew exactly which aerial photos of which map squares he needed to request from the Imperial War Museum.

I was hoping that the photos would simply show me ground that looked interesting in terms of diggings. It was just a starting point ... something to use as a base. I had a broad idea of where to look. For example, there was no point looking behind the Sugar Loaf because we knew none of the Diggers ever got there.

When he received the first photos from London, Lambis was stunned. A comparison between an aerial taken on 17 June 1916 (a month before the battle), another taken a week after the battle on 29 July, and a third on 1 August threw up an immediate area of interest. The area was at the southern end of the distinctively shaped wood just below Fromelles village. The pre-battle aerial showed no sign of any major excavations but the aerials taken after the battle clearly showed that a large patch of the ground had been disturbed. Closer examination showed the disturbance was a series of large open pits. They were in a rectangular plot of land, about 30 metres wide and 150 metres long, sitting on the southern end of the wood.

Lambis sought more aerials from the Imperial War Museum, and when he received one dated 20 December 1916 he could easily see eight large pits dug in two lines along the southern border of the tree-line below the wood. This shot showed that five of the pits had been filled in. A final aerial which arrived some time later and was taken on 16 September 1918, two months before the Armistice, showed that the five filled pits had blended into the surrounding paddock but that the remaining three pits were still open and empty.

The findings buoyed Lambis enormously. He had sought the aerials purely on a gut feeling and his hunch had proved correct. He felt he was on the right trail. Re-reading Corfield's treasure-trove of research gave him another clue. It had been there all along, hidden in a story about two great mates, Private Walter Vaile and Lieutenant Jack

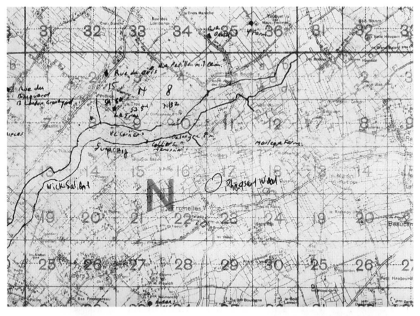

A copy of the British Army trench map of 1916, with the approximate Allied and German front lines drawn in. Pheasant Wood is shown in map square N17, the Sugar Loaf at the bottom of square N8 and Fromelles village in N22. Each numbered square is 500 yards square. (SOURCE CHRIS BRYETT)

Bowden, who had both died in the battle. Bowden's body had never been found and was one of those classified as missing in action. His family made persistent enquiries about his fate. Initially they brought confusion. Because Bowden was listed as a private, although he had been recently commissioned, his family was told that he apparently 'died of wounds while a prisoner of war'. They had no record of where he had died or where he was buried. But by 1918, Corfield reported, the story had changed and the family was advised:

> *Officially reported as killed in action 19 July 1916. There is no question of his ever having been taken prisoner of war, this belief must have risen from the circumstances of his personal effects being picked up by the Germans in the field. There is a possibility that his body was buried by the enemy though we have never received any information to this effect.*

Lieutenant Jack Bowden, one of the missing, whose Red Cross file provided a vital clue to the final resting place of the Fromelles missing. (PHOTO COURTESY JENNY INGHAM)

After the war the Red Cross in Berlin confirmed that it did have a record of Bowden and so Corfield then added:

> the confusion, if there was confusion, resulted from the Germans believing him to be **among those they buried in one of five large British Collective Graves outside Fasanenwäldchen, Pheasants Wood or in a collective grave at Fournes.** (emphasis added)

Lambis checked German trench maps from the time and found that Fasanen Wäldchen was included in them. It was the name of the wood where he had discovered the excavations in the British aerials! Another piece of the puzzle had fallen into place: Lambis now had the name of the wood in his aerial, Pheasant Wood (or, as the Germans knew it, Fasanen Wäldchen). Indeed, when he started to go through the records and other accounts, he found that Pheasant Wood appeared without fanfare a number of times. The pits in the aerials were surely the mass graves.

> When I think back, Martial mentioned something about Pheasant Wood to me when I was at Fromelles in 2002. I walked past it every day on my way to the battlefields but it didn't mean anything to me then. And the work into the missing was all done after I returned in May 2002.

Lambis was certain that this was a major validation of his theory and he started making enquiries in the official channels, sending all his findings to the Australian Army and the Department of Veterans' Affairs. All he met were roadblocks: dead ends and prevarication.

> All I got was 'piss off, go away, they're all accounted for' responses and replies. It was very frustrating and eventually I realised I needed

to give the thing a push to get it taken seriously so I went to the press, even though I'm usually reluctant to do that. I spoke to Neil Wilson of the Herald-Sun and ultimately to Jonathan King, who broke the story on the day before the anniversary of 2003.

17

GOING PUBLIC

The shortest and surest way of arriving at real knowledge is to unlearn the lessons we have been taught, to mount the first principles, and take nobody's word about them.

HENRY BOLINGBROKE

Jonathan King's article was published in the *Australian* on 18 July 2003 (appropriately, the eve of the 87th anniversary of the battle) under the headline 'Mass Grave of Australian 'Diggers' in France?'.

A Mass grave containing the remains of 250 missing Australian soldiers is believed to have been found in a French field, 87 years after they were killed in the battle of Fromelles – one of the bloodiest encounters of World War I.

A noted WWI historian, Dr John Williams, was quoted in the article:

We know there are remains of many Australian soldiers buried in mass graves near Fromelles and it would be good to recognise this site. If the Government doubts Mr Englezos they could commission an official search to prove or disprove his hypothesis, once and for all.

(In the light of subsequent events, Williams' initial enthusiasm and support seems strange. He later changed his mind and wrote a disparaging report on the likelihood of the Pheasant Wood containing a mass grave. More of that later.)

Elsewhere in the article, King said that Lambis planned to lobby the Commonwealth War Graves Commission to erect a memorial at Pheasant Wood, with flowering gum trees around the perimeter. Robin Corfield agreed that at the least the site should be marked with a 'cairn' so that descendants of the missing could make pilgrimages to pay their respects.

But King then quoted Michael Seal, Director of the Commonwealth War Grave Commission in Arras, near Lille, who cautioned that it was not his commission's job to search for new remains, that they were short of funds and so a 'watertight case' was essential before they could consider any memorial. In any case, he said the memorials at VC Corner and Peter Corlet's Cobbers statue in the Australian Memorial Park in Fromelles already commemorated the battle and those who died there without any known grave.

Lambis was adamant:

If the Commonwealth War Graves Commission refuses to respect the memories of these lying in that paddock near Fromelles then we will build a memorial to them at the Shrine of Remembrance in Melbourne – where at least there is some support.

Typical of the responses Lambis received to his enquiries in these early stages was this reply, dated 3 December 2004, to an email he sent to the Director of the Office of War Graves, Air Vice-Marshal Gary Beck, in which Lambis had listed all the names of those he believed to be the Missing:

Lambis,

Every one of these names is listed as buried at VC Corner Australian Cemetery Fromelles.

Commission information on VC Corner includes: 'It contains the graves of over 400 Australian soldiers who died in the attack at Fromelles and whose bodies were found on the battlefield, but not a single body could be identified.'

We are checking CWGC [Commonwealth War Graves Commission] records to see if any more information about the state of the bodies is available. However, given that not a single one could be identified suggests they had already been interfered with, eg, hastily buried by Germans and tags removed and reported to Red Cross.

If this is so, then that should lay to rest your belief they still remain at Pheasant Wood. Lambis, you will have to let this one go, or find some evidence for your belief.

If we learn anything new, I will be in touch. Would you please distribute this message to your friends and maybe one of them can convince you as I don't seem to be able to.

Lambis replied to Ward Selby and his team succinctly:

Hello Ward, he has missed the point completely ... amazing ... bye for now, Lambis

Jonathan King's article contained some inaccuracies but it clearly put the mystery of the missing on the public agenda and prompted questions from the media, the veterans' community and the Federal opposition. Eventually responding to the groundswell of interest, Gary Beck confirmed (in a brief provided to Defence Minister Senator Hill to allow him to answer a question from Senator Mark Bishop in a Senate Estimates Committee) that 163 Diggers had been gathered by the Germans and buried.

Lambis was gobsmacked! He was initially taken back that he was wrong with his guesstimate of 250. But he was elated that at last he had official confirmation that the 'missing' actually existed. They had obviously been there all the time. No-one had asked about them.

The Office of War Graves had done the simple maths:

        1299 names with no known graves on the VC Corner Wall
(less)   5 bodies found in the 1920s (after cemeteries established)
(less)   1131 bodies buried at VC Corner and other cemeteries
(equals) 163 'The Missing'

The figure of 1131 unidentified bodies known to be buried at other cemeteries was calculated by adding:

410	VC Corner Cemetery
266	Rue David Military Cemetery
142	Ration Farm Military Cemetery
120	Aubers Ridge British Cemetery
72	'Y' Farm Military Cemetery
52	Le Trou Aid Post Cemetery
27	Rue du Bois Military Cemetery
22	Rue Petillon Military Cemetery
10	Anzac Cemetery
10	Sailly-sur-la-Lys Canadian Cemetery

"It is no longer possible to establish with absolute
certainty whether Lieutenant J.C.Bowden of the 59th Aust.Batt, and
Private John Charles Bowden of the 59th Aust Batt.are identical.
The possibility of it rests on the fact that the report of the death
of the Lieutenant J.C.Bowden was only made on the receipt of the
paybook.   His identity Disc may quite well have read Private John
Charles Bowden, as it is possible that, as an Officer recently promoted
he had not yet renewed his disc.
           After the battle near Fromelles on the 19.7.16.
the identity Discs were removed from all the fallen men and sent in
The name of Bowden is not reported in the lists of graves. It may be
assumed that possibly Lieutenant Bowden was buried in one of the five
large British collective graves before the Fasanen, Wäldchen
(Pheasants Wood) near Fromelles, or in the collective grave (No.1 M.4.3)
in the Military Cemetery at Fournes.
           There are no materials here for further investigations
concerning those buried in the graves mentioned.

                    Prisoners Care Department.
                    (Sgd) V.Grusingen.
                         26.1.19.

Translated copy of a letter sent by the German Red Cross in 1918 replying to a
query by Jack Bowden's family and advising that he was likely to have been buried
at Pheasant Wood.

Not long after this, Jeroen Huygelier, a Belgian archivist and one
of Lambis' growing international support network, referred Lambis to
the records of the International Red Cross. Huygelier explained that
the records were thorough and extensive and had been invaluable to
him many times in the past. Lambis had not been aware of them.
Huygelier pointed out that the Red Cross had created them in late
1915, through its Wounded and Missing Enquiry Bureau, and that they
contained around 30,000 individual case files of Australians reported
as wounded or missing during World War I.

Lambis attacked them like a dog at a bone. And his timing was spot on. The Australian War Memorial had only digitised the records two years earlier and they were now available online via the AWM's excellent website.

These records were a revelation to Lambis. The Red Cross investigated and responded to enquiries about the fate of missing Australian personnel. In a Herculean performance, the organisation managed to investigate most of those posted as wounded and missing on official army lists and to reply in writing to relatives and friends of those missing. Usually, each soldier's file included a searcher's report, eyewitness accounts from friends or comrades of the place and circumstances of the death or wounding of the individual and, where possible, his place of burial, together with letters from friends or relatives and responses by the Red Cross.

Lambis now returned to Robin Corfield's *Don't Forget Me, Cobber!* as a base-line reference, and painstakingly went through the honour roll of all those who died at the Battle of Fromelles and cross-referenced each name against the Red Cross records.

The turning point came when he viewed Jack Bowden's file. Lambis' heart missed a beat as he read a translation of a letter dated 21 January 1918 from the Red Cross in Berlin to the organisation's headquarters in Geneva responding to a query from Bowden's family seeking his final resting place. One paragraph jumped out at Lambis:

> *After the battle near Fromelles on the 19.7.16 the identity discs were removed from all the fallen men and sent in. The name of Bowden is not reported in the list of graves.* **It may be assumed that possibly Lieutenant Bowden was buried in one of the five large British collective graves before the Fasanen Wäldchen (Pheasants Wood) near Fromelles, or in the collective grave (No.1 M.4.3) in the Military Cemetery at Fournes.** *(emphasis added)*

Another piece in the jigsaw puzzle – and a corner piece too! Lambis realised that he was effectively piecing together the German death list from the Battle of Fromelles – all the Australian dead who had been collected by the Germans after the battle, placed on their light railway carriages and taken to the pits they had dug at Pheasant Wood. There, with the efficiency and meticulousness for which their army is renowned, the Germans had sorted the dead by nationality, taken their identification tags and then listed their details before burying the remains in the mass graves.

The identity discs worn by Australian soldiers in World War I comprised two fibreboard (compressed cardboard) discs, one round and one octagonal. They were stamped with the soldier's name, service or regimental number, religion, and his unit. The octagonal disc, often coloured green, was to remain on the body even after burial, so the remains could be identified should they need to be exhumed. The circular disc, sometimes coloured red, was used to identify the belongings of the soldier and be sent home. According to the Australian War Memorial, the colours were to help soldiers to remember which tag went where:

red meant blood and was to be taken, since the soldier was dead;
green meant grass and was to stay with the body.

Working long into the night over the next months, Lambis patiently cross-checked the honour roll names with those on the German death list and eventually came up with 161 names of soldiers who were recorded as having been gathered by the Germans and buried. It was close enough to Beck's figure of 163. Lambis had even discounted one name because, although he saw his name on the death list, his file did not have the documentation confirming that he'd been one of those gathered and buried by the Germans. Lambis was growing in confidence in his theory:

> *If there are 163 dead unaccounted for and the records tell us the Germans buried 161 of them, clearly that's around the figure. So it was a very strong link. The really super-critical file was Bowden from the 59th Battalion because in that one particular document, it mentions that we buried them in five pits before Pheasant Wood and in mass grave IM.4.3 at Fournes, the German General Cemetery, about five k's back of Fromelles. The next question to be answered was: were there records somewhere to suggest that these bodies had been subsequently found and re-buried somewhere else?*

As he worked, Lambis found that the demand for some action from the army and the Federal government was growing. On 13 March 2005, the *Canberra Times* ran a piece which represented the prevailing view: that Lambis had made a sufficiently substantive case so that the next logical step was a proper examination of the Pheasant Wood site:

> *Opposition spokesman on veterans' affairs Mark Bishop is among a growing group who believe a technical examination should be made of the likely mass grave sites around Fromelles. Such agitation has previously met with bureaucratic reluctance, but Bishop is hopeful that Defence Minster Robert Hill will authorise examinations, and has been heartened by the attitude of the Chief of Army Lieutenant-General Peter Leahy.*

Senator Bishop claimed that while the Office of War Graves had confirmed that 163 bodies remained unaccounted for, Lambis had established that 161 names appeared on the German Red Cross files as having been buried by the Germans in a manner that

Team Lambis member, John Fielding, and Fromelles resident and Commonwealth War Graves Commission officer, Martial Delebarre, at the Fromelles Museum. (JOHN FIELDING PHOTO)

The southern end of Pheasant Wood, looking north. The mass graves dug by the Germans after the Battle of Fromelles were situated in the grassed area in front of the tree line, in the right half of the shot. (PATRICK LINDSAY PHOTO)

could not otherwise be explained [other than by burial by the Germans in mass graves]. I believe this matter is now at a stage where it can be said that a strong prima facie case exists for a technical examination of the sites referred to.

The senator welcomed the decision of the Chief of the Australian Army, General Peter Leahy, to examine the material that Lambis had referred to him. He said he hoped the army and the government would formally approach the French government and the local authorities at Fromelles seeking permission for a 'ground scan' of the site. Bishop kept up the pressure by concluding:

At official level in Canberra, the existence of the Pheasant Wood site has been denied by the Office of Australian War Graves, but the evidence is now building.

In September 2004, John Fielding was due to take another school tour to the Western Front so Lambis gave him his orders: he needed someone to survey the ground, get some photographs and give him a first-hand assessment of the ground at Pheasant Wood. Fielding was delighted.

I went over there, armed with all these maps. I went with my son and he and we did a Boy's Own Annual trip: Agincourt, Waterloo, World War One, World War Two, D-Day – all in about three weeks. We had a great time.

When we got to Fromelles, we knew exactly where to go. We walked the ground, photographed it all, panoramas and stuff. But at that stage we were labouring under a misapprehension: we thought those three empty pits which showed up on the 1918 aerial were the pits, you see. So I concentrated on the right-hand side, or the eastern side of Pheasant Wood, when in fact the pits were really more in the centre.

The lawn was newly mown when I was there and therefore you could really see the undulations quite clearly. Then I returned and I emailed those off to Lambis who was delighted.

18

THE PANEL

Knowledge speaks, but wisdom listens.

Jimi Hendrix

Lambis was even more upbeat some months later when he called John Fielding. He told him it was 'action stations' because he'd just received word from Roger Lee, Head of the Australian Army History Unit, that he'd been instructed to establish a Panel of Investigation to examine Lambis' claims. Lambis told John that they had to be ready to present their case to the panel at the Defence Department's Campbell Offices Headquarters in a month's time. The team – Lambis, John and Ward Selby – then focussed all their energies on preparing their presentation. They would only have one chance to persuade the panel they had a genuine case that demanded their action.

As he honed his presentation, Lambis took some satisfaction from the fact that his quest had gathered such momentum and the pressure had paid off. The Panel of Investigation would examine the evidence and decide whether it was strong enough to warrant a proper examination of the Pheasant Wood site. The panel would comprise Roger Lee (as Chairman); Dr John Williams, nominated as an independent expert; Professor Bill Gammage, author and historian from the Australian National University; Associate Professor Iain Spence from the University of New England; Professor Jeffrey Grey from the Australian Defence Force Academy; Dr Bruce Scates from the University of New South Wales; Dr Peter Stanley, Garth Pratten and Craig Tibbitts from the Australian War Memorial; Air Vice-Marshal Gary Beck and Kathy Upton-Mitchell from the Office of War Graves; Keith Knight from the Defence Imagery and Geospatial Organisation; and Bill Houston, Brian Manns and Emma Robertson from the Army History Unit.

It was a high-powered assembly and a testament to the case that Lambis and his team had painstakingly built and substantiated. Lambis spent hours with John and Ward on their presentation. They revisited all their research and distilled it to its essentials. They selected the photos that best illustrated it and wove their argument into a PowerPoint presentation. The team was satisfied their case was powerful and John and Ward knew they had a secret weapon: Lambis' passion. For his part, Lambis was in turmoil. He was comfortable presenting to a room full of people. It was his bread and butter; he did it with his students every day. But this was a very different room full of experts in their various fields. The more he thought about it, the more he built up to it like a dental appointment.

But when he found himself outside conference room CP4-2-66 in the Department of Defence's massive bunker-like Campbell Offices in Canberra on Friday 10 June 2005, Lambis felt strangely calm.

I know it sounds wanky but I felt I was there honouring a duty to those who are waiting for us to return to find them where they've been waiting for 90 years. I had faith in the process and I was confident that the members of the panel that I knew had good hearts. My only fear was that my passion would make me get carried away.

At ten to nine, Roger Lee officially opened the meeting and outlined the panel's purpose and duties, which came down to establishing whether

there is sufficient and compelling evidence to warrant Army's conducting further investigation of Mr Englezos' claim that Australian missing remain buried in three grave sites near Fromelles, France.

Lee explained that the resolution of the panel would culminate in a brief he would prepare for the Chief of the Army to hand to the Minister, outlining the panel's views and setting out any recommendations. He pointed out that the Chief of the Army had already undertaken that

if there is sufficient and compelling evidence to support the existence of mass graves of Australians in the Fromelles region, he will proceed with further action so that our dead are properly honoured.

Lee concluded by telling the panel that, as their decision would be likely to create a precedent, they should proceed with caution. He then turned to Lambis and invited him to make his case.

Ward Selby manned the laptop computer and switched through the PowerPoint pages while Lambis spoke. During the last week, Team Lambis had decided to expand their submission to include two other sites in addition to Pheasant Wood: Fournes Cemetery (which had been mentioned in many of the sources as an alternative to Pheasant Wood) and another which had shown up as having some fresh excavations on the aerial photographs, Marlaque Farm. They had decided to include Marlaque Farm, which stood about a kilometre north-east of Pheasant Wood, because of what they believed were pits dug there on an aerial photo dated 11 December 1916. But they had agreed that their main thrust would be to convince the panel that their case for Pheasant Wood was irresistibly strong and demanded further physical investigation.

Lambis began by referring to a table of unidentified Diggers known to have been buried in the cemeteries in the Fromelles area from the Battle of Fromelles. On the screen the panel saw that of the total of 1294 Australian soldiers missing from the battle, 1131 were shown from cemetery records to have been buried in VC Corner and the nine other surrounding cemeteries. That left 163 unaccounted for – the missing Diggers of Fromelles.

Then Ward called up an aerial photograph from the Australian War Memorial collection. Numbered E05990, the photo is simply described as: 'Oblique of Fromelles area, from the air, showing Australian and German lines'. But as most of the experts on the panel knew – and Lambis enthusiastically pointed out – the shot shows virtually the entire Australian battlefield as it was on 19 July 1916. It is a stunning shot and in a snapshot it captures almost all the key elements of the battle. Taken from an oblique angle looking across the Australian position from a position roughly in line with the Sugar Loaf salient, it clearly shows the Australian and German front lines, with no-man's land between them, and then looks south-east across the German-held territory as far as the Aubers ridgeline.

There is something magnificently evocative about the image. At a glance it shows the futility of the attack: the relentlessly flat terrain, the strength of the German defences, the dominance of the Sugar Loaf and the great variance in no-man's land from its widest part in front of the Sugar Loaf, to its narrowest in front of the 8th Brigade on the Australian left flank.

This remarkable aerial shot by the Royal Flying Corps shows virtually the entire Australian battlefield at Fromelles as it was on 19 July 1916. Taken from an oblique angle, it captures almost all the key elements of the battle from a position roughly in line with the Sugar Loaf salient (bottom right). From the bottom of the frame, it shows the Australian, then German front lines, with no-man's land between them, and looks south-east across the German-held territory as far as the Aubers ridgeline. The Fromelles township is in the centre about a third of the way down the photo, with Pheasant Wood just to the left in front of the town. (AWM PHOTO E05990)

Ward Selby and John Fielding had carefully marked the aerial to show all the key elements of the battle and Lambis orientated the panel by showing them the Sugar Loaf, where the Australian Memorial Park stands just inside the German front lines, how the River Laies snakes across no-man's land, where the Delangré Farm stronghold defied the men of the 8th Brigade and where the township of Fromelles stood to the rear.

With a click of the mouse Ward Selby overlaid the position of Pheasant Wood, just to the rear of Delangré Farm. The battlefield logic of Lambis' argument was clear as he showed where the light railway line ran from behind the German lines, around Rouges Bancs and then cut across the south-western corner of Pheasant Wood.

As Lambis warmed to his task, John Fielding scanned the room looking at the way Lambis was being received. He felt the room was pretty much divided 50-50 although the negativity from some parts of it was palpable. He was particularly disappointed to overhear some snide remarks about Lambis' appearance. But Lambis was on a roll and ignored them.

He was explaining the sequential discovery of their evidence and was telling the panel about the vital importance of Jack Bowden's Red Cross Record. On the screen, a copy of the original German card recording Bowden's details on the 'Death Voucher' Number 10064/ W225, from the Inquiry Officer at the Army Korps 6 to the Royal Prussian War Office: Medical Section, Central Office for Lost Property, Berlin:

Lieutenant Bowden J. C. of the 59th Battalion fell in the neighbourhood of Fromelles on 19/7/16.

Lambis now had the panel's full attention. He went on to explain that he had reviewed each of the 1299 names of Diggers listed as missing on the wall at VC Corner. The next page on the screen revealed a list of the names of the 161 soldiers whose names were recorded on that list and who also had German Red Cross files showing they were gathered at Fromelles and buried by the Germans. Suddenly the missing were no longer nameless numbers, they were soldiers with

£ano	England Totekiſten Ur. 10064 ▼ /225		
Name Abſchrift	B o w d e n , John Charles		
Dienſtgrad	Sold.	Ur. der Erk-Marke	1929
Cruppenteil	59.Batl.		
Zeit u. Ort der Gefangennahme	Soldbuch wurde vom N.O.A.O.K.6		
Aufenthaltsort	überwiesen .17.8.16.		
Bemerkungen Verwundung Heimatsort			

£and	England Totekiſten Ur. 10064		▼225
Name Abſchrift	B o w d e n , John Charles		
Dienſtgrad	Sold.	Ur. der Erk-Marke	1929
Cruppenteil	59.Batl.		
Zeit u. Ort der Gefangennahme	Soldbuch wurde vom N.O.A.O.K.6		
Aufenthaltsort	überwiesen.17.9.16.		
Bemerkungen Verwundung Heimatsort			

Bowden's record of death from the German archives. (AWM)

names, regimental numbers, ranks and battalions. As the panel members took this in, Lambis emphasised the synchronicity of this number and the number calculated by subtracting the total of unidentified Australians listed as buried in all the nearby cemeteries from the total missing from the battle – 161 on the German death list and 163 with no record of a place of burial.

Then the next slide showed a letter from the Central Committee of the German Red Cross Societies No. VII, in German on one side and then translated on the other. The first paragraph dealt with some early confusion over Jack Bowden's rank: how he'd been promoted to lieutenant shortly before the battle yet his ID tag still had him as a private. The next paragraph contained the twist:

After the battle near Fromelles on the 19.7.16 the identity discs were removed from all the fallen men and sent in. The name of Bowden is not reported in the list of graves. It may be assumed that possibly Lieutenant Bowden was buried in one of the five large British collective graves before the Fasanen Wäldchen (Pheasants Wood) near Fromelles, or in the collective grave (No. 1 M.4.3) in the Military Cemetery at Fournes.

Lambis offered further confirmation of the Pheasant Wood graves with the next image on the screen: extracts from the Regimental History of the Bavarian Reserve Infantry Regiments opposed to the Australians at Fromelles, as supplied by the Bavarian Main State Archive in Munich in July 2004:

July 20 1916 ... there are 399 dead in the section of our regiment alone and in the area in front of our section there are also several 100, where they have been laying for weeks and polluting the air until our patrols regardless of the hostile fire gradually put chlorinated lime and then soil on them ... **for the fallen enemies we are preparing mass graves behind the Fasanen-Wäldchen** *[emphasis added]. We have also started to fill in two sappen which the enemy built in the night from the 19th to the 20th July, from his position up to ours and is now full of dead enemies ...*

Lambis followed this up with the photo of the flat-top carriage of the German light rail piled high with dead bodies with German troops

Battle of Fromelles, 19–20 July 1916

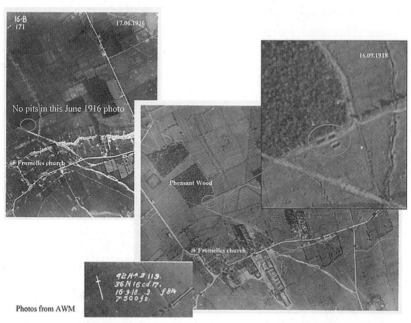

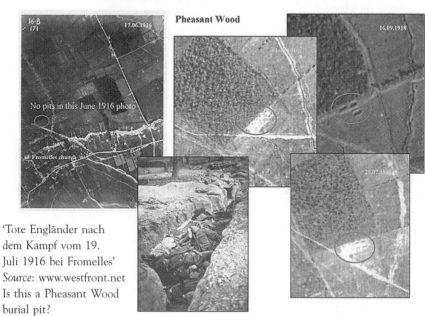

'Tote Engländer nach
dem Kampf vom 19.
Juli 1916 bei Fromelles'
Source: www.westfront.net
Is this a Pheasant Wood
burial pit?

Aerial photograph of Pheasant Wood taken in 1918.

standing around it. It was from the Unit History of the 16BRIR and credited to photographer Hans Bauer. Lambis read the caption:

Casualties of the battle of 19/20 July 1916. Bodies of dead English are taken from Fromelles to Fournes by field railway.

He pointed out that the Germans called all those who fought against them at Fromelles 'English' and then he quoted a passage from Robin Corfield's *Don't Forget Me, Cobber!*:

We know that they collected many bodies and loaded them on a train, photographed them, and then took the dead to mass graves at Pheasant Wood and elsewhere over the days after the battle.

Lambis expanded on the way that the Germans had used their field railway to transport the bodies they collected behind their lines. He referred to German maps on which the light rail line was marked as moving from behind the German front lines through the south-east corner of Pheasant Wood, on its way to Fournes. He suggested that the simplest way for the Germans to have disposed of their dead enemies' bodies, which would pose a health threat as they decomposed where they fell, would have been to load them on to the field railway and take them to the open pits at Pheasant Wood where they could be offloaded and buried.

At this point Gary Beck challenged Lambis' logic. He said this assumption was ridiculous. Pointing to the map, Beck indicated where the train line ran and where the Pheasant Wood pits were sited, noting that the three empty pits were furthest away from the rail line. Common sense would dictate they would have taken the bodies and carried them to the furthest pit and buried them there until each pit was full and then moved back. That's not what's happened so it's clearly not the case.

John Fielding had not said a word to this point. But now he could not resist and intervened:

I don't know, Mr Beck, what sort of soldiers or troops you've ever commanded but the guys that I command, if they were faced with the task of carrying rotted corpses, would pick the line of least resistance. They would drop them in the first hole they could and, if that became full, they'd be forced to then go to the next hole. So, I don't know where you get your idea from.

Lambis filled the awkward silence that followed by speaking to the next page, which showed two German trench maps from the Bavarian RIR unit history, also included in Corfield's book. He pointed out where Pheasant Wood (Fasanen Wäldchen) was clearly marked on each of them.

Next, Lambis turned to the Royal Flying Corps aerial photographs of Pheasant Wood before and after the battle. Ward Selby and John Fielding had prepared a montage and Lambis took the panel through the different photos, emphasising where the land was untouched as at 17 June yet obviously excavated by the shot dated 29 July, a week after the battle. He showed how the three empty pits were still clearly visible in September 1918.

John Fielding later recalled how he and his team-mates were secretly delighted on their arrival to meet the panel when they were shown an aerial that had been presented to the panel by the Army History

Testament to the desperate fighting behind the German lines, bodies of Australian and German dead lie intermingled on the morning after the action. One of the series of photos taken by a German officer and given to Australian POW, Captain Charles Mills, at the war's end. (AWM PHOTO A01557)

Unit. Team Lambis had been unaware of its existence. It came, not from the Imperial War Museum, but from the Australian War Memorial files and it showed clearly five freshly filled-in pits and three that had been dug and were still empty.

It was one of the biggest breaks we got. The Army History Unit had tabled an aerial photograph, taken just after the battle. In it you could actually clearly see the empty pits and then where the filled-in pits were. We then realised this is where they were.

Lambis then moved on to the work his team had done to try to discover whether the post-war Graves Recovery Unit (GRU) had found the Pheasant Wood mass grave site and perhaps exhumed the bodies there and reburied them elsewhere. The GRU kept records of all the bodies they recovered. They recorded where they found the remains, noted them according to the map square reference, and then the details of the cemeteries where they reburied them. Lambis explained that he had requested that the Commonwealth War Graves Commission search the records of all the possible 12 surrounding cemeteries for remains that had been recovered from the map reference for Pheasant Wood – Map 36N, Square 17c. He reported to the panel that the result came back: 'nil returns' for bodies recovered in that area.

At this point Lambis introduced a series of modern-day photographs of Fromelles and the Pheasant Wood site. He started with a colour satellite image that showed that Pheasant Wood remained identical in size and shape to the Royal Flying Corps aerials taken around the time of the battle. Then he handed over to John Fielding to speak about the photos he took in October 2004 of the burial site at Pheasant Wood. Fielding also emphasised how little the land had changed down the years and how easily he found it.

Think my photos were probably the first taken by anyone who actually knew that he was photographing the site of the mass graves. I explained that I could clearly see undulations where we believed the pits were dug.

Lambis again took over and argued that an aerial of nearby Marlaque Farm, taken by the British on 11 December 1916, showed what he believed were further burial pits. He supported this contention by quoting from Private Bill Barry's memoir where he wrote that, after being taken prisoner, he found himself 'sitting on the edge of a hole' into which 'the dead were being thrown without any fuss or respect'.

It was Lambis' belief that Barry was writing about Marlaque Farm and he supported this proposition by showing blow-ups of the aerials with what he claimed were open pits and German photos of dead enemy piled against a wall of rough bricks and timber. He followed with a similar argument centred on Fournes Cemetery, supporting it with aerials and extracts from Commonwealth War Graves records that showed that in 1920 they had exhumed six graves from under a German cross that read that they were casualties killed on 19 and 20 July 1916. Only one of these bodies was subsequently identified – as a British soldier from the Machine Gun Corps.

Lambis continued to explain that in July 1923, the Commonwealth War Graves team returned and exhumed another 176 remains which had various dates of death. Amongst them was a plot marked 'large trench grave No. I.M.4.3', that stated it contained 51 British soldiers buried between 23 and 25 July 1916. During the exhumation one further body was identified by an ID tag that the Germans had apparently missed – Private Patrick Gearing, Regimental Number 3501, from the 53rd Battalion.

The members of the panel clearly showed that they had little faith in these claims and Lambis eventually drew the presentation to a close with his final request:

I believe that a non-intrusive, geophysical investigation of the burial sites near Fromelles is warranted.

He said he was not seeking a full-scale excavation or reburial of the remains at this stage but, rather, in the first instance, he was seeking preliminary field studies including a professional archaeological geo-radar survey and, possibly the digging of test pits. The aim would be to establish the exact location and extent of the site with a view to considering the possibility of large-scale excavation or reburials after the results of the preliminary field work.

After Lambis finished, the panel members raised their queries: could the pits have been dug by the Germans for a completely different purpose, for example, an ammunition store for the impending battle or perhaps as positions for trench mortars or other artillery pieces? They expressed their surprise that a grave apparently containing so many bodies could have been missed by the graves registration units, especially when it was seemingly known. They asked what the land has been used for since the war and whether records existed at the local level of any activity since the Armistice of any evidence of mass graves or remains being found.

Lambis and the team answered the queries as best they could and then left the panel to its deliberations.

While Lambis Englezos, Ward Selby and John Fielding wound down with a tour of Parliament House, the panel members deliberated and reached their conclusion. They rejected Lambis' proposition that there were mass graves at either Marlaque Farm or Fournes Military Cemetery as having 'no compelling or unequivocal evidence' to support it. But on Pheasant Wood their conclusion was:

> It was agreed that while not conclusive, sufficient evidence does exist to warrant further investigation of records pertaining to the Pheasant's [sic] Wood site. Field studies are not recommended unless more compelling documentary evidence is located to support the contention that the site was used as a mass grave by the Germans in July 1916. Should more compelling evidence be discovered, the Panel agreed to reconvene, consider the new evidence and prepare an appropriate recommendation to the Minister for further action.

The panel went on to recommend that they contract a researcher to investigate the military records of the Bavarian Division opposing the attackers at Fromelles to find out how the dead were collected and interred after the battle. It also agreed that the Australian Army should approach their British counterparts and examine the area's intelligence assessments to find out what activity occurred there during the two years after the battle in 1916. Finally, the panel asked the army to try to locate the maps and reports of the Graves Registration Unit for the area after the war to find out whether they revealed any remains recovered from the site after the war.

19

THE GROUNDSWELL

*It is error alone which needs the support of
government. Truth can stand by itself.*

THOMAS JEFFERSON

On 15 June 2005, Senator Mark Bishop (Labor, Western Australia) rose
in the Senate on an adjournment debate and again spoke on Fromelles:

> *I raise this matter again simply because the Fromelles story, as I
> term it, has ignited a response I could never have imagined. In
> Western Australia, for example, my home state, the West Australian
> newspaper, to its credit, published the names of 18 Western Australians
> on the German list of Australians buried by them.*
>
> *Responses from family members made it quite clear that until this
> time they had had no idea what had happened to their uncle or great
> uncle, as it may have been. They simply knew that an uncle or great
> uncle had been killed, but no information had ever been provided by*

the relevant authorities. Inquiries to the Army by bereaved mothers were met with mute response. Mothers went to their graves never knowing what had happened to their sons, husbands and brothers.

Bishop pointed to the groundswell of interest by Australian families in their forebears and noted that, of the many families who had a relative missing from Fromelles, none would be aware that their loved one was actually buried by a Bavarian unit of the German army in a mass grave outside the town of Fromelles.

The senator then expanded on the remarkable response to the story from families across Australia. The *Adelaide Advertiser* published the names of 23 South Australians and one man from Broken Hill among the 163, while a similar story in the Hunter Valley revealed that 1000 men from the region fought in the battle from the 30th, 31st, 53rd, 54th, 55th and 56th Battalions. Of these, 59 were killed or died later of their wounds and eight Hunter Valley men's names appear on the German death list.

After the article appeared in the *Newcastle Herald* and the *Maitland Mercury*, fourteen people called in to identify themselves as relatives of those eight missing men and only a few were aware of their relatives' fate.

Bishop told how a number of grief-stricken relatives of the missing men had travelled to France on fruitless searches for them in the years immediately after the war. One family treasured their loved one's personal diary with its final entry on the afternoon before the battle and a letter to the family from a mate that concluded:

Well ... I am sorry I could not get our comrade into our lines as it was entirely impossible as we were surrounded. Some of our boys had to fight their way back that is when I got wounded. So your son would be buried behind German lines, but I hear that they had every respect given them.

Bishop also echoed and answered the obvious question: Why was nothing done after the war to find the burial site?

The reason simply was that the task of recovering bodies was enormous. Resources too were limited, and financial pressure no doubt caused work to be limited. Further, communications with the Germans were not good, as one can imagine. Access to German records was therefore difficult.

The senator ended with a simple request:

As all families conclude, the dead soldier cannot be brought back, but at least we should be able to mark the spot where he is buried.

Lambis Englezos and his team were delighted to hear Bishop was maintaining the pressure on the government, but they were more concerned to hear what the panel had decided. After they returned from Canberra, they waited. And waited. And waited. Lambis decided the only option he had while he waited was to work on strengthening his case.

In the adjournment debate in the Senate on 10 August, Mark Bishop again raised the issue of the missing of Fromelles. He referred to the recent ceremonial burial of four Diggers found near Merris in northern France. They had been unearthed by a farmer in 2003 and re-interred in the presence of the Chief of the Army Lieutenant General Peter Leahy, the Australian Ambassador to France Ms Penny Wensley and French officials and representatives. Two of the Diggers were likely to be Lieutenant Christopher Champion and Corporal Ernest Corby, who were reported missing in the area. The other remains could not be identified. All four were re-interred at Outtersteene Communal Cemetery Extension in Bailleul near where they were discovered. Senator Bishop praised the army and the Office of War Graves for the 'spirit of respect' they showed in this instance and in a number of other recent examples of discoveries of Australian servicemen from World War II. But he contrasted this spirit with the 'ongoing saga' relating to Fromelles.

Bishop referred to Lambis' presentation to the Panel of Investigation and called on the Minister to resolve the mystery before the following year's 90th anniversary of the Battle of Fromelles. He suggested:

The Fromelles Café today, showing the lasting connection to Australia. (PATRICK LINDSAY PHOTO)

A simple answer in this case would be to simply examine the site with ground-penetrating radar. This would reveal the presence of organic matter. That, though, it seems would be too easy.

The senator also noted that he understood that the panel had recommended that John Williams, Sydney author and academic and a member of the panel, be appointed to investigate the records of the Bavarian Division at Fromelles.

Later that month Lambis received a letter from the then Minister for Veterans' Affairs, De-Anne Kelly, dated 25 August. She delivered the verdict of the Panel of Investigation. They had dismissed the contention that Marlaque Farm or Fournes Cemetery contained any of the missing.

As to Pheasant Wood, the panel was more positive, but hardly enthusiastic:

The evidence in relation to the Pheasant Wood site is less clear. The panel was of the view that, while not convincing, there is sufficient doubt to warrant further documentary research. It posed two questions that it considers need to be resolved before any further action should be taken. Clearer evidence is needed that the Bavarian Division did use pits or mass graves to deal with the dead from the Battle of Fromelles and that, if they did, the site you have identified is indeed the site they used. If there was a mass grave, what evidence is there that it was not found and all remains in it recovered and re-interred in the numerous war cemeteries in the area after the cessation of hostilities.

The Minister concluded by informing Lambis that she had asked the army to attempt to answer these questions and that she had asked the Commonwealth War Graves Commission to make further inquiries 'about the origins of unknown soldiers already buried in existing cemeteries':

> *Clearly, if the Commonwealth War Graves Commission does discover evidence of remains recovered from the Pheasant Wood site and re-buried in another cemetery, the issue will be resolved.*
>
> *When I have received the results of these inquiries, I will write and inform you of the results and what actions, if any, I propose to take as a result.*

Lambis was not happy that the Minister had effectively asked his team to prove a negative: to find evidence that the Pheasant Wood site had not been found and the remains from it re-interred in other cemeteries. But at least the letter signalled some form of progress.

Rather than leave things entirely in the hands of the army and the Commonwealth War Graves Commission, Lambis and his team set about covering the ground themselves. Once they had extended their coverage and again worked their way through the war graves records, they were surprised to find an additional nine names of soldiers missing from the Battle of Fromelles. They were listed on the memorial wall at another famous Australian battle site, Villers-Bretonneux, about 80 kilometres to the south in the Somme. The nine Diggers listed there all also appeared in the Red Cross files showing they were gathered, not at Villers-Bretonneux, but at Fromelles on 19 July 1916 and buried by the Germans. This brought the total missing, buried by the Germans, to 170.

One of these new names was Lieutenant Robert David Burns of the 14th Machine Gun Company. When Lambis opened Burns' Red Cross record, it yielded another clue. Burns had been one of the last to try to withdraw from behind the German lines. He broke up his machine gun so the enemy couldn't use it and tried to fight his way back to the Australian lines but was killed, probably in no-man's land. He was the heir to the vast Burns Philp fortune – one of the biggest trading companies in the Pacific – and his Sydney-based father had called on his company's London executives to try to find his son's grave.

A reference in Burns' file led Lambis to an official internal inquiry held in 1920 by the Australian War Graves Service. The findings are now held in the National Archives. The inquiry was established to investigate claims that civilians had been present at the exhumation of loved ones' remains, something that was prohibited by the British regulations at the time. The investigation was prompted because a Burns Philp executive, named as Mr C.A. Smith, apparently had been present at the Fournes Military Cemetery, near Fromelles, when a grave believed to contain Australian dead from the Battle of Fromelles was exhumed in 1919. Major G.L. Philips, Officer Commanding Australian Graves Services, swore an affidavit that caught Lambis' eye from its opening paragraph:

The records in Australia House [in London] show that a letter dated the 12th day of March 1919, was received from the Officer in Charge of Records, Administrative Headquarters, AIF, London, addressed to the Corps Burial Officer of the Australian Graves Registration Section France and relative to Lieutenant R.D. Burns, 14th Machine Gun Corps, killed in action on 20/7/16. This letter referred to an inquiry which had been received asking for the place of burial of this officer, further that records show that Lieutenant Burns was killed during the action at Fromelles on 20/7/16. It was also stated that **a communication was received from Germany giving the information that there were five large collective British graves before Pheasant Wood** *[emphasis added] and also a German Military Cemetery at Fournes. It was asked that a search be made and Australian Headquarters, London, be advised of the result. A digest of these facts was forwarded to Major Allen, then*

inspector of the AIF Graves Section in France, and instructions were
given that a search be made.

So, once again, Lambis had confirmation that the Germans
buried Australian dead in mass graves at Pheasant Wood. In another
affidavit in the file, by Major A. Allen, Inspector of Australian
Graves Services, Northern Section (responsible for the Fromelles
area), Lambis found:

Before any question of the exhumation of Lieutenant Burns' body
arose **I made an exhaustive search all around Fromelles,**
Pheasant Wood and a portion of Fournes *[emphasis added]. I*

An Australian chaplain prays at the burial of a Digger on the Western Front in
August 1916. It was a respect sadly denied to many of those who fell at Fromelles.
(AWM PHOTO EZ0064)

traced where a cross had been removed, the inscription giving the exact date of death, and I was informed a British Officer had been 'lifted' by the Germans and removed but no one knew where, and after a further search I located this cross in Fournes Cemetery, the only cross of its kind with the date of death and the word 'Fromelles' on the cross.

The inquiry went on to explain that the grave marked by the cross at Fournes was exhumed in May 1920. Mr Smith of Burns Philp was present but they could find no trace of Lieutenant Burns' remains. The British working party dug up the ground beneath the cross and found no remains. Extending their dig a little wider, they initially found some clothing and, under that, they found five or six bodies. They were all identified by their clothing as British soldiers. They could not find any trace of any Australian remains.

To Lambis, the importance of this inquiry was that it revealed that Major Allen, the representative of the Australian War Graves Service, did in fact search the Pheasant Wood area seeking evidence of buried Australians and that he found no trace of the graves. Lambis now believed his team had established that the Germans had buried the missing Australians at Pheasant Wood in 1916 but that, as late as 1920, the War Graves teams had not located the mass graves there. It followed therefore that they could not have re-interred the remains at Pheasant Wood at one of the official cemeteries.

During this period, Team Lambis gradually added to the weight of evidence that the Germans had buried the Australians at Pheasant Wood. One confirmation came from letters that Charles Bean wrote to his friend, Leslie Chinner, about Chinner's brother Lieutenant Eric Chinner, who had died heroically in the enemy lines with the advanced men of the 32nd Battalion. Leslie Chinner had asked Bean to try to do what he could to find where his brother was buried. Bean wrote back to Leslie Chinner on 21 September 1927:

> As to obtaining any trace from the German side, the only course that I could suggest would be to search the cemeteries on the spot. There is little likelihood, however, of your brother having been placed in a separate grave unless he reached hospital. The History of the 21st Bavarian Regiment, which was opposed to him, says: 'For the fallen enemy, mass graves behind Fasanen Wood were arranged'. This means 'Pheasant Wood' or 'Pheasant Copse' (for the German word means 'little wood'). The German dead were buried in the cemetery Beaucamps. I think your brother would probably have been buried behind Pheasant Copse; whether this grave has been discovered by the British graves authorities, I do not know, but if so his remains have probably been removed to VC Corner.

Bean advised Chinner that he had written to Major Phillips, the officer who swore the affidavit in the 1920 inquiry, if he knew of Pheasant Wood and if remains had been recovered from there. Bean wrote back to Chinner with Phillips' response in January 1928. Phillips told Bean that he believed Lieutenant Chinner had been stated by the Germans to have been buried by them in the vicinity of Fromelles in a trench grave – that is, presumably, a common grave. Bean believed it was likely that Chinner had been buried by the Germans in the common grave dug by the Germans at Delangré Farm. Bean explained that, under Major Phillips' instructions, all those buried at Delangré Farm were exhumed and reburied at VC Corner and he pointed out that Chinner's name is commemorated there. He makes no further mention of Pheasant Wood.

Lambis also sought expert advice from Dr Tony Pollard from the Centre of Battlefield Archaeology at the University of Glasgow about the way the earth on the Pheasant Wood site would have behaved in the years since the pits were filled in. Lambis noted that the pits appear to have subsided to their present state of slight depressions. Pollard reported that it was quite common for earth mounds, as high a metre, to subside in the first two or three years after burial because of the partial decay of the bodies in them:

Indeed, over time graves previously known to have mounds may reduce to the extent that they represent a slightly sunken hollow, in effect a reversed impression of their former manifestation.

This, Lambis believed, would explain why the graves were no longer obvious, nor even recognisable as such, when the people of Fromelles returned to the village two and a half years after the Germans filled them in. The Graves Registration Units may have similarly missed them and the townsfolk may have simply seen the remaining empty pits and used them as handy receptacles to dispose of the battlefield junk that littered the area and then gone about recovering their fields for use in cropping, as happened all over the French battlefields.

To his growing update on the original submission to the panel, Lambis also added the statement made by Australian Prime Minister Billy Hughes in 1921. After hearing a report that the British were considering halting the exhumation of any more of their war dead in France, Hughes (nicknamed 'The Little Digger') promised that his government would authorise

whatever expenditure is necessary for the recovery of Australian bodies.

Lambis was well aware that the main thrust of the panel was to try to prove that any bodies buried at Pheasant Wood had later been re-interred elsewhere. He tried to take a similar approach to play the devil's advocate to his own case:

> We tried our best but all we ever found is evidence to suggest that the mass grave has not been found and therefore any remains there have not been recovered. We gathered information and we forwarded it to the chairperson of the panel and Roger has circulated it and sought information and done the rest.

20

THE MAN IN THE BLACK HAT

*If a man does not keep pace with his companions, perhaps it is
because he hears a different drummer. Let him step to the music
which he hears, however measured or far away.*

HENRY DAVID THOREAU

If Lambis Englezos was the cowboy in the white hat in this story, then
the man wearing the black Stetson rode into town in late 2005. Sydney
lawyer and amateur military historian, Chris Bryett, had just capped
a lifelong fascination with Australia's military history with an emotional
tour of the Western Front battlefields of World War I.

Bryett had watched Lambis' work with fascination from afar but
came home determined to help him get some resolution. He offered
to help in any way he could. Lambis sent him the presentation
document to the Army Panel of Investigation.

The first thing that struck Chris Bryett was the number of the
missing. The lawyer emerged and he quizzed Lambis on how he had

Dead lie in the German trenches the day after the battle at Fromelles.

substantiated the final number. Chris was concerned at the method Lambis had used:

I thought he really needed to start to firm up the numbers because it was how we could make the case more compelling, by shoring up all the little bits. Lambis was already starting to make enquiries in other areas. So I started to work on the numbers from scratch.

The original figures came from a spreadsheet that Senator Hill had handed over to the Senate Estimates Committee. It had originated from the Office of War Graves, which had apparently got it from the Commonwealth War Graves Commission. Chris went back to first principles:

I started to verify those numbers by visiting the State Library in Sydney, copying a register at a time and then sitting on the bus and reading the register and ticking them off. I checked each cemetery register as to who was in what cemetery and compared it with the spreadsheet that Senator Hill had given to the Senate Estimates Committee.

Chris knew that Lambis had gone through the 1299 listed in the Honour Roll of the Fromelles dead and missing in Corfield's book and checked them off against the Red Cross records. Where they had mention of a German death list, he included them in and all else went out.

However, Chris came at the numbers from a different angle. The spreadsheet listed the numbers of Australians from the Battle of Fromelles buried in eight regional cemeteries. He then went through those one by one and cross-matched them by battalions from the 5th Division and the dates of their deaths. If they died on the 19th or 20th he included them. Then he eliminated those recorded as being buried somewhere and came down to the number of those with no record of being buried. He spoke to Lambis.

Sydney solicitor, Chris Bryett, founder of Recovering Overseas Australian Missing Inc. (ROAM), was determined that if the Australian authorities failed to search for the missing Diggers of Fromelles, he would do so without them. (PATRICK LINDSAY PHOTO)

We got to a point where I said yeah I've done it and I'm reasonably comfortable with the number. He said how many do you reckon there is? And I said 170. It might go a little higher or lower but for everyone that goes higher you could probably find one that makes it go lower, so it's going to stay around 170 in my view. And he said that's amazing. I asked why and he said well we've just done this exercise with the Red Cross Wounded and Missing Records and we've come to 170.

So, in essence, Lambis and Chris had corroborated the missing by counting them in two ways: Lambis counted those the Germans claimed to have buried; Chris added up all bodies actually recorded as being buried at all the regional cemeteries and then subtracted that from the total known to have been killed or missing after the battle. Lambis claimed 169 were buried by the Germans, Chris reckoned 170 were missing from the cemeteries. They were elated.

Though both in their mid-fifties and captivated by the same passion, Chris Bryett and Lambis Englezos came to it by quite different paths and were contrasting characters. Chris' love of the military started during cadets at Blacktown Boys High in Sydney's north-west. He spent five years in the Cadet Corps and emerged as the senior cadet under officer of the unit in his final year:

I often laugh when I think that we had 143 .303 rifles. We had our own rifle range, we had three Bren guns and a mortar. And I had the key to the lot ... and I was 17! Imagine that happening today. But they gave us that responsibility then and we lived up to it.

At one point Chris had even considered joining the army and studying law there, but they didn't have structures for that in those days. So he studied law, became a solicitor and specialised in commercial litigation. He married and raised a family and his real reconnection with things military was around 2001, when he and his wife Linda took a holiday in New Zealand. Looking for something to read, he picked up a book on Passchendaele, billed as New Zealand's worst massacre and written by a New Zealand military historian named Glen Harper. Chris was hooked and started reading a series of books on the battle:

> I got another one and another one and then I'd pretty much read all about Passchendaele from every angle and then I started reading about other parts of the Western Front, other battles and I started collecting books, and more books, and more books from all over the place. I started collecting Bean's volumes and I started collecting first editions because I thought that was a wonderful thing to collect. Then I found out he'd actually corrected things in later volumes and maybe betting the first editions wasn't the smartest move. I actually had some imported from Alaska and all over the place to create a set of first editions of Bean which I only recently completed.

Before long Chris reached the point where his family had trained his four-year-old grandson to say, 'no more books, Grandad!' every time he brought out a new one.

> We were running out of places to store them. Eventually, when my daughter moved out, I reclaimed my study and started storing them in there.

In time, Chris decided he should study one battle in detail rather than try to cover the entire Western Front:

> It seemed to me that it was logical to look at the first one and the first one, of course, was Fromelles. Also it had some things that

fascinated me. I had formed a view about British generals being somewhat incompetent and it had that aspect to it so I kind of enjoyed that. It also had Hitler, which always has some interest for everybody. And then I stumbled on to the Pheasant Wood burial pits mystery.

Chris first saw the Pheasant Wood references on a World War I internet forum. Lambis was mentioned and he made contact. Then he started gathering material on the battle.

I think I probably have almost every possible reference there is available on Fromelles and I've read all of it. Lambis and I were on a parallel path.

His interest in Fromelles was cemented when he visited the area on his Western Front battlefield tour in March 2006. It was a tightly scheduled tour but he managed to see VC Corner Cemetery and the Cobbers statue, and then he had a brief chance to visit Pheasant Wood. Tour leader, Englishman Mike Kelly, was urging Chris to be as quick as possible as they were bound for the Menin Gate at Ypres in Belgium, about 30 kilometres away.

We got down there and we had a look. We couldn't get out of the car because we were all so rushed. I took a couple of photos from the road. That was as close as I got. We just packed up and went and I told everybody the story of the missing on the journey to Menin Gate.

Chatting over a few drinks with Mike Kelly that evening, Chris learnt that Mike was involved in a project to find the site where the legendary American World War I hero, Sergeant Alvin York, won his Congressional Medal of Honor in 1918. Mike's friend Tom Nowlan, a geoscientist, was writing his PhD thesis on York and was currently director of the Laboratory of Spatial Technology at Middle Tennessee University. They had gathered together a world-class team of historians, battlefield archaeologists and related experts and they planned to start work on the 'dig' within months. The project was independent of government, self-funded and had secured all the necessary permissions and the support of the local French authorities. It set Chris thinking about the possibilities at Fromelles.

At that stage Chris Bryett was only aware that there were apparently 163 Diggers who were supposedly missing and they were probably in the pits at Pheasant Wood. The lawyer in him started thinking about how to cut through the red tape and find them.

21

THE WILLIAMS REPORT

The Mystery Battle of the AIF.

Fromelles Digger, speaking after the war

In November 2005, John Williams visited Pheasant Wood to conduct his inquiries for the Panel of Investigation. Williams has had a varied and colourful career, blending photography and the fine arts and history. He has a Bachelor of Technical Science from the University of New South Wales, a Master of Arts in visual arts from the Sydney College of the Arts and a PhD in Modern History from Macquarie University. He has held many exhibitions of his photography in Australia and overseas since the 1970s and has written a number of books, including *Anzacs, the Media and the Great War* published in 1999, *German Anzacs and the First World War* in 2003 and *Corporal Hitler and the Great War, 1914–1918: the List Regiment* in 2005.

In the first of those books, Williams devoted a chapter to Fromelles, titled 'A Lively Skirmish' (from an account in the *Sydney Morning*

Dead lie in a portion of the German 2nd line at Fromelles the day after the battle.
(AWM PHOTO A01558)

Herald of 19 July 1919 by Senior Chaplain James Green). Williams quotes a soldier who fought there as calling Fromelles 'the Mystery Battle of the AIF' and he writes of it:

> *Since it involved but three relatively mediocre divisions (two British and one German) and took place over one night, the 'subsidiary action' at Fromelles could not be expected to rate highly in the subsequent official histories of the senior powers.*
>
> *On a mythic-historical plane, however, it would play an important role, not just in how the Anzac legend evolved, but also – since one of the combatant forces was Adolf Hitler's 16th Reserve Infantry Regiment 'List' (16RIR) – in interwar Nazi mythology.*

After giving a potted history of the lead up to the battle and the causes of its failure Williams says:

Huge numbers of dead and wounded lay in no-man's land and an informal truce, later abandoned, enabled stretcher bearers to bring in many of the wounded. During the late afternoon German light railways carried truckloads of Australian dead to the rear for burial.

Williams believed Charles Bean 'sanitised' Fromelles in his official history:

Bean threw a camouflage net over the horror of Fromelles. His account reeks of tragedy and indignation but is sparing of precise judgements, particularly of those sharing responsibilities for the debacle.

And later:

Bean hedged opinions with 'probably', 'possibly', 'somewhat' and 'seem'. His diary entries and notebooks reveal far more trenchant opinions of the causes of the disaster.

Williams went on to claim that the Germans were also 'fabricating mythical history out of Fromelles'. He believed that Hitler's List Regiment saw the battle as evidence that the unit discarded its 'trench troops' label there and laid claim to being a bona fide assault infantry unit. He summed up by saying:

A battle which saw the decimation of a division which then represented one-quarter of all Australian troops on the Western Front was always destined to figure prominently in mythical and military Australian histories. But in Germany, too, albeit for quite different reasons, Fromelles assumed a cultural relevance disproportionate to its global military significance.

Thus, John Williams had studied Fromelles and formed views on it before he travelled there to further investigate Lambis Englezos' and his team's claims on behalf of the Expert Panel. In Fromelles Williams met Martial Delebarre, who showed him around the battlefield and the Pheasant Wood site. Williams later reported to the panel that he saw 'nothing unusual, at least to my layman's eye'.

Williams took a curious view on the evidence of the mass grave at Pheasant Wood. Without referring to any supporting evidence, he seems to have jumped to the conclusion that the pits were dug by the Germans before the battle:

On the surface, the idea that men could be spared – with a major enemy offensive due any moment – for the digging of mass graves in which the enemy's dead may be interred seems preposterous. Even assuming men were available, how could the Germans possibly know how many Allied troops would be killed in their trenches?; especially so given the tactics of the defending division were, as in May 1915, to repulse the attacking troops before they penetrated German trenches.

According to Williams, the only source that suggested the presence of the mass graves was the unit history of the 21BRIR which appeared in 1923. He quoted the official British historian, Sir James Edmonds, as telling Bean:

It won't do to rely on regimental and divisional histories: they are nearly all written by 'hacks' ... who wanted to earn their fees as quickly as possible, without research or investigation.

Williams told the panel that he visited a French historian named Baileul-Catignies in Sainghin-en-Weppes in the company of Martial Delebarre. Baileul was researching a history of all the German regiments that fought in the Armentières region and claimed to have the 'war record of every German soldier buried on the plain of Weppes between 1914 and 1918'. Williams said he had examined a German map showing all graves dug in the sector during the war and could find no reference to any near Pheasant Wood. He did not address the question of whether the German grave map referred to all graves dug by the Germans or simply those dug for Germans. He concluded:

M. Baileul believes, as I now tend to believe, that the constructions by Pheasant Wood were military and defensive in nature – possibly a heavy minenwerfer [trench mortar] emplacement carried out in accordance with Falkenhayn's orders – and which may or may not have been completed by 19 July 1916.

Williams backed up this view with a suggestion that when writing the 21RIR unit history, the author may have confused the German word for grave 'das Grab' with the similar word for trench 'der Graben'.

He went on to suggest that if there were remains in the pits at Pheasant Wood they were likely to be those of Portuguese soldiers killed in the area in early 1918:

They may even have dumped some of these in the rectangular works by Pheasant Wood, for the minenwerfern which one suspects were

Some of the more than 44,000 Australians killed from 1916 to 1918 on the Western Front. At Fromelles alone, in a single night, almost 2000 Australians lost their lives. (PATRICK LINDSAY PHOTO)

installed there, would have been de-installed so as to follow the storm troops. But that is pure conjecture.

If human remains do exist underfoot in the vicinity of Pheasant Wood, the likelihood seems to favour their being Portuguese.

Williams then downplayed the overall importance of the Australians' contribution to the war in the area by claiming the Australian dead would represent little more than 5 per cent of the 20,000 'Germans, Britons, Frenchmen, Indians, Anzacs, Canadians and Portuguese killed during the war in fighting around Fromelles', adding: 'Only a fraction of those men have known graves'.

John Williams developed his alternative theory that the Pheasant Wood pits were for German trench mortars by claiming that the absence of the site on the German graves map was 'surely convincing evidence'. He proposed to the panel that whatever remains, if any, were in the pits at Pheasant Wood should be 'left to rest in peace'. He pointed out that it was against the French law to use metal detectors on the battlefields and that the official policy was to let unknown war victims lie in peace:

A minimum of 1,300,000 French soldiers died in the First World War; over a million of them on the Western Front. The Germans lost almost 2,000,000 men in the war, of whom, once more, over a million fell on the Western Front. British Empire losses account for perhaps another half million. Less than half of these have known graves, suggesting that the last resting place of almost one and a half million men is unknown.

What's good for an Australian is good for a German or Frenchman. If we have a right to go fossicking for the last resting place of dead Australians, then so do the families of the million and a half men who are not Australian. And that, simply, is why French and Belgian law is as it is.

When Lambis gave Chris Bryett a copy of John Williams' eleven-page report it was like a red rag to a bull.

To say I was disappointed was a massive understatement. He got the names of battalions and sources wrong, basic facts that should never have been wrong. His supposition that the pits had been dug before the battle was without any foundation. And it just occurred to me at that time that he wasn't making a lot of headway. I made some enquiries about Williams' suggestions that the Pheasant Wood pits were probably for German trench mortars. The experts I consulted said it was very unlikely. They also gave me some clues on where the records would be. It wasn't where the Panel was looking. I thought there's no way in the world they're going to find anything that's useful. This is going to drift forever.

While Chris was near his boiling point, Lambis remained staunch in his belief that the proper process must be followed and that it would eventually prove his theories correct. However, Chris was fast becoming disillusioned at the growing delay as the process dragged on. The stance taken by Williams' report weighed heavily in his subsequent actions.

22

THE BREAKAWAY

*Insanity: doing the same thing over and over again
and expecting different results.*

ALBERT EINSTEIN

Chris Bryett's lawyer genes began to assert themselves as the time
passed. His instinct was to find an expert – the best in his field in
the world who could not be challenged – to decide the merits of the
Pheasant Wood site.

*Around Anzac Day of 2006, I formed the opinion that the Panel
wasn't ever going to come back with a conclusion that was useful to
Lambis. And that the only way we would ever get the Panel to do
anything useful or positive or helpful, so far as we would assess it,
would be if we got a private dig running.*

Lambis Englezos was wary but understanding when Chris told him his thoughts. He sympathised with Chris' feelings but he decided to 'stay with the process'. Chris headed in a different direction:

From Anzac Day 2006, I became the man in the Black Hat … the baddie in the process. Lambis understood from day one that he had to stay with the process and be the White Hat guy. But I said there's two possibilities: I'm going to make some noise and look like we're going to do something and therefore they will do it because they will want to get control, they won't want us having control; or they'll do nothing … and we'll go and do it. One way or the other, we'll have this solved. And neither of us cared who was going to go and do it, as long as it got done.

Chris started getting serious about putting a team together during May through to July. He created an association he called ROAM (Recovering Overseas Australia's Missing Inc.). Progress was relatively slow until he started contacting the world archaeological community in July of 2006. He found an expert website where you can seek comment or help on projects. His email explaining the situation at Pheasant Wood brought a dozen responses.

Two of them said, if you don't pick me, Richard Wright is your boy. I'd never heard of him, didn't know him from a bar of soap. I saw he was a professor and I thought, professor, that's going to be a bit hard. But he also responded so I made contact … and mass graves are his bag.

Richard Vernon Stafford Wright is Emeritus Professor of Anthropology at the University of Sydney, where he had taught since 1961 after returning as an honours graduate from Cambridge. He had extensive experience in mass grave investigations in Bosnia and Croatia and was regarded as a world expert in the field. He had been engaged by the Australian government.

Chris visited Wright at his home and took him through the Pheasant Wood mystery with his photos and files. He asked for Wright's advice and his help.

He said he was interested. I thought that's a bloody good win. We've got this guy who's a professor and he's got excellent experience in this area. His interest is the dig. My interest is in identifying and closure.

Richard Wright gives a fascinating insight into the mind and motivation of the forensic archaeologist. He uses the Holocaust as an example:

Without the material evidence of the Holocaust, the deniers of the Holocaust can set up a contest where we argue over the meaning of lines of text in historical documents and argue over the integrity of people's memories. Of course scholarship and memories are critical. But we also need to look at the powerful evidence of the bodies.

They are there, somebody shot them. They demand an explanation. And explanations must come through the eyes of unbiased forensic professionals.

Wright is often asked how he can handle his work. He believes he 'unravels into two strands':

The work is often dangerous and disgusting but, frankly, it's not distressing, not emotionally distressing in a way that would keep a psychological counsellor in business.

Stress for me as a forensic archaeologist comes long before the bodies are uncovered. Stress comes at the start of the field work: Am I going to find the grave? Am I going to let down the waiting team? Am I going to let down the case investigators who have invested months of work looking into the background to the killing? Am I going to let down the people at head office in Sydney or The Hague?

According to Wright, the real stress in the job comes with dealing with the relatives and friends of the dead. He recalls working on the Srebrenica massacre in Bosnia where hundreds of men and boys had been killed in a Kravica warehouse in July 1995. They had been herded into the warehouse and killed with machine guns and grenades. By the time he started working on the mass grave of this killing, Wright had worked for four years in Bosnia and had never lost control of his emotions. That changed when he opened a wallet of one of the dead:

Now he was reduced to a pair of jeans and a denim jacket, filled with shattered bones, mummified flesh and hair. Inside the wallet was a licence, with a smiling Polaroid photo of the young owner of the wallet. I looked at his date of birth. I said to my scene-of-crime officer: 'This lad is the same age as my daughter. I mean was the same age.'

That 'was the same age' was too much for the emotions. I had to take deep breaths and go for a walk in the abandoned orchards before returning to work.

Even while he was assembling the ROAM team, Chris Bryett was still trying to help Lambis navigate through the official channels. He secured a copy of the official army orders detailing the evidentiary standard required before it must act on information to recover the remains of soldiers lost in battle. Vietnam War MIA (Missing In Action) investigator, former Lieutenant Colonel Jim Burke's Operation Aussies Home had acquired the orders under a Freedom of Information application and posted it on its website. The minimum evidentiary standard required was 'strong circumstantial evidence'.

> I said to Lambis, you've already hit the mark. They're making you go through hoops you don't need to go through. You are already at 'strong circumstantial evidence'. You had William Barry's account out of Corfield, you had the aerials which are pretty strong, then you got Chinner towards the end from the Bean letter. You've already reached the standard.

As Chris Bryett thought through his plan of action, he began to widen his aims:

> I realised that if we only located the missing, then I would call that to my own standard, a very limited win. What are you going to do with them, pick them up, cart them down the road, shovel them into some hole down at VC Corner where they're already on the plaque? Why would you bother? I thought why are you wasting your time doing that, just leave them where they are, stick a cairn up and we'll all go home. That's not good enough. You have to do something with them. The army then has to go and get them.

Chris' overriding concern was that the army may not invoke the option of forensic testing to try to identify the remains. He was worried that the logistic problems and the cost of forensic testing of 170 sets of Australian remains, together with as many as 300 British remains which may also be in the Pheasant Wood site, may prove too big an obstacle. Chris decided the best way to ensure the DNA testing happened was to create a team capable of doing it all themselves. His aim was to ensure that the Australian Army could not say later that they could not get DNA and therefore not try to identify the remains. Professor Wright was concerned about the quality of DNA that could be recovered from the remains. Chris persuaded him that ROAM needed to find the best expert available to handle the task.

Wright referred Chris to Jon Sterenberg, a British forensic archaeologist who had extensive experience in mass-grave identification and recovery in Sierra Leone, Bosnia, Yugoslavia, Serbia, Iraq and East Timor. Sterenberg was then the Director of Excavations and Examinations for the International Commission on Missing Persons in Bosnia.

Weeping willows frame the entrance to Rue Petillon Military Cemetery where many of the victims of Fromelles are buried. (PATRICK LINDSAY PHOTO)

Jon has said he thought we would be able to recover and he arranged with the International Commission on Missing Persons to do ten free tests if we could get DNA sampling. Jon assured me that if a 3D survey were done before removal of a bone it could later be placed back in its previous position with its original skeleton.

Chris learned from Alan Cooper from the Centre for Ancient DNA in Adelaide of the difficulties in acquiring DNA samples from a grave like that in Fromelles. Cooper warned that the biggest problems often started with the way the material was collected. DNA can often be found in the roots of teeth and in bones like the hip joint, but it can be contaminated by those collecting it. Cooper counselled that proper preparation by the collecting team was essential. They must wear gloves and the collected bones could not be washed. Properly collected DNA can be preserved for centuries, even millennia. Cooper had successfully acquired DNA 5000 years old. He also advised that the high water table at Fromelles need not necessarily be a negative. The problem wasn't whether the remains stayed wet or remained dry. The damage was caused when the remains are caught in a cycle of wet-dry, wet-dry. This can leach protein, therefore DNA, from the remains.

The high water table which we thought would be a problem in fact could become a saving feature. The DNA in the remains that have stayed in water constantly is probably still there. Those remains that are under water are OK … In other words, not every set of remains will be able to rely on DNA identification. They'll probably have a significant number in which they can find DNA but there may be others where they can't find any.

As he progressed with the development of the ROAM team, Chris became aware of some sites where important discoveries had been either compromised or even stolen by vandals. He realised site security was going to be a crucial element. While still searching for the security team member, Chris connected with another British archaeologist, Martin Brown. Brown had appeared in a number of British radio and television programs centred on the World War I battlefields, including *Trench Detectives* on Channel 5 and *Finding the Fallen* on Discovery Channel. He was also one of a small band of archaeological advisers to the British Parliamentary All Party Group on Battlefield Heritage and War Graves. He agreed to become ROAM's battlefield archaeologist.

> *Martin then raised the question of whether we had an EOD and I raised the question back of what was an EOD. He said it was an Explosive Ordnance Disposal officer. He made the very important point that if you don't have one and you find ammunition or explosives then the dig stops and you sit around until you can find one and that might take a week.*

Brown referred Chris to Rod Scott, who did work for the British Ministry of Defence and the army.

> *He's a warrant officer and an archaeologist, and he is pretty much the best on WWI ordnance in the British Army and is the only one the French EOD will let work with them. So we had been so lucky that on almost each and every occasion we've hit the best at what they do.*

All the while, Mike Kelly, the tour guide, had been helping Chris connect with the various experts he needed for the team. He realised how valuable Mike was, with his wide knowledge of the field and his practical experience on the ground in France. Mike agreed to be the team's logistics manager. So Chris now had his team. He believed that the panel of investigation had stalled. He determined to start prodding and poking until he energised the situation.

23

PRIME TIME

Yes, yes lots of men gave their lives for our freedom
... and some are still there.

MARTIAL DELEBARRE, FROMELLES

Chris Bryett was working on his ROAM presentation document when
Lambis called to tell him that *60 Minutes* wanted to do a story on the
missing of Fromelles. On Sunday 16 July 2006 almost two million
Australians looked up from their dinners to see veteran reporter Ray
Martin tease them with the traditional *60 Minutes'* studio
introduction:

> *It's one of the darkest, most heroic days in Australian history. Yet*
> *it barely rates a mention in our history books.*
>
> *It all happened in the tiny French village of Fromelles. There, in*
> *the first battle after Gallipoli, nearly 2000 young Diggers died in a*
> *single, awful night back in 1916.*

But there's also an intriguing twist to the story. At least 170 Australians vanished that night without a trace – one of the great unsolved mysteries of the First World War.

And now a couple of Frenchmen and a Greek-born schoolteacher from Melbourne are determined it will not be forgotten. Determined to honour those who died on that faraway battlefield, 90 years ago this Wednesday.

The story opened with three chilling quotes – from French battlefield tour guide Yves Fohlen, from Lambis Englezos and from Martial Delebarre – that summed up the story of the missing of Fromelles brilliantly:

YVES FOHLEN: *Gallipoli was a picnic. Here it was the slaughterhouse.*
LAMBIS ENGLEZOS: *There was a sacrifice and it was a bloody disaster.*
RAY MARTIN: *Do you come back here at night and feel the spirits?*
MARTIAL DELEBARRE: *Yes, yes lots of men gave their lives for our freedom … and some are still there.*

The program examined all major aspects of the battle and its subsequent cover-up. It showed the deep respect with which the Diggers are still held in the area:

RAY MARTIN: *You're a Frenchman. Can you understand why these men came 12,000 miles across the ocean?*
YVES FOHLEN: *No.*
RAY MARTIN: *To fight for your country?*

YVES FOHLEN: No, no. For myself it is a mystery, but it is so wonderful. It is the most beautiful Australian mystery. Yes.

And it canvassed the mystery of the missing Diggers, whom it pointed out, may still be lying in mass graves at Pheasant Wood. Lambis made his case and closed with a telling quote to the effect that while he had experienced considerable resistance to his attempts to have the site investigated,

I'd hate to think that our missing war dead were an inconvenience.

Spurred on by the program, Chris Bryett completed ROAM's presentation document and developed a plan of action, aimed at mobilising support for an independent non-invasive examination of the Pheasant Wood site, provided the initial investigation showed sufficient evidence of the mass graves.

We had a document, we had a team – one with wonderful experiences and qualifications. What we needed was some way of funding the project. Then, just at the perfect moment, a bloke named George Jones booked a tour of the Western Front battlefields with Mike Kelly.

George Jones is a remarkable man. He was brought up in an orphanage from the age of five, after the authorities removed him from his alcoholic mother and stepfather. He has never known who his biological father was. He struck out on his own at fifteen and ended up joining the army. He volunteered for Vietnam and served there in 1968 and 1969 attached to the Royal Australian Electrical and Mechanical Engineers as a motor mechanic. After five years in khaki, most spent pushing around large amounts of dirt, George resigned and joined the bank where he found he had a penchant for financing mining ventures. He studied at night and emerged with a Bachelor of Business degree from Curtin University.

I had a feeling for mining. After ten years I left the bank and that's what I've been doing ever since. Initially, advising people on how to do it and now doing it myself. It just evolved.

George used his great success with mining projects in Western Australia to build a growing reputation as a philanthropist. In the second half of 2006 he and his wife Penny took a European holiday and decided to visit the Western Front battlefields. George was captivated from the start, overwhelmed by the scale of the losses and the poignancy of the cemeteries dotted throughout the countryside. One cemetery in particular, near Fromelles, tugged at his heart.

We were walking down the line of tombstones. I noticed one that read 'an unknown Australian soldier'. The next one was 'an unknown New Zealander' and then an unknown British soldier. And then the next one was an 'unknown unknown'. I was very moved by it. The guide then read a poem he told me had been written after the poet had visited a similar cemetery.

The poem was written by Michael Edwards and is called 'The Visitor'.

I half awoke to a strange new calm
And a sleep that would not clear
For this was the sleep to cure all harm
And which freezes all from fear.

Shot had come from left and right
With shrapnel, shell and flame
And turned my sunlit days to night
Where now none would call my name.

Years passed me by as I waited,
Missed the generations yet to come,
Sadly knew I would not be fated
To be a father, hold a son.

I heard again the sounds of war
When twenty years of sleep had gone,
For five long years, maybe more,
Till peace once more at last had come.

More years passed, new voices came,
The stones and trenches to explore,
But no-one ever called my name
So I wished and waited ever more.

Each time I thought, perhaps, perhaps,
Perhaps this time they must call me,
But they only called for other chaps,
No-one ever called to set me free.

Through years of lonely vigil kept,
To look for me they never came,
None ever searched or even wept,
Nobody stayed to speak my name.

Until that summer day I heard
Some voices soft and strained with tears,
Then I knew that they had come
To roll away those wasted years.

Their hearts felt out to hold me,
Made me whole like other men,
But they had come just me to see,
Drawing me back home with them.

Now I am at peace and free to roam
Where 'ere my family speak my name,
That day my soul was called back home
For on that day my family came.

One of many surviving German concrete blockhouses along Aubers Ridge that formed a powerful defensive line protecting the German reserve troops and allowing them to be deployed at short notice to provide counter-attacks to any assault. (PATRICK LINDSAY PHOTO)

The interior of a surviving German concrete blockhouse along Aubers Ridge overlooking Fromelles, showing the massive reinforced concrete walls. (PATRICK LINDSAY PHOTO)

A German machine-gunner's point of view through the gun port of a concrete blockhouse near Fromelles. (PATRICK LINDSAY PHOTO

Over the following three days as they travelled, Mike Kelly told George about ROAM and the story of the missing Diggers of Fromelles. He said they had a world-class team, all of whom were prepared to work without pay. All they needed was a benefactor who could cover the team's expenses. It would cost around $50,000. George Jones acted immediately:

When they told me the story of the team, the quality of it, and that the people don't want to be paid but they needed money for expenses, I couldn't refuse to do it.

So Chris Bryett's ROAM team now had their missing piece – a sponsor. With George Jones on board, Bryett set about doing what old soldiers used to call 'energising the situation'. More than fifteen months had dragged by since Lambis and his team had made their presentation to the Panel of Investigation and they had heard nothing of substance in reply. Bryett had formed the firm view that the panel was marking time. He fired his opening shots in a series of emails to Kathy Upton-Mitchell, Deputy Director of the Office of Australian War Graves.

In mid-October 2006, Bryett began by asking whether the Office of Australian War Graves (OAWG) was involved with the recovery and identification of five World War I soldiers whose remains had recently been discovered near Ypres in Belgium. He also asked how the soldiers would be identified and whether people outside OAWG would be involved in the process. Upton-Mitchell replied that when remains of Australian military personnel from either world war were recovered the OAWG's role was to provide 'ongoing commemoration' while the Department of Defence was charged with identification and funeral arrangements.

Bryett followed up with an inquiry about how the army was notified to start those processes. Upton-Mitchell responded that a Defence

Adviser at the Australian Embassy in Paris acted as the liaison. Her curiosity piqued, she then asked:

Why are you so worried about processes? Do you have a relative missing in action in Belgium?

The following week, Bryett came clean:

My interest is that we have assembled a world class team of archaeologists and other important folk to form a team to go and conduct a test dig at Fromelles as a privately funded dig. Naturally, we need French Government approval. Frankly, we would like to have Australian Government blessing just as the Government has done with the Vietnam missing through Operation Aussies Home Inc. Are you aware of any distinction between Vietnam missing and WW1 missing? We have the funding conditionally available so no need to worry about the DVA budget yet. Our view has been for some time that the Panel has been terminally stalled and thus the need for this project to be privately convened. Therefore Lambis and we diverge on this aspect. We say this with great respect for the eminent members of the Panel.

Bryett added that ROAM was concerned that, assuming it won the necessary approvals and found Australian remains at Fromelles, the French authority, the Prefect du Nord, would then exhume the bodies and hand them to the Commonwealth War Graves Commission, which would, in turn, notify OAWG and the Embassy in Paris.

Bryett also asked what OAWG would do to identify the remains, bearing in mind that it was his understanding that under Australian Defence Forces protocol forensic testing was at the discretion of the

Surgeon General. He hoped the remains would not simply be classified
as 'known unto god':

> To understand what might happen, and how the Surgeon General
> might exercise his discretion, we are watching what procedures are
> followed in relation to the Westhoek (Zonnebeke) 5. That would
> give us a heads up on what to expect.
>
> With the greatest respect for all concerned our expectations are
> that we will meet Sir Humphrey face to face as we believe Lambis
> has already done. We think Australia can do better than delay the
> inevitable. Let's get some closure for the families?
>
> This will be a wonderful opportunity for DVA to get on board.
> We assure you they are most sincerely welcome!
>
> I'll bet I can write your reply already. I do hope I am wrong. I
> apologise if I have been too abrupt or rude it is not intended.

Not surprisingly, perhaps, Upton-Mitchell took almost a week to
digest this message and reply, noting that she wanted to 'consult and
consider carefully'. She began by explaining that the government's
chosen path for investigating the claim that remains are located near
Fromelles by forming an expert panel was made after careful
consideration and with appropriate sensitivity to the other nations
who fought in the area. The panel had been tasked to investigate the
possibility that those 'working in the field after WWI may have
overlooked a mass grave'.

> The Australian Government is proceeding with appropriate concern
> for all those who lost their lives. If there are any Australian dead in
> the Pheasant Wood area, a period of careful historical and archival
> study hardly constitutes unacceptable delay in locating them. I believe

Mr Englezos and his group are aware that progress has not 'terminally stalled'.

Upton-Mitchell went on to explain that the panel was awaiting the results of a search through the German Archives and possible information from France and UK, then added:

It is entirely your affair if you and your group wish to approach the French Government seeking permission to undertake a test dig on the site. Given the process in place, I could not recommend that the Government support you in this action.

She also pointed out that Bryett was misguided in drawing a comparison between the situation in Fromelles and Operation Aussies Home (a private search for MIA in Vietnam):

After each conflict in which Australia has fought there has been, with one exception, a post war operation to search for and recover remains. Graves Recovery Units or other units with different names but essentially similar functions – scoured the battlefields, interviewed combatants of both sides and local civilians and checked medical unit and other unit records to locate battlefield burial sites. Any remains discovered were then exhumed and concentrated in war cemeteries. One reason the Government is following the process it is on Fromelles is that it is difficult to see how a mass grave of the alleged scale of Pheasant Wood could have been overlooked given this process.

Vietnam was different. We were not in a position to conduct the usual post conflict search for remains. I am advised that an Army team visited Vietnam in the early 1980s in an attempt to find the missing remains but the political climate was not good and they were unable to access the areas in which our missing were killed. The

286

political climate has now changed and the Vietnamese authorities are supportive. The search that we would normally have undertaken in the early 1970s can now be done. Consequently I do not believe there is a direct comparison between the activity in Vietnam and your proposed activity in France.

Upton-Mitchell warned Bryett against 'promoting confidence in the ability of DNA to identify remains':

DNA is a useful tool but it has major limitations. There may be multiple remains recovered, often only parts of the long bones and skulls are evident after almost 90 years. Records do not exist or one set of remains may be very similar to another with no distinguishing factors. Both Defence and OAWG approach the task of examining remains with the aim of achieving identification if at all practical. The analysis is thorough and expert and forensic evidence is obtained to assist the process. The fact remains, though, that in many cases identification is not possible.

In conclusion, Upton-Mitchell noted that information on the remains of the soldiers discovered in Belgium would be released once the reports were provided by Belgian authorities:

You can be assured that the process is in accordance with the law as it relates to these matters but, even more importantly, we have a strong commitment to look after our war dead and will ensure that the appropriate actions are taken.

Bryett initially wrote a short inflammatory reply. He conceded the point of Vietnam but lamented that the panel hadn't been able to make a 'positive response', queried that it hadn't consulted the 'world's best trench map expert', then launched a broadside at what he saw as the inefficiency of the post-war recovery units:

> *Look at the 410 found on the wire at the end of the war and now in the rose garden at VC Corner. Compare that 410 to the 5 found between CWGC registers. All 5 identified, not one of the 410 identified. It beggars belief that only the men with letters home or cigarette cases with their initials were found after the first CWGC register was created.*
>
> *If the GRU [Graves Recovery Unit] were so efficient why are so many bodies still turning up. Why is there no record of recoveries from Pheasant Wood where Bean said there were burials there.*
>
> *Look, Kathy, at a personal level, I must be missing something. I know your [sic] as well meaning as I am. To me this isn't too hard. Why stall? If there [sic] not there it costs you nothing to find out and the mystery is solved and goes away and OAWG are seen as abundantly helpful.*
>
> *We both know the Panel won't achieve anything.*

On 8 November 2006, Bryett followed up with his main barrage – a point-by-point consideration of Upton-Mitchell's earlier email. He started by saying that when the government appointed the panel, it wasn't aware that an alternative was available, the ROAM plan for a private dig at no cost to the public purse. He challenged what he saw as the 'gaps' in the panel's expertise: the lack of a mass-grave archaeologist and of a World War I trench expert. He questioned whether members, especially the eminent historians, would be able to publish their individual opinions should they differ from the majority. He queried the number of times the panel had met and suggested that an independent panel would have more credibility.

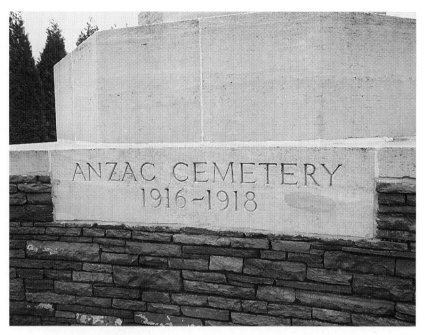

The Anzac Cemetery at Sailly-sur-la-Lys near Fromelles was started as a direct result of the Battle of Fromelles in July 1916. It contains 111 named Australians from the battle, including Captain Norman Gibbins, of the 55th Battalion, one of the heroes of the rearguard action. It also includes many men of the 31st Battalion who died in the battle but have their deaths incorrectly noted as 21 July 1916. (PATRICK LINDSAY PHOTO)

Bryett pointed out that the question of the other nationalities involved in Fromelles would be met by the substantial number of British members in the ROAM team. He claimed that a sufficiently compelling case for an investigation of the Pheasant Wood site had already been made:

> The evidence that they are burial pits for Australian WW1 soldiers is compelling and beyond strong circumstantial evidence which is the requisite standard. See for example, Bean's letter to Lt Chinner's

brother. There are no Graves Recovery Unit records indicating recoveries from that area. True it is that no one has found any evidence of a report of a successful recovery which became lost. Surely that is an illogical line of argument lacking in any intellectual merit? I believe that we are faced with the compelling conclusion that our Diggers are still there. At the least the evidence is so compelling that a dig should be conducted.

As to Upton-Mitchell's assertion that the government would not support ROAM's attempt to seek permission from the French authorities to undertake an investigation:

That is a very disappointing position for you to take. My team is privately funded and will not be a drag on the public purse. It will resolve the issue conclusively.

Bryett also challenged Upton-Mitchell's assertion that Vietnam was the sole exception to the rule on speculative searching by the Australian Defence Force:

But I believe your argument is deficient in that it does not take into account the ADF Forensic Recovery Team. My understanding is that they have at the very least looked for missing Australian Defence personnel in the Christmas Island (most recently), the highlands of Papua New Guinea, the Indonesian Island of Buru and New Britain.

As I understand the position, the Government approves and financially supports the private search for and recovery of the remains of Vietnam veterans; sends its own ADF Forensic Recovery Team to recover the remains of WW2 veterans (even one veteran at a time) and conducts a Panel of Investigation in relation to WW1 veterans (even where the site's location is known without doubt [depressions in the ground] and up to 170 veterans could be there).

On the question of identification, Bryett submitted that the ADF Forensic Recovery Team successfully identified 21 veterans out of 23 recoveries. He believed they would be likely to find artefacts that would provide identification for many, citing the fact that since the first cemetery register for VC Corner five Australians' remains had been found and all were identified:

It will take time and money to optimise the result. Our experts expect to recover DNA from a great many of the remains. Our mass grave archaeologists have the skills and the equipment to give identification the very best chance.

Upton-Mitchell had raised the issue of treating the remains of the war dead with respect, saying it was the primary aim of her office. Bryett replied by saying that in ROAM's view that meant the dead had to be given the very best chance of identification:

The reverential recovery of the remains of WW1 veterans and giving them individual graves with family generated epitaphs are my highest priorities.

Bryett concluded that ROAM's driving motivation was solving the mystery of the missing Diggers of Fromelles and that they were happy to help the panel in any way it could to resolve the issue:

I believe my plan provides the best prospect in providing closure for many families and is the best way to discharge our sacred duty to locate and honour the missing Diggers of Fromelles.

Clearly, Upton-Mitchell and the government didn't share Bryett's view. Bryett was under no illusion that they would change their mind:

I thought well that's all right, she's telling us to go do it. We've got a right to go and do it. We'll go and do it.

Around this time, Mike Kelly's Sergeant York project was in full swing in the Ardennes Forest, finding the exact spot where York had won the Congressional Medal of Honor. Kelly referred Chris Bryett to the team's archaeologist, a Frenchman named Alain Jacques. Jacques agreed to intercede on ROAM's behalf with the French authorities in Lille to seek permission for access for the private dig. Bryett was delighted with the progress and soon had what he believed was 'approval in principle'.

What Bryett didn't know was the impact that his team's intervention was having behind the scenes in the bureaucracy and the government. From the outside they may have appeared to be, in army vernacular, slowly 'lining up the ducks', but under the waterline those ducks were paddling like crazy.

24

PHEASANT WOOD

The wood at the bottom of the village.

PIERRE JEAN GEORGES DEMASSIET

It is November 2006 and frost etches the outlines of the short grass on the killing fields. In the dull early light they seem impregnated with memories. The old shell holes have long been ploughed flat but otherwise they are unchanged since the carnage. I look across the old no-man's land to the Cobbers statue in the Australian Memorial Park. In the background the Fromelles church dominates the higher ground and, in front of it, I can see the tree tops of Pheasant Wood.

This morning, my daughter Sarah and I are accompanying our friend, the local historian Martial Delebarre, to visit the owners of the land on which we believe the Germans buried the missing Diggers, along with many more British troops, after the Battle of Fromelles. Sarah speaks fluent French and will act as my interpreter. We have come to no-man's land to walk once again in the footsteps of the missing before our meeting. It strengthens our resolve to play our small part in finding them.

Yesterday, we visited the Mayor of Fromelles, Hubert Huchette, at la mairie (the town hall) in Rue de Verdun to try to locate the owner of the burial site. In my ignorance, I expected this would be a difficult task. I thought it would mean long hours trawling through old documents. Instead, Monsieur Huchette simply turned to his computer screen and pulled up a graphic program revealing a plan of the town and its surrounds. He began clicking through it and soon the screen revealed the owner of the wood as Hubert Leon Dimbre of Mons-en-Baroeul. Another click on the plot of land at its southern edge, plot #454, and the screen showed the owners as Pierre Jean Georges Demassiet and his wife, Marie-Paule.

The Pheasant Wood mass grave site, looking west to the village church. (PATRICK LINDSAY PHOTO)

When we arrive at the Demassiets' house in the main street out of Fromelles, we find they are an old French provincial farming couple straight out of Central Casting. Pierre is 78 and Marie-Paule is 77. Their weathered faces brim with character, good humour and the wisdom of long experience. Pierre is a small powerful man with wispy white hair, high cheekbones and dancing impish eyes. His well-worn jumper is tucked into his working pants and secured with a thick black leather belt. Marie-Paule wears a floral dress over her woollen skivvy as she prepares vegetables from their garden for this Sunday's Mass of the Patron Saint at the Fromelles church. The Demassiets are proud farmers. They both have the strong hands of those who have spent a lifetime working the land.

They listened in silence as Martial Delebarre told them of the remarkable history of their plot of land adjacent to Pheasant Wood. They call it 'the wood at the bottom of the village' rather than Pheasant Wood. They are clearly amazed at the story as it unfolds. They had no inkling of their land's dark history. They exchange knowing looks as they mention, almost as a throwaway line, that the land always refused to grow anything useful, just grass.

Pierre excuses himself and heads off to another room in their small sturdy cottage. He returns after a few minutes with a cardboard file full of old papers and draws out his title deed and the plans showing the boundaries of his land. Using the plan and the aerials we have brought with us, Martial carefully explains how, after the battle, the Germans collected the dead enemy soldiers, placed them on the light railway and took them to the pits they had dug on the Demassiets' land. We have brought some of Team Lambis' composite aerials and photographs and Martial and Sarah explain how Lambis found the pits. It makes sense to Pierre. He mentions the undulations and says he always thought something was strange about the plot.

Pierre Jean Georges Demassiet and his wife Marie-Paul, owners of the land alongside Pheasant Wood where the Germans buried the missing Australian and British soldiers in mass graves after the Battle of Fromelles. (PATRICK LINDSAY PHOTO)

Madame Demassiet has been silent as she listened to the unfolding story. Now she tells of her family's losses in the Great War. She lost two uncles – Charles and Louis Beaussart – both commemorated on the Fromelles church memorial. One was taken hostage by the Germans and was subsequently killed; the other went missing at the Battle of Chemin des Dames in 1917. The body of the uncle taken hostage was discovered in 1928, identified, and was buried in the family plot in Fromelles church cemetery. The other uncle remained one of the many missing.

Marie-Paul Demassiet quietly explains that she understands completely the feelings of the Australian and British families whose loved ones may be among the missing at Pheasant Wood. Like countless other French families, hers has suffered the gnawing pain of sending off one of their sons to war, never to hear of him again. She understands the enduring loss, magnified by not knowing his fate or having a final resting place where his descendants can find some closure.

The Demassiets ask what is to be done about the graves. Martial explains that the Australian Army has appointed a panel of experts to investigate the claims that the graves are at Pheasant Wood. If the panel accepts the evidence, the army will approach the French authorities, and the Demassiets, for permission to investigate the site, firstly without disturbing the ground, and later, if the signs indicate it, to dig to finally discover whether the missing are still there. Pierre and Marie-Paule Demassiet have no hesitation. They are happy to give their consent to the investigations of their land. They hope it will mean the missing will soon rest in peace. We are delighted to report back to Lambis, Chris Bryett and Roger Lee and the Australian authorities that another potential hurdle in the journey – approval from the Pheasant Wood landowners – has been surmounted.

25

UNDERGROUND

You know, the proof of absence isn't the
absence-of-proof argument.

BRUCE BILLSON, MINISTER FOR VETERANS' AFFAIRS

Around this time, Chris Bryett learnt that a NATO gas pipeline crossed part of the Pheasant Wood site. Aware that it could prove a major impediment to any digging at the site, he began quietly researching the exact position of the pipe and the protocol for seeking permission to dig near it. Some months later he had navigated through the NATO bureaucracy and found a sub-contractor who sought and obtained approval.

All the while, the email exchanges between Bryett, the Army History Unit and the Office of Australian War Graves continued and grew in intensity.

They kept writing to me and I kept writing back showing why I thought what they were saying didn't make a whole lot of sense. In the end they stopped writing to me.

During this period, relations between Bryett and Roger Lee, Head of the Army History Unit, stretched to breaking point. Bryett recalled one phone call he made to Lee in early December 2006 where Lee began by saying 'I don't know if I should talk to you'. He did and they discussed ROAM's submissions to the panel on geophysical survey, limited excavation, ROAM's team members, costs, consequences of delay, other countries, the evidence, the defence instruction, and their conclusion.

In mid-December Bryett decided to break the deadlock by taking pre-emptive action. He delivered a submission to the Army History Unit setting out ROAM's detailed proposition about how it would conduct its private investigation of the site.

I was convinced that they were going to meet and they were going to steamroll us and they were going to not give us a fair go. What the submission effectively said, which probably got up their nose, was we're going to go and do the investigation but we're happy to do it for you as well if you like while we're there if you give us a blessing.

On 15 December, the day the panel was due to meet, Roger Lee responded to a Bryett email saying be couldn't predict what the Expert Panel may or may not recommend to the Minister and concluding:

Finally, I suspect the panel would take some offence at the implications in your final question. Can I say that you are not the sole authority on, nor gateway to the sole world experts, on this topic. I know who your team members are and, as I said, I respect their expertise and experience. They are not the only experts available to us and we have been receiving advice from others also qualified in the field. And before you ask, the names of these other experts will be included in the material provided to the Minister who may or may not choose to make such details public.

Bryett replied saying he intended no offence to individual members of the panel and asked Lee to forgive his 'regular enthusiasm'. Bryett made the point that

at least I bring any beef to your face. I haven't encouraged any newspaper article or mention in parliament and our offer is one of genuine assistance.

At the time, Bryett believed he really didn't need the Australian authorities' approval because he had already secured approval in

The Cobbers statue in the Australian Memorial Park at Fromelles, based on the exploits of Sergeant Simon Fraser in rescuing the wounded after the battle. (PATRICK LINDSAY PHOTO)

principle from the French authorities. Roger Lee agreed to circulate ROAM's submission to the members of the Panel of Investigation and he told Bryett that the panel would be reconvened before the end of the year.

It may have been circulated but we got no reply and they ignored us forever after that.

In the following days, Bryett spoke to Alain Jacques from the French authorities in Arras. Jacques was very helpful and told Bryett that ROAM would not need police approval for their investigation of Pheasant Wood. He advised that he thought official French approval would take between one and two months to come through.

The next thing the players knew about the process came when the Minister for Veterans' Affairs, Bruce Billson, gave an interview to reporter Neil Wilson from Melbourne's *Herald-Sun* newspaper and disclosed that he was negotiating with a British academic, Dr Tony Pollard of Glasgow University, who had earlier advised Lambis Englezos, to carry out an investigation of the Pheasant Wood site.

Bruce Frederick Billson was elected to represent the Victorian seat of Dunkley at the age of 30 when the Howard Government first came to power in 1996. Born in Albury in southern NSW and educated in Frankston, Victoria and at the Royal Melbourne Institute of Technology, he worked for the Hastings Shire and was a ministerial advisor at State and Federal level before standing for Federal parliament. He began his rise to the ministerial ranks in mid 2004, serving first as Parliamentary Secretary to the Minister for Foreign Affairs, then to the Minister for Immigration before being appointed Minister for Veterans' Affairs in January 2006. Billson's family history played a substantial role in his accession to Minister for Veterans' Affairs.

My grandfather served up in Papua New Guinea in the Second World War. He never talked about it much but he made a great impression on me. I sought the role of Veterans' Affairs Minister in part because of that experience. Veterans' Affairs can be a very demanding portfolio. There's a lot expected of you and there's a readiness and a robustness to point out your deficiencies wherever they might emerge. And I think that's great because I think that reflects the nation's view that we have a special duty to the people that have served our country.

Since his appointment, Billson has maintained a watching brief on the search for the missing Diggers of Fromelles and, in an interview with the author, he expressed his admiration for Lambis Englezos:

One of the things that struck me since being appointed is people's conviction. I suppose from my point of view I see a real moral obligation, wherever there is a legitimate basis, to carry out investigations – to do so with care because we're also mindful that there are many descendants for whom there will never be any leads, there will be never be any opportunity for closure so we need to manage that with great care so as not to get ahead of the actual work that we're doing. Being very committed to this work, but being very measured, being optimistic but not overly, not excessively promoting the possibility is a balancing act that we take very seriously as well.

As to Lambis' many years of advocacy, I have great admiration for that.

Where we've got a legitimate basis I see it as part of our special duty to those who have served our nation, particularly those we've put in harm's way … That's only tempered by a great deal of care about managing expectations. And I say that all the way through because this is something that handled poorly would give false hope and unjustified promise to people already coming to terms with a loss in their life and empty chapter to their family history. We've seen that through this work, the work we've done on Christmas Island [the exhumation of a WWII sailor from HMAS Sydney], the work we're doing with MIAs in Vietnam, even the work we're doing with submariners, the AE1 and AE2. I take this very seriously.

Billson followed up his newspaper interview with a press release on 6 February 2007 confirming that the Australian Army was negotiating with Pollard with a view to commissioning his team to investigate

a site near Fromelles village in northern France, to confirm if the remains of First World War Diggers are still buried there.

Both Team Lambis and ROAM saw this as a victory. Team Lambis felt vindicated, both because it represented the first step toward their aim of investigating the Pheasant Wood site to confirm their contention that it was the site of mass graves containing missing Diggers and because it validated Lambis' belief that the 'system' worked. Chris Bryett and ROAM saw it as a victory because they believed that their intervention and their provision of an alternative 'private' dig had acted as a catalyst, prompting the eventual decision to commission an investigation. For both teams it represented the first official acknowledgement that the missing Diggers of Fromelles had been buried by the Germans at Pheasant Wood after the battle in July 1916, as they had maintained for some years. Billson's release went on:

Army has asked Dr Pollard's team to carry out a non-invasive investigation of the site at Pheasant Wood, possibly using ground-

penetrating radar, to determine whether there was a mass grave at the site and the likelihood that remains are still there.

Billson acknowledged that Lambis' and his Friends of the 15th Brigade had been the driving force behind the decision. Then he launched a thinly veiled broadside at Chris Bryett and ROAM:

While the Government appreciates the work and interest of such groups [Lambis' and his team], unauthorised digs and physical searches are both reckless and counter-productive. The investigation of possible war graves and dealing with the remains of Australian war dead is a sensitive matter, and should be handled on an official basis.

The following morning, speaking on ABC Radio's 'The World Today', Billson used some unaccustomed 'ownership' language:

What's been established through a team of experts here in Australia and drawing from that international research is clearly there were graves dug in the vicinity of Pheasant Wood, we've been able to establish that from aerial photography of the time, and from German instructions to their troops in that area.

Billson backed himself each-way with a comment about the difficulty of establishing whether or not the bodies, having been buried at Pheasant Wood, were later exhumed and re-buried after the Armistice:

Records about the extensive program of post-war recovery and re-interment of remains are patchy – not least of all because many records kept in London were destroyed by German bombing during the Blitz. As a result, the expert panel recommended this further investigation be carried out on-site.

So the official line was that, as yet, there was no definitive answer as to whether the missing were still buried at Pheasant Wood. Working on advice from Roger Lee and the Army History Unit, the Minister had commissioned a team from Glasgow University under Tony Pollard to test the site to determine what happened after the original burial of the dead in 1916:

That's why we're calibrating our action because we're not at the stage where we can go to the French authorities or our other allies.

We're approaching this not only as a committed and compassionate national government but also recognising that we're part of an international community with a very deep and abiding interest in this.

So we've said: well we're pretty certain this is what's happened on the spread of information that's available. We're not so sure, or we can't satisfy ourselves to any degree of certainty, that the recovery operations were completed. It would be at odds with behaviour that is evidenced everywhere else for it not to have happened there but whilst there is a doubt let's go to the next stage and do some further investigative work, do the non-intrusive analysis to see what further insights can be gained. You know, the proof of absence isn't the absence of proof argument. But let's go to that next stage.

26

THE TURNING POINT

If the facts don't fit the theory, change the facts.

ALBERT EINSTEIN

The Minister's media statement omitted the two real reasons that the Panel of Investigation changed tack from a stance of scepticism to a position of acceptance that an on-site investigation was warranted. The first came in the form of two documents from the German archives: a report by the 21BRIR (the German regiment facing the Australians at Fromelles) and an extract from the 21BRIR's war diary. The second reason was the activities of Chris Bryett and his ROAM team.

The two German archival documents were the 'smoking gun' that cast aside all doubts about whether the missing Diggers of Fromelles had been buried by the Germans at Pheasant Wood. The documents were unearthed from the German archives in Munich after inquiries by the Office of Australian War Graves, prompted by Lambis Englezos' earlier requests. They are a stunning corroboration of the evidence put before the Panel of Investigation by Lambis and his team.

The first of the documents is an order from Major General Julius Ritter von Braun of the 21BRIR to his men in the field, dated 21 July 1916, two days after the battle. It is headed 'Taking of construction materials to the front and retrieval of bodies' and assigns one non-commissioned officer and 24 men from the unit's medical company for 'rescuing the injured and salvaging the corpses'. It provides a fascinating insight into the attention to detail and the remarkable record-keeping practised by the Germans, even under the many pressures of active service in the field.

The order outlines in minute detail how three lorries will carry 'long iron rotating stakes, rolls of wire and long posts' from Brulle to the light railway track east of Fromelles. There, they will be unloaded and then the lorries will be loaded with German corpses from near the 'regimental conveyance post' which will be taken to the 'south-east section of the Beaucamps cemetery'. At the cemetery, men from the regiment's music corps, under the supervision of a medical officer, will lay out the bodies in the presence of sergeants.

> *They remove the papers and identity tags in such a way that the personal belongings and the identity tag are removed from each body individually and immediately tied up in a sandbag provided with a strip of cardboard or strong paper label [address tag] on which the number and company of the identification tag is marked.*

Once identified, each body will be laid in one of the mass graves, accommodating about 300 bodies.

> *They will be separated on the basis of their unit, though laid out beside one another. The officers are to be laid separately in the centre.*

For the burial of the English bodies, H-Company is building mass graves for about 400 war dead. H-Company has to date only been deployed on restorative work at the post.

The order declares that the doctor in charge will ensure that each layer of bodies is immediately covered with a layer of earth mixed with chloride of lime and that, once full, the grave is to be immediately covered.

The blessing of the bodies and the graves will take place later.

The order also stipulates that strips of canvas can be used to transport the bodies but not for laying them in the grave. Individual body parts are to be wrapped and buried in cloth. The light railway is also to be used to carry the bodies as far as the Beaucamps stop, with stretchers to be used to carry them to the graves.

A dead German soldier in a makeshift grave near Fromelles.

The sites for depositing the bodies are to be laid sideways and fenced off by barbed wire at an appropriate distance. The Music Regiment corps is setting up alternating guard posts for this purpose.

The civilian population is forbidden to loiter and gape at the bodies.

The recovery and burial of the German dead in Beaucamps is to proceed in four-hourly shifts until specific arrival times are clarified, according to the order, which then goes on to provide the corroboration for which Lambis and his team had been hoping:

The bodies of English soldiers are being interred in mass graves directly south of Fasanenwäld (Pheasants' Wood) *[emphasis added]. H-Company, supported by one medical NCO and four men of the regiment on the orders of the regimental doctor, is responsible for the removal of belongings and the identification tags in exactly the same way as for German bodies.*

In order to expedite the rapid return of bodies, the corpses are separated by nationality and suitably laid in piles close to the railway, Grashof and Christuskreuz.

The removal of even the most insignificant property pertaining to a body (German or English) is deemed to be theft from corpses and is severely punishable. The sergeants in Beaucamps or a soldier of sable rank from H-Company are the only persons authorised to collect belongings, as ordered above, at Pheasants' Wood. The 3rd Battalion is despatching a relief group to Beaucamps to assist.

The document was a turning point, an irresistible affirmation of Team Lambis' claims. The German orders – made at the time of the action – confirm that, after the battle, the Australian and British dead in enemy territory were gathered in piles near the light railway, at

Dead soldiers in the German second lines, on the Australian left flank, on the morning after the battle. (AWM photo A01554)

Grashof and Christuskreuz (strong points behind Rouges Bancs and near Pheasant Wood respectively). They were then loaded on the light rail and taken to the mass graves prepared by the Germans behind Pheasant Wood.

The second German document comprised a series of extracts from the 21BRIR war diaries on the day of the battle and the following days. It begins with an entry timed at 7 pm on 19 July:

> *Several enemy divisions are attacking the three left units of the division. In the third unit the attack is being completely repulsed; in the fourth unit it is only temporarily successful. On the other hand, the enemy is managing to penetrate the second unit ...*

It goes on to explain how the Germans reacted to the Australian attack, holding the Diggers off with accurate artillery and small arms fire until their reserves could be deployed to counter-attack:

> *The difficulty in communicating in pitch blackness, made all the more uncertain by the smoke from exploding shells, as well as the heavy deployment of hand grenades, is initially slowing progress. Only after the pioneers move in new munitions does the attack proceed, slowly at first, then more fiercely despite all the resistance of the enemy who have entrenched themselves and are bringing in fresh forces.*

The German counter-attacks gradually drove the Australians back and the entry for 20 July, written some weeks later, reads:

> *Towards 7 am the entire position is once again totally under our control ...*

The fog also prevented a large section of the enemy forces from surveying the situation. Having left it too late, they are now finding their retreat path blocked.

Later, it deals with the casualties on both sides:

Our losses are heavy, especially in the 3rd Battalion, totalling seven officers and deputy officers. Among the dead are Lieutenants Baumgartel, Keim, Wolf and Wagner, 288 NCOs and their teams. Eight officers and 377 men are wounded. One officer and 94 men are missing, most of whom were probably buried under collapsed breastworks.

Much higher are enemy losses. In the regimental area alone, 399 men lie dead, in the front terrain another 100 men, where they contaminate the air for weeks on end until, despite enemy fire, our forces sprinkle them with chloride of lime and cover them with soil.

In addition, the enemy have in our zone alone lost over 200 men as POWs, eight machine gunners and a large number of weapons, munitions, supplies and other equipment, the salvaging of which will take many days.

The point is made that, apart from the many artillery batteries that were rushed in to support them, the regiment repulsed the attack without the need to call on reinforcements from other units. It could have called on the 3rd Infantry Reserve Regiment 104 and the 134 Machine-Gun Company. It notes that, despite the continuing enemy artillery bombardment which continued until around midday, the unit had already begun to rescue the wounded and to withdraw prisoners to the rear. It had also started the massive repairs needed to the forward defences and the light rail lines that were extensively damaged by its own mortars and artillery during the counter-attack.

The entry for the night of 21 July reveals that the recovery of the fallen is continuing and their number means that the 'big cemetery at Beaucamps' will have to be 'significantly enlarged yet again':

For the enemy dead, mass graves are being constructed behind Fasanen-Wäldchen (Pheasant Wood). The work must be commenced by filling in two saps which the enemy built during the night of 19/20.7 from its position to ours and which are now full of enemy dead. As usual, the enemy has not bothered to salvage them.

The final sentence presumably refers to the German view of the British toward recovery of their dead for, as we know, the Australians had only recently taken their position in the line.

The diary notes that on 25 July the extension of the Beaucamps cemetery was consecrated and the German dead from the battle were solemnly interred there. Two days later the regiment paraded in front of 'His Majesty Crown Prince Rupprecht of Bavaria who greeted the soldiers engaged in the battle of 19 and 20.7 and paid tribute to their achievements'.

The Diggers' continuing efforts to recover and identify their fallen mates are underlined by an entry for 12 August:

Bringing in of two Australians who were captured by our forces after a brief battle, while they were attempting to remove letters and identification tags from the British bodies still lying in the front terrain.

These Diggers were likely to be trying to recover or identify some of their dead mates from no-man's land when they were overpowered and captured.

Although they had been out-manoeuvred and had lost the first round, the initial investigation of the site, Chris Bryett and his ROAM team had played a pivotal role in the panel's change of heart. Documents obtained under a Freedom of Information order clearly show that ROAM's activities had acted as an important catalyst in persuading the panel and the army to advise the Minister to call for a physical examination of the site.

And a briefing note from Roger Lee to the Chief of the Army on 14 February 2007 left little doubt as to Team Lambis' impact:

The Friends [of the 15th Brigade] conducted their campaign through the media and **eventually placed army in the position where it could not avoid considering the case.** *(emphasis added)*

The Expert Panel had made five 'General Recommendations' and three 'Findings'. The first two recommendations noted that 'all issues' relating to the remains of Australian service personnel overseas, including their recovery and 'all scientific and forensic processes', were the responsibility of the Australian government. The third called for the reaffirmation of the general principle that the 'government does not search for, nor will it support private individuals searching for, the unrecovered remains of our war dead'. The fourth noted that the post-war recovery of remains of war dead was not 'infallible' and called on the government to establish a formal structure to examine allegations of unrecovered war remains. The fifth recommendation called on the Minister to refer such allegations to a panel of experts to decide whether the allegation was compelling enough to justify official examination.

The panel made three specific findings on the evidence before it on Pheasant Wood.

Studio portrait of 1804 Private Alfred Ernest Phillips, 7th Battalion, of Richmond, Victoria. Phillips enlisted on 5 August 1914 and was killed in action on 19 July 1916 at Fromelles, while serving with the 59th Battalion. His brother, 1743 Private Edwin John Phillips, 60th Battalion, enlisted on 3 March 1916 and was killed in action on the same day in the same battle. Twelve sets of brothers died at Fromelles, and two sets of fathers and sons. (AWM PHOTO DA08081)

On the one hand, it agreed (with some members dissenting) that the evidence supported the contention that Diggers were buried after the Battle of Fromelles in a mass grave behind Pheasant Wood.

On the other hand it held that the evidence as to whether these remains had been recovered and re-interred at other cemeteries was

minimal and vague and did not support the contention that the remains had not been recovered.

The Panel agreed that the argument in support of the contention that remains were still on the site relied on circumstantial and unreliable evidence and was insufficient to justify an excavation of the site.

Finally, it found, again with some of its members dissenting,

that as the evidence relating to the question of whether remains had been recovered was so inadequate, further research should be undertaken, including a non-invasive survey of the site to establish whether sufficient data could be obtained to warrant a physical examination of the site.

The Panel was aware of the perception that the research phase had dragged on and was conscious that this needed to be concluded as quickly as possible.

The Panel recommended that, as Dr Tony Pollard and his group at the University of Glasgow had the experience necessary to provide the specific answers the Panel was seeking, had a proven track record in these matters and included a French archaeologist on his team who was familiar with French law and processes, he should be approached to undertake this next research step.

The ministerial minute, prepared by Brigadier Bowen for Minister Billson, revealed the rationale underpinning the Minister's actions. The minute identified two 'key issues':

1. *The level of public and media interest in this subject continues to grow.*
2. *The core of the issue is whether or not Governments and/or concerned citizens should search for the remains of missing in action. We understand that shortly after the end of World War One, an agreement was signed between all combatant nations that once the comprehensive battlefield clearance process was complete, there would be no more speculative searching for remains. While this appears to be the basis of the policy for all Governments (except recent US MIA policy), neither the British authorities nor the Commonwealth War Graves Commission have been able to locate this document (searching continues).*

The minute goes on to brief the Minister on the Expert Panel's findings: that the panel had agreed with Team Lambis' proposition that the evidence supported their claim that Australian dead were buried in mass graves, but that the evidence supporting the claim that these remains were not recovered after the war was 'much less convincing'. The panel was divided on this issue and some members dissented from the majority view that the evidence was 'insufficient, on historical grounds, to support any further investigation of the site'.

The minute further advised that this finding would not be likely to satisfy 'the public interest groups' and that the media would

be unlikely to provide sufficient public exposure to the Panel's reasoning to protect the Army and Government from uninformed criticism.

It then revealed the driving force giving impetus to the final decisions:

(d) *The Panel also noted that the more extremist of the public interest groups was, through its media campaign, in danger of 'hijacking' the management of Australia's war dead and were unanimously of the view that this must remain a function of Government.*
(e) *In view of this, the Panel recommended that a further step in the investigation – namely a physical examination of the site, but excluding the possibility of a 'dig' – be undertaken. The Panel recommended that this be done by an assessment team acceptable and familiar with French Government requirements.*

A few lines later came another reaction to ROAM's intervention:

The Panel was particularly concerned that a group of Australian citizens was prepared to ignore Australian Government intentions on this matter and act unilaterally. Advice from France is that they are claiming to have full Australian Government backing to their proposal to conduct a physical excavation of Pheasant Wood. Apart from the strong ethical consideration that this could be seen as a desecration of a grave, such precipitate action has the potential to cause considerable embarrassment for the French and Australian Governments if important objects or other clues necessary for any future identification are disturbed or damaged. The Government also has concerns to ensure that Australia's dead are not used for commercial or personal aggrandisement purposes.

When the minute went on to consider the issue of 'sensitivity', it did so purely from the point of view of the government, the army and

the bureaucracy. It did not address the sensitivity of the relatives of
the missing Diggers of Fromelles.

> *This issue is quite sensitive. There is considerable public interest,
> re-invigorated by the recent discovery of other remains in Belgium,
> and a number of journalists have taken it on as a 'crusade'.*
>
> *The potential for the group (from Sydney) to do something
> precipitate and cause widespread embarrassment to the Government
> is assessed as high – they appear already to have misrepresented their
> status to the French authorities (who took them at their word and
> were on the verge of granting permission to undertake a 'dig').*
>
> *The Office of Australian War Graves is already receiving
> correspondence from the families of men still missing in France and
> Belgium supporting the search.*

Finally, the minute dealt with the likely cost of the recommended
site examination. An indicative estimate was $75,000 for a small
examination and $150,000 for a 'more widespread survey'. It noted
that should the examination reveal large numbers of remains, the army
would need to seek 'supplementation' of the extra costs.

Another ministerial minute, this time from the Deputy Chief of
the Army, Major General John Cantwell, and dated 7 January 2007
advised Minister Billson that the Australian Army had begun
negotiations with Dr Tony Pollard from the Centre for Battlefield
Archaeology at Glasgow University to undertake a non-invasive
examination of Pheasant Wood.

Once again, ROAM's activities occupied the writer's mind. One
of the key issues General Cantwell referred to the Minister was:

> *The group of Australian citizens that was prepared to ignore Australian
> Government intentions on this matter and act unilaterally continues*

Some of the many German blockhouses still dotted around the fields near Fromelles. These three show how hard it would have been for attackers to approach them across open ground. (PATRICK LINDSAY PHOTO)

to plan for an excavation of the site in July 2007. Army has advised the relevant French authorities that this group does not have official Australian status.

On the 'sensitivity' aspect, the minute claimed that:

The extremist group (from Sydney) is currently circulating rumours among the relevant public interest groups that the Government and the Army will 'go slow' on the announced investigation of the site. They are continuing with their plans to undertake a 'dig' in July 2007. When they become aware of Army's response to the relevant

French authorities clarifying their unofficial status, they may resort to a public campaign to attempt to overturn this advice.

An email from Dr Tony Pollard to Roger Lee, sent on 15 December 2006, may reveal the basis for the claims made in the ministerial minutes that Chris Bryett had misrepresented ROAM's status to the French authorities. Pollard's email centres on providing 'ball-park' cost estimates for the investigation of Pheasant Wood. But it starts off by reporting some second-hand claims sourced by Pollard to Peter Barton, British military historian, then in France:

Peter Barton is in Arras today (Thurs) discussing the issue with Alain Jacques and another couple of people who have responsibility for the area. They were just about to grant permission for the ROAM project as they were informed by them that they had the full backing of the Australian government (as I understand it from a phone conversation with Peter this afternoon). They are quite content to not grant permission but they would like a written instruction from the Australian authorities as to where they stand with the ROAM proposal (i.e. if you say you don't want it to go ahead they will deny permission).

Clearly, Pollard had the inside running for the gig, as a later reference in the email revealed:

Peter and myself had a successful meeting with the All Party Parliamentary War Graves and Battlefields Heritage Group chaired by Lord Falconer in the House of Lords on Tuesday. Much interest was shown in the issue and I think it is safe to say we have support for the proposal previously discussed – Anglo-French initiative with Australian collaboration at our initiation (though I would not presume to say as much without much more official communication with those at a higher level than myself).

Roger Lee, in his briefing note to the Chief of the Army on 14 February 2007, picks up Pollard's claim about ROAM:

The French authorities at first thought ROAM were an official group authorised by the Australian Army. In response to an indirect inquiry by the French, DCA [Deputy Chief of the Army] wrote to them in December clarifying the status of ROAM.

For Chris Bryett, this explained why their negotiations with the French, which had been progressing smoothly, suddenly ran into problems. Bryett had received approval in principle from the authorities in Lille for ROAM's investigation at Pheasant Wood. He had acknowledgments from both Kathy Upton-Mitchell of the Office of Australian War Graves and Roger Lee, effectively saying that if ROAM wanted to conduct a private investigation that was its business but it would not receive Australian government support. Now he realised that, not only did ROAM not have Australian government support, it also had it running interference against ROAM's actions.

On 21 January, ROAM received a letter from Gerard Fosse, the curator of the French Archaeological Service at Lille, saying they had been contacted by the Australian government notifying them that it didn't want a dig. Therefore the French authorities would not issue approval for one. They would nevertheless be inclined to approve ROAM's team conducting a non-invasive geophysical examination.

So we ended up with approval in principle for geophysics. But Pollard team was going to do geophysics – we could have duelling geophysics. We could all turn up the same days and have a party. That in itself *is bizarre and stupid. In our offer that we put to our government, we said we could do geophysics and do the dig, so that we would actually do the right geophysics that would be useful and a dig.*

Understandably, Chris Bryett is disappointed and angry at the allegation made by Peter Barton and repeated by Tony Pollard and Roger Lee that he misrepresented ROAM's status to the French authorities.

The allegation is that Alain Jacques of the French Archaeological Service which is part of the Prefect du Nord [or Police Department North] told Peter Barton (who became a team member of the GUARD team) who in turn told Tony Pollard (the Director of GUARD our competitor for the job) that I had told Alain that my team ROAM had the 'full backing of the Australian Government'. I believe that is called second-hand hearsay and is normally inadmissible as evidence of anything. Certainly no weight should be put on it without testing the allegation thoroughly such as asking me if I made such a misrepresentation.

Since I was in regular contact with Army on the project I would have thought that procedural fairness or natural justice would require that I be asked before it was relied upon by Army to select GUARD over ROAM.

Bryett pointed out that when he approached Jacques it was as a result of the British historical tour leader, Mike Kelly, talking to him while he was on site with the Sergeant York project. As that project was private and had proceeded without the need for US government approval, Bryett could see no reason why ROAM would need Australian government approval. Indeed, in his first email to Jacques he explained that ROAM's project was private and he subsequently told Jacques that it was privately funded.

Since I was practically invited by Cathy Upton-Mitchell of the Office of Australian War Graves and Roger Lee of Army to go do it myself, if I could, I did it. At no time did I indicate to them that I had the 'full backing of the Australian Government'.

In fact Bryett points out that ROAM had nothing to gain by making such a statement:

Frankly, I didn't need to. The French Archaeological Service was keen to see that I had appropriate archaeologists on the team. Of course, I did, I had some of the world's best on the ROAM Team. I certainly had some of the world's best mass grave archaeologists and after all it is the largest non-genocide mass grave since WW1.

In Bryett's view it was ROAM's proposed test dig that was opposed by the French Archaeological Service.

That is what they stopped us from doing once Tony Pollard told Roger Lee that our approval by the French would be withdrawn if the Australian government said so. Our approval in principle for the non-intrusive test dig was withdrawn. However, in that letter withdrawing consent the French Archaeological Service indicated approval to geophysical survey by ROAM. If we had made such a large scale misrepresentation why would they leave that door open to us?

After the Minister's decision, ROAM began researching Tony Pollard and his experience. They believed that he had limited mass grave experience and concluded from his appointment that Roger Lee and the army weren't going to deal with Pheasant Wood as a mass grave, but rather as if it were a single recovery.

> *We felt they had taken the view that, if GUARD were capable of doing a dig, they were capable of doing all things. That's, of course, not quite the case. Our team had genuine mass-grave recovery experience.*

ROAM based its approach on Professor Wright's and Jon Sterenberg's mass-grave methodology. They advocated scraping the top layer of soil on the site to delineate the extent and outline of the pits. Then they planned to dig a sump hole away from the main burial pit. The sump would be connected by a trench up to the edge of the burial pit, allowing the water to drain from the pit to the sump hole and permitting observation of the pit without the need to dig into it. In ROAM's application to the French authorities, it had actually gone further, and had sought a secondary permission to take ten samples of remains from the burial pits so they could test them for DNA. ROAM had previously arranged with the International Commission on Missing Persons to have ten samples examined free of charge.

> *We wanted to establish whether it was possible to get DNA from the remains. If we could establish that you could get DNA from these remains, then army had no excuse: when they came up to the exhumation stage pursuant to their instruction, they would have to do DNA. They couldn't say it's problematic, we can't get any. That was the purpose of all of that. A 3D survey was to be done of the side of the burial pit so that the bones could be returned to the correct skeleton.*

Bryett then wrote to Veterans' Affairs Minister, Bruce Billson, seeking permission to proceed with a parallel investigation. An earlier letter he had written in the first week of September 2006 had gone unanswered. Phone enquiries of Billson's office had eventually met with the response that the inquiry had to go to the army.

It was going to float around and bounce around and some time in my lifetime they might come back to me and tell me what the answer was.

On 21 January 2007 Bryett again emailed to Minister Billson, following up on his earlier request asking that he reconsider the plans to commission the British team and instead consider appointing what he called ROAM's international team to the task.

I was concerned that he was going to make a press statement on this issue and he would galvanise himself to Glasgow and it would be really, really hard to try to get him to move away from that once he'd gone public on it.

The following day Bryett received an email from Cameron Hooke with a letter attached signed by Minister Billson advising that the government had decided to commission the team from Glasgow University to carry out the initial investigation of Pheasant Wood. The attached letter was dated 8 January, but by the content Bryett concluded it was written in early December, before the panel met, because it said the panel would probably meet 'soon'. It also talked about Jim Burke going to Vietnam 'next year'.

In response Bryett turned his attack to the cost of the Pollard investigation, reportedly around $150,000. Bryett checked with British

Western Front archaeological expert Martin Brown on what sort of investigation you could carry out for the figure.

> *I said would you get a dig and GPR? He said yeah that's probably about the right money. So I assumed there was a dig in it. There are two choices: there's either a dig in it or he paid five times the commercial price. I assumed he hadn't paid five times the commercial price, so it had to be a dig but I was wrong.*

ROAM took the view that the government had erred in snubbing the available Australian mass-grave 'know-how' in favour of Tony Pollard's British team. They conceded that Pollard had excellent archaeological skills, particularly in British battlefield conflict. Their point was that the Pheasant Wood site potentially contained the remains of 170 Australians and 327 British soldiers – the largest non-genocide mass grave yet discovered in Western Europe. The Australian experience centred on mass-grave archaeology in digging and geophysics. ROAM questioned whether the British team could match this mass-grave experience. In addition, they pointed out, the British team would cost $150,000; the Australian team's work would be at no cost to the taxpayer.

ROAM also believed (mistakenly it would transpire) that Pollard's team would only use ground-penetrating radar (GPR) for their investigation, not the other non-invasive methods available like resistivity and magnetometry. Chris Bryett's main concern was the possibility of a negative result from ground-penetrating radar.

> *Some on the Panel of Investigation believe that the soldiers were reburied after the war. If the investigation only uses GPR and returns a negative result, we won't know if it is true negative, meaning they were reburied, or a false negative, perhaps caused by the high*

water table. The bottom line is that the Diggers may still be there in the pits.

Bryett pointed to a case in Bosnia where a mass grave containing 120 bodies was missed using ground-penetrating radar. The remains were verified by a subsequent dig. For Bryett and ROAM, the only sensible approach was a dig:

Anything less is wasting money, time and it's shy of what's required for this site.

When Bryett could not get the Minister to reply to his queries he went to the media, resulting in a story that the Minister had snubbed Australian know-how and noting that the Americans and British recovered their own war dead: they didn't let others do it. It was followed by a subsequent article featuring ROAM's benefactor, George Jones, and his philanthropic motives.

Bryett was intrigued to discover soon after that Tony Pollard's British television series, *Two Men in a Trench*, which had previously concentrated on British sites, had announced its next series would cover World War I battlefields.

27

THE WILD CARD

Even God cannot change the past.

AGATHON (AROUND 440 BC)

From the start of their quest, one name has thrown a scare into both Lambis Englezos and Chris Bryett: Ration Farm. It's an unassuming cemetery about kilometre and a half north of Pheasant Wood. For most of the war the original Ration Farm was around a kilometre back from the British front line at the end of a communications trench. It served as a staging post for rations that were being transported to the troops in the front line. The first burials at the farm were by the 1st Leinster Regiment as early as November 1914. Three months later, the first cemetery, Ration Farm Old Military Cemetery, was created. It was used until October 1915, chiefly by units of the 6th Division and at the time of the Armistice it held 73 graves. These were transferred in April 1923 to the present Ration Farm Cemetery, which had been opened in October 1915 and had been in use until October 1918.

After the Armistice, it was used as a 'concentration cemetery' – that is, one where isolated graves and small plots were re-interred. Among the isolated graves brought in are many of Australian soldiers who fell in the attack at Fromelles; and among the small graveyards concentrated were Chapel Farm Cemetery, Fleurbaix (1.6 kilometres west of Bois-Grenier, containing eleven British graves of 1915 and 1916, and Ferme-du-Biez Military Cemetery, La Chapelle d'Armentières (1.6 kilometres south-east of that village, containing 36 British graves of 1915 and 1918). The cemetery covers an area of 5016 square metres and is enclosed by a brick wall.

Chris Bryett stumbled across it during his early research:

When I did the original missing numbers with Lambis, my searches alerted me to one area that I told Lambis could be our left field. He said: what is it? I said Ration Farm, that's the potential problem. He said: why? I said: there are hundreds of 'Known to Gods' in there. I said they could absorb our 170 and still keep going.

Ration Farm was one of the British 'receiving cemeteries' from the Battle of Fromelles. The name emerged from enquiries from the Commonwealth War Graves Commission about which cemeteries were used to bury remains recovered from no-man's land at Fromelles. A comment in one of the email exchanges mentioned Ration Farm Cemetery and Anzac Cemetery, indicating that the original source records may not be available.

In late 2006 Bryett discovered that many of the Graves Recovery Unit diaries had been lost in the intervening years. Fortunately, the GRU had noted the map references of their recoveries and these source records were handed over and became part of the various cemetery records. Therefore each cemetery's records reveal the source of its dead through the map references of the places where the bodies were found

Ration Farm Cemetery. (PATRICK LINDSAY PHOTO)

… all the relevant Fromelles cemeteries, that is, except two: Ration Farm and Anzac Cemetery. The numbers involved at those cemeteries alarmed Bryett immediately:

> *The numbers almost match identically. There are about 132 Australians and hundreds of 'Soldiers of the Great War Known Unto God'. If you add them you get close to about 500 and if you add 169 Australians and 327 British, you come to about 500. It's almost the perfect match. Anzac is irrelevant because it's only 24 so you can discard it. But Ration Farm is another matter. In fact, I got to the point where I believed that, if our missing were not at Pheasant Wood, the most likely spot is Ration Farm.*

Bryett worked off a spread sheet using the data Senator Hill had given to the Senate Estimates Committee. They led him to Ration Farm.

What we were told by the Commonwealth War Graves Commission was, you should look to see where the 'knowns' came from at each cemetery. That will give you a clue where the 'unknowns' came from. So Lambis and I started a scurry-on through the Ration Farm names and the first one I looked at – the very first one, I can't remember his name – but the first one I looked at was on a German death list.

I said to Lambis, we've got a really big problem. But there wasn't another one that had German death list on it, indicating that he had died behind the German lines – just that first one I hit. Many identified Diggers in Ration Farm were from the Battle of Fromelles.

When Bryett told Lambis of his findings, he immediately began to visualise his ultimate nightmare. Chris Bryett was sufficiently unsettled by the find that he reported it to ROAM's potential sponsor, George Jones.

There was no way I was going to take the man's money without him knowing all the facts. Next time he came over was when Richard [Wright] was introduced to him and I explained it to him that they may be in Ration Farm, we thought there was a possibility. Certainly, if they're not at Pheasant Wood we believed they would be at Ration Farm but only a dig at Pheasant Wood will confirm things definitely. George understood and he was comfortable and didn't bat an eyelid.

Chris Bryett started off being unshakeably confident that the missing were buried at Pheasant Wood, but is no longer so sure:

I would say I was more than 80 per cent certain at least and I wasn't listening to anybody who said anything different. Now I reckon it's an each-way bet, in fact, I'd almost be more inclined to think they're in Ration Farm. A lot will depend on the preliminary investigation of the Pheasant Wood site. Let's just say, I still believe they're at Pheasant Wood where the Germans buried them but if they've subsequently been re-buried, I reckon they're at Ration Farm.

28

ON THE GROUND

I said g'day boys. I know it's been a long time but be patient,
don't worry, we'll get you.

Lambis Englezos at Pheasant Wood

It is May 2007 and Lambis Englezos is sitting in the shade of the
Cobbers statue on Rue Delvas outside Fromelles. He has been in
Fromelles for five days now. He has visited the battlefield every day
yet he has not been able to bring himself to visit Pheasant Wood.

Each day Lambis has walked along Rue Delvas and down the hill
out of the village passing Pheasant Wood as he heads toward Rouges
Bancs and the battlefield, the Australian Memorial Park and VC Corner
Cemetery. He sucks in the history as he walks. He can visualise the
chaos of the battle around him as he walks, like some kind of cosmic
time traveller. He can hear the cannonades and smell the cordite. He
looks across the field at the wood as he walks and he thinks of the
men waiting there for him but he cannot go to them yet.

In two days Tony Pollard and his team of investigators will arrive from Glasgow. Lambis knew he had to be there when they came to check out the site. For five years he has thought about that day. He knew they weren't going to dig. He knew that it was to be a non-invasive search, with new-fangled technology, but he knew he had to be there. So he took his long-service leave and made the trip.

The last time Lambis visited Fromelles, in 2002, he walked past Pheasant Wood every day without realising its significance. In fact, he has never been to Pheasant Wood. Despite all that has happened, with so much of his life centred on this stretch of ground, Lambis has never set foot on it:

> I'm not sure why I didn't go there straight away. I'm sure the locals were a bit curious about me, standing there on Rue Delvas looking across. I walked all around the place but I didn't go there. Something was holding me back. For some reason I felt that the time had to be right for me to visit.

The next day, Lambis visited the cemetery at Rue Petillon. It was a long walk on a hot day and he was ready for a rest by the time he opened the wrought-iron gate and moved through the beautiful triple-arched stone entrance. The willows draping the arches hung limply in the stillness. Lambis knew the place well. It is home to 291 Diggers and 1216 souls from other nations. Many of the men from the 58th Battalion lie here, including Sergeant George Challis, a member of the 1915 Carlton Premiership-winning Australian Rules team. Robin Corfield quotes from Private Bill Barry's account of carrying supplies across no-man's land at the height of the battle:

> When I was making my second trip in I passed a chap carrying something wrapped up in a blanket and when he was asked what he

had he answered with a gloomy look on his face 'This is all we could find of George Challis, Carlton champion footballer'. He had been blown to pieces.

Being a passionate Carlton man, Lambis well knew the story. He also knew that the last of the Diggers brought to rest at Rue Petillon was Major Roy Harrison, company commander of the 54th Battalion, who was killed in no-man's land early in the battle but whose remains were not found until a farmer unearthed them in 1921. Roy Harrison was identified by his silver cigarette case.

As Lambis slowly walked down the line of headstones, a strange feeling crept over him. He could feel the aura of the young men who slept there. He noticed by the dates in the stone that he was passing the headstones of many of the men of the 58th Battalion who had died in a German raid on 15 July, four days before the big attack at Fromelles. He paused at Roy Harrison's headstone. He felt at home with these men. A feeling of calm washed over him as he read and remembered their names. The heat caught up with him and he moved to the side and sat down on the prickly grass. When he looked up he saw that he was sitting in front of the headstone of one of his favourite characters from the battle, the Reverend Spencer Maxted, the beloved Chaplain of the 54th Battalion.

A Church of England minister from Pymble on Sydney's North Shore, Maxted left his wife Gertrude and his young family to enlist as a private soldier. He served as a stretcher-bearer at Gallipoli and then in Egypt he was transferred to the Chaplain's Department and promoted to Captain. The measure of the man was seen during the infamous desert march to the canal when, although he was entitled to a horse, he marched with the men. At Fromelles, he worked himself to a standstill helping recover and tend to the wounded after the battle, making many trips out into no-man's land. He had been working

A view of the German front line after the battle at Fromelles. In the foreground Australian dead lie covered with blankets or coats by the Germans. This photo was taken on the morning of 20 July as the Germans reclaimed their positions. (AWM PHOTO A01560)

for 24 hours non-stop, mainly as a stretcher-bearer, when he fell asleep exhausted and was killed as he slept by a stray shell. He was later awarded a Military Cross for his bravery in recovering the wounded. Bean wrote that Maxted provided 'services of mercy never to be forgotten by those who benefited from them'.

Lambis soon found himself in conversation with Maxted:

It took me by surprise a bit and I sat there and lay down on the grass. I sat there and had a chat with the Reverend and sought his counsel and perhaps a blessing. I know it all sounds a bit fanciful but I've had a lot to do with Fromelles and I was quite emotional.

I may have been dazed by the heat but I felt very comfortable there and I felt he gave me his blessing.

The next evening Lambis walked down from the church, through the narrow laneway behind it, and on to the field leading out to Pheasant Wood. As he approached it he began to feel the same wave of emotions he experienced at Rue Petillon Cemetery. At first glance, the tract of land that runs along the southern boundary of the wood seems unexceptional enough – 100 metres or so in width, flat, rich deep green knee-high grass, set against a dense tree-line of even height, perhaps ten metres high. As he came closer Lambis could sense the aura of those who had been waiting for him for so long. He could see the undulations in the ground where the earth had subsided along the row of pits.

It was quite moving when I got there. I walked along the ground between the pits and the wood and I had more conversations. I said g'day boys. I know it's been a long time but be patient, don't worry, we'll get you. I felt very drawn to the place. You get a gut feeling. I've always been confident that they were there. I had some wonderful conversations with the boys there.

In the failing light Lambis bade them farewell, promising to return the next day and to stay with them until the investigating team came to find them at last. As he wandered slowly back, he continued to wrestle with the question that has troubled him from the start of his quest: should he be searching for the missing Diggers or should he leave them in peace.

In my heart I believe we must find them but out of respect to them I worry whether we should leave them where they are untouched or

338

whether we should do everything we possibly can to recover them. After visiting them, I think I was right in my initial thoughts: I believe we should recover them.

Standing on the high ground looking back at Pheasant Wood, Lambis found himself comparing it with Bullecourt, the site of another disastrous one-day slaughter of Australians on 11 April 1917.

Bullecourt always felt like the nastiest place in France that I've ever been to. It's a benign-looking, flat place but it scared the shit out of me. Talk about feelings, just knowing that I was going there and just standing in the field, it felt like the most dreadful place I'd ever been to. At Pheasant Wood I felt I was in good and comfortable company.

After his first visit to Pheasant Wood, Lambis returned, as he had promised, each day. He knew it so well from the aerial photos, from his studies, from the satellite images, but every day he grew to know it better. Every time he arrived he said g'day to the boys there, reassuring them that now he had found them, he would not abandon them.

As he counted down the hours until the investigation team arrived Lambis had to fight back his emotions. All the time, he drew on his mental picture of those buried there. Lambis knew the faces of many of the missing from the archives in the Australian War Memorial and from descendants who have sent him photographs. In fact, even during his current visit he had met and chatted with Australian families who had come to VC Corner Cemetery and had left messages with photographs of their loved ones there. He often dreamed of building up a photo library of those at Fromelles so future visitors could put faces to the names.

The memorial wall at VC Corner Cemetery, just outside Fromelles. It is the only all-Australian cemetery on the Western Front. The wall commemorates 1299 Diggers listed as missing after the battle. (PATRICK LINDSAY PHOTO)

I've read all the Red Cross letters. I've read every file of the 1299 missing. I've read Jack Bowden's sister Mary's letters, trying to find out about Jack and you can't help being touched by that – the pleas from the families back in Australia wanting to know anything, any information at all, about their loved ones. It would be wonderful if visitors could see those who rest here as real people with faces and families, rather than as names carved into stone.

Lambis' hopes continued to grow: maybe when they finally do the recovery work, it will all become tangible, not just scattered debris from Fromelles but the remains of the men who've waited so patiently.

I have a mental picture of exactly who's buried there at Pheasant Wood. I will still contend that it's the 14th and 15th Brigade site. I hope that when they do dig, there's fabric there and colour patches because that will help in terms of identification. If my contention is correct I hope we will see the faded green and red colour patches of the 14th and 15th Brigades somewhere.

29

VINDICATION

Truth sits upon the lips of dying men.

MATTHEW ARNOLD

Dr Tony Pollard and his team of six from Glasgow University Archaeological Research Division (GUARD) arrived at Fromelles on 16 May 2007. For the next twelve days they cast their expert eyes and sophisticated state-of-the-art equipment over the sus-pected Pheasant Wood mass grave site. They came armed with Team Lambis' 'hand-up brief' to the original Australian Army Panel of Investigation, which they confirmed with their own archival enquiries in Australia, Britain, France and Germany, both before and after their site testing.

The GUARD team's enquiries of the British military records revealed that an intelligence report on the 'country east of the line Armentières-Arras, 1916' described Pheasant Wood at the time as

The grass had to be mown and baled before the GUARD Team could begin their non-invasive investigation of the Pheasant Wood site in mid 2007. (LAMBIS ENGLEZOS PHOTO)

Lambis Englezos with GUARD Team member Iain Banks at Pheasant Wood during the investigation. (LAMBIS ENGLEZOS PHOTO)

an immature plantation of young oaks, the trunks being about the thickness of a man's arm.

They noted that their initial inspection of the Wood today revealed that several of the trees still in the wood were

of wartime vintage, being of no use for timber because of steel splinters still embedded deep within.

They also confirmed that the roads, tracks, field boundaries and ditches and, of course, the wood itself all

follow the same trace as those shown in the aerial photos of the time.

As we've seen, a satellite view of the area shows it virtually unchanged from the 1916 aerials.

The GUARD team noted that a geological section of the Fromelles sector, done by the British Royal Engineers in 1922, revealed the soil layers which give it its high water table. A layer, between 2.5 metres and 5 metres thick, of 'Quaternary water-bearing river alluvials and surface loams and clays' overlaying a 20-metre layer of 'pure blue Ypresian clay' combine to hold the water table close to the surface.

GUARD set itself a series of general aims and specific objectives to fulfil its commission by Roger Lee's Australian Army History Unit.

The general aims were to verify the presence of the pits shown in the aerial photographs taken between 1916 and 1918; to ascertain their size and condition; to establish whether Allied troops were buried in them; to consider whether if there is evidence of such burials, whether there is further evidence of recovery and re-interment of these remains at cemeteries elsewhere; and to provide a 'detailed historical framework' for the events which occurred at Fromelles and Pheasant Wood in 1916.

The team's specific objectives included: a full topographic survey of the site at one-metre intervals (to reveal changes in the topography relating to the presence of the pits); a geophysical survey, using resistivity meter and gradiometer (to identify underground archaeological features like the pits and the wartime railway); a ground-penetrating radar survey (to provide additional information like the depth of the underground features); a metal detector survey (to recover artefacts and give evidence of the site's wartime history); and an extensive archival documentary search (to seek any evidence of post-war recovery and reburial of the remains).

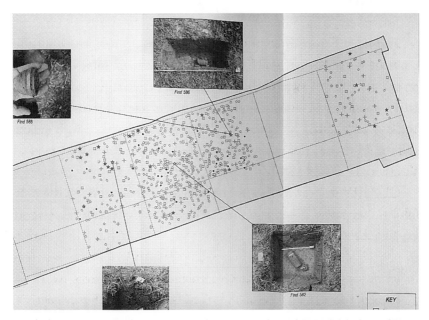

The results of the metal detector survey conducted by the GUARD Team during their investigation of the Pheasant Wood site. (TONY POLLARD PHOTO)

The GUARD team's first task was to deal with the waist-high grass on the site which had been cut, as arranged by M. Serge Desruelles, the farmer leasing the land from Madame Marie-Paule Demassiet (sadly, her husband Pierre had died in January, a few months after we met him). Unfortunately, recent wet weather had prevented the grass cutting until a day or so before the team arrived and it was still lying on the land when they began their work. By day three of their work, Tony Pollard had arranged for the grass to be baled and the undulations across the site became clearly evident.

While the GUARD team went about its work, Lambis Englezos watched fascinated but determined to stay out of their hair. He offered his services as a 'convict labourer'. These were graciously accepted by Tony Pollard and Lambis soon tagged along as a 'silent' member of the group, helping with the manual labour but assiduously holding his tongue, even though his curiosity would sometimes almost drive him to distraction.

The team began by setting the survey grids against which all the other measurements would be based. The geophysical survey was based on grids 20 metres square while the ground-penetrating radar worked off 15-square-metre grids. The team members marked them out using bamboo canes at each corner, the 20-metre grids marked with yellow and the 15-metre grids with purple, while common canes were marked with both.

GUARD first carried out its topographic survey and fed the data into its computers. Then it turned to its resistivity testing. The report explained that it works:

on the basis that the resistance encountered by a current passed between two sets of probes in the soil will vary across a survey area, and that some of the variation will reflect past human activity. Human activity affects the compaction of the soil and the level of moisture present. Where a hole or trench has been dug and then backfilled or silted, the fill of the hole or trench will never be as compact as the surrounding undisturbed soil. The fill will always contain more water and more oxygen than its surroundings.

Pollard explained that resistivity tests can establish a picture of the features buried in the soil but he cautioned that the kind of soil at Pheasant Wood, with its predominance of fine-particle clay, can be a problem:

The particle size means that there is frequently little differentiation between disturbed and undisturbed soils after the passage of time.

The next tests used a magnetometer to detect alterations in the strength of the earth's magnetic field.

Such variations come from a range of causes: heating the soil (through hearths, kilns etc.) will increase the thermoremnant magnetism of the soil; backfilling negative features will cause a disturbance to the alignment of the magnetic fields of the soil particles; topsoil and subsoil will have different levels of magnetic susceptibility, so that backfilled features will have a different magnetic signature than either; and the presence of iron-rich materials in greater concentration than under natural conditions.

It was followed by ground-penetrating radar which sends a series of pulses into the ground at the speed of light.

16 horizontal receivers collect the data and images are generated in 3D to show where the ground may have been disturbed, or indicate the presence of buried objects, buried metal, cavities and water.

Finally, the team ran a sophisticated metal detector across the site, aiming at locating any buried metal objects and artefacts. The machine is generally effective to about half a metre deep. Surprisingly perhaps, Pollard noted:

> *this is one of the first occasions that a systematic metal detector survey has been executed on a First World War site on the Western Front.*

The team swept both east–west and then north–south across the entire site. Lambis stood quietly, barely containing his growing excite-ment as the machine beeped away, metre by metre, across the site. The machine had been set so only large metal objects would register because, based on its earlier battlefield experience, the team anticipated metal would be there 'in high quantities'. The men worked in two-man teams: one sweeping, the other using a spade to find and carefully remove the object and place it into a plastic bag which was then pinned at the spot it was found. The number of strikes meant that it took an average of two days to complete each 20 × 20 metre grid square.

The two medallions found by the GUARD Team during their investigation of the Pheasant Wood site. (TONY POLLARD PHOTO)

The metal detector survey took the most time but it also provided the most dramatic results. The time and effort were more than repaid by the discovery of two small objects: two copper-alloy medallions.

The first medallion was a 3.8 × 2.4 centimetre heart-shaped pendant bearing the letters 'ANZAC' embossed across its top, above the Australian coat of arms. Under the crest it had 'Oct 15' and beneath that '1915'.

The second medallion was 2.9 × 2.3 centimetres and in the shape of an inverted horseshoe. It featured the letters 'AIF' and inside the horseshoe letters reading 'Shire of Alberton' and the date '1914'. This medallion still retained traces of its original red, white and blue enamel.

Pollard was unable to locate other examples of the objects but he points out:

> a wide variety of medallions were produced during the First World War and not all of them by the military. It was not uncommon for wives and sweethearts to purchase medallions and present them to their loved ones – hence the term 'sweetheart badges'.

Dr Tony Pollard delivered GUARD's report on the findings of its investigation at Pheasant Wood to Roger Lee in mid-July 2007. The report was considered by the Army History Unit's Expert Panel on 25 July. In the meantime, Pollard pre-empted its release in an interview with the *Sydney Morning Herald* on 24 July in which he was quoted as saying:

> These men were lost to history. We now have an order from the commander of the Bavarian troops in the area that grave pits were to be dug to accommodate 400 Allied dead and our survey has

*identified exactly where these pits are. We think the bodies are still
in there.*

The next day, the Minister for Veterans' Affairs, Bruce Billson,
issued a press release confirming his support of further examination of
Pheasant Wood in the light of the GUARD Report's findings. He said
the report revealed

> *subsurface anomalies in the soil that coincide with war time aerial
> photos and confirm the presence of a series of pits. Other evidence,
> including water pooling discovered in the pits, led Dr Pollard to
> conclude that 'it was beyond doubt' that the site was used as a burial
> ground.*
>
> *The survey concluded that the soil had not been disturbed since
> a 1918 counter-attack and advance by the British Army, casting
> doubt on the likelihood that the remains were recovered in post-war
> battlefield clearance operations. The pattern and distribution of bullets,
> shrapnel and other debris of battle suggests the soil was undisturbed
> after the end of the war.*

Billson noted that the Expert Panel had recommended a formal
approach to French authorities seeking approval for further examination
of the site and added:

> *Even with full French cooperation, any further significant work on
> site would most likely have to wait until the next northern summer
> when the soil has dried out. The water table is very close to the
> surface which makes the risk of cave-ins very high.*

The Minister also added that there was only a remote likelihood
that any remains found could be identified.

*The high water table, the acidity of the soil, the German practice of
using heavy doses of lime when burying the dead and the high
probability of co-mingling of the remains would make individual
identification, even using the latest techniques, extremely difficult.*

The GUARD Report's executive summary set out the details of its
commission from the Australian Army and notes that Lambis and
others in Australia suggested between 60 and 170 Australian soldiers,
listed as missing after the Battle of Fromelles, may have been buried
at Pheasant Wood. In its fourth paragraph the report highlighted the
fact that the metal detector survey's discovery of the two medallions

*bearing ANZAC and AIF insignia clearly indicated that Australians
had been present on the site, probably as bodies brought from the
front line by the German light railway which ran alongside the pits
(as detailed in the German orders). The metal detector survey also
recovered a number of buttons, some of which may have become
detached from clothes and accoutrements worn by the dead. In
addition, bullets, both fired and unfired and various elements from
shells, including shrapnel balls, shell fragments, pusher plates and
shell casings were recovered from across the site.*

The report then moved to its most important finding:

*The apparently intact nature of the metal artefact scatter, which
includes material dating to the final Allied advance in Autumn 1918,
along with the relatively undisturbed nature of the pit fills suggested
by the geophysical surveys, in addition to the lack of any documentary
evidence for exhumation, **pushes the weight of evidence in favour
of the bodies still being in situ in the pits** [emphasis added].
However, a trial trenching evaluation would be required to establish*

beyond doubt whether or not this was the case – any such exercise should also be supported by an exhaustive programme of archival research to establish the full character of the documentary record, as relating to the identification of individuals and the activities of German burial and allied exhumation parties.

GUARD traced the Shire of Alberton to a now-defunct council region in Victoria's Gippsland area. On inspection of Lambis' list of the missing, they found only one with an association to the district, Private Henry Victor Willis, whose parents John and Janet Willis lived in Alberton. Pollard concluded:

It is tempting to claim that Willis was the owner of horseshoe medallion and was buried in pit 4 at Pheasant Wood but not all names in the archives have their place of recruitment or native place listed so this association of an individual with the object and the site, compelling as it may seem, must therefore remain just a possibility.

Lambis knew of Harry Willis. He was the great great uncle of one of Team Lambis' keenest members. Tim Whitford had joined the team in mid-2006. After Ward Selby moved to Britain, he became Lambis' technical support man. (As Lambis' mate and team member John Fielding would say: 'When it comes to technology, Lambis is a man behind his times'!) Tim Whitford and Lambis had become fast friends as they worked together on the quest.

Lambis was the first to tell Tim Whitford of GUARD's discovery of the Alberton medallion. Lambis and Tim have subsequently spoken to a large number of Harry Willis' descendants and they believe the odds heavily favour the medallion being his. The family was something of a fixture in the early days of Alberton, with many recorded as early

A studio portrait of Henry Victor Willis of D Company, 31st Battalion, from Alberton, Victoria, who was killed at Fromelles and is one of the missing Diggers from the battle. The GUARD Team found a medallion from the Shire of Alberton during their investigation – a possible link with Willis as he appears to be the only missing Digger from the district. (AWM PHOTO DA11372)

students at the local Alberton Public School in the years before the turn of the twentieth century.

Tim Whitford was about eight years old when his nan, Marjorie Whitford, who was babysitting him, sat him down at the kitchen table at the home where his parents still live in Victoria's Gippsland district and asked him what he wanted to be when he grew up.

When I said I wanted to be a soldier her mood changed instantly. A look of dread or sorrow came over her face. I remember it vividly. She said: don't you dare be a soldier! You'll be killed like my Uncle Harry! It was a moment that has stuck with me ever since. As I

Henry Willis' enlistment permission form. The Willis family has always believed that Henry, who was under age, forged his mother's signature to sign up.

*got older I developed this abiding interest in Harry – who he was
and where he came from.*

Tim's nan told him the story that had been passed down to her:
that Harry had been given a white feather because he hadn't joined
up, even though he was only sixteen. She explained how Harry had
lied about his age and had gone off to war, where, in her words, he
'got shot up and we don't know where he is'.

The Willis family was a huge one – fourteen kids – and they were
battlers from Gippsland in rural Victoria. Four of Harry's other brothers
also joined up. While training at Broadmeadows Dave Willis contracted
meningitis and died at Royal Park Camp before he even had a chance
to go overseas. Brother Syd went to Gallipoli, after surviving the
sinking of his troopship *Southland,* and he was later wounded but made
it home.

Tim only found out a few years back that Syd had named his
first-born son Harry, after the brother he lost at Fromelles.

*I still call him Young Harry. He's an ex-WWII Digger who lives in
Melbourne, aged 84. He pulled me aside one day before I came to
Fromelles and said: 'I'll tell you something me old man said. Harry
and me old man met up in France as Harry was coming up for the
attack and they snatched a couple of moments, because they were
in different units. They shook hands, as brothers do, and they both
knew what Harry was going into. They were under no illusions that
he would come out.' Young Harry told me that Syd was a bitter
man for the rest of his life, hated the Poms, hated the bastards who'd
sent his brother to his death.*

Young Harry had to live with the legacy of his late uncle Harry all
his life. So had Tim. For as long as he could remember, he had been

told that he looked like his lost great great Uncle Harry. For his part, Tim believes he sees the original Harry growing old in Young Harry:

If Harry Willis had lived to an old age, there he is in Young Harry ... the spitting image, a cheeky bastard and a funny bloke.

Tim grew up and ignored his nan's advice. He joined the Army and served for fourteen years, rising to sergeant and commanding a battle tank in the Royal Australian Armoured Corps. Over the years he tried to find out as much as he could about Harry Willis. In the days before the internet, Tim visited Central Army Records and pulled out Harry's file and read it through and through. That was when he first learned that he was killed at Fromelles.

In the mid-1990s when Tim was seconded to the British Army in Germany, he regularly visited Fromelles. He would spend the weekend walking around the battlefield and he'd find himself asking why they left Harry's name off the wall at VC Corner and why they put it on the wall at Villers-Bretonneux instead.

I eventually decided that because most of the blokes that are on the wall at Villers-Bretonneux are 31st Battalion blokes it was just one of those clerical anomalies. They were trying to recover from the most horrific battle the battalion ever had and for whatever reason the returns didn't go in or something and he got left off. But, in many ways, that made it even worse. We didn't know where he was buried and his name wasn't commemorated at VC Corner with his mates.

Tim told his nan what he found out but she could add nothing further and his research hit a series of dead ends. Then, in mid-2006, he saw Lambis and his story on *60 Minutes*.

I don't normally watch it, but I was bolt upright watching this bloke with his theory. I said to my wife Liz: this bloke's nailed it! I reckon I was on to the phone to him about five minutes later. I dialled into the 60 Mins web and left my name and said if Lambis wants to get in touch with me I'm a descendant. He was straight on the phone.

Lambis invited Tim to a commemorative service being held by the Friends of the 15th Brigade the next day. Tim was in with both feet from then on.

Tim's nan, Harry's niece, is still alive in her early nineties. Harry's sister, who was Tim's great grandmother, lost her brother Dave as well as Harry, while their brother Bert came back with his health ruined by gas. A fourth brother, Syd, who had been wounded many times, also returned a deeply changed man. The war had ripped the Willis family apart. Harry's mother, Janet, never recovered from the loss of her two sons. As a little girl, Marjorie Whitford remembers her as stern and without joy. She had to be careful not to disturb Syd and had to listen as Bert coughed his lungs out. All that was left of her Uncle Harry was his ID disc, returned via the International Red Cross, and a picture on the wall.

A search of Henry Willis' personnel file shows that his family was advised of a number of reports of his death. One of his comrades from his machine-gun section in 31st Battalion, Private Henry Rogers, a 20-year-old draper from Taree, said he believed Harry was shot through the jaw during the battle. Another 31st Battalion man, Private Bert Hickson, a labourer

I knew Willis. He was in the same tent as myself. He was a stout fair man about 21 years of age. He came from Yarram, Gippsland, Victoria. He was killed at Fleurbaix in 'No man's land'. I saw his

body 13 hours later lying dead. We had to retire and leave our dead there.

Perhaps the most poignant entry in the file is a handwritten note, dated 'Alberton 10/7/15':

I am quite agreeable that my son may enlist for active service abroad (signed) Janet Willis.

I certify that the above signature is genuine. [signed] H.V. Willis

Tim Whitford's subsequent research has confirmed that Harry Willis was indeed under-age when he enlisted, but he was eighteen, not sixteen, and was twenty-one when he died. Nevertheless, he would still have needed his parent's permission to join up.

Looking at Henry Willis' enlistment permission slip, it's certainly possible that he forged his mother's signature to join up. Elsewhere in his file where his mum, Janet Willis, confirmed receipt of her late son's Star Medal her signature looked to be in a much stronger hand. Perhaps the permission slip betrayed some evidence of 'forger's shake', where the copier writes at a much slower and less assured speed than the original.

Like many of the missing Diggers' families, Tim Whitford was understandably delighted at the prospect of finally finding his relative's resting place. He wrote to Tony Pollard of his excitement after reading of the Alberton medallion:

You have no idea how much I love your work mate. Ever had one of those days when you thought your work doesn't matter??? Today ain't one of them. Well done!

My 7 year old daughter Alexandra took the newspaper article to school today ... beaming that her daddy and her soldier-uncle had made the paper ... His name will live on.

Harry Willis' birthplace of Alberton in South Gippsland is still a tiny village today, as Tim Whitford attests:

My Nan grew up on tales of Harry as a little girl and still lives just 4 km from Alberton. Harry has descendants in the Whitford, Willis, Morse, Noonan, and Farley families. There would be literally hundreds of South Gippslanders who could trace a link to him ... We are from the shallow end of the gene pool if you know what I mean ... As far as I know, Nan is his closest living relative.

While the circumstantial evidence from GUARD's metal detector survey strongly suggested that Henry Willis and his comrades were buried by the Germans in the mass graves at Pheasant Wood, GUARD believed that what makes it even more compelling was the array of results from the other tests they carried out.

The GUARD Report described the medallions as 'two items of unequivocal Australian provenance' that 'provide very compelling evidence that allied troops were buried on the site in 1916'. Pollard concluded that the position in which the medallions were found (on either side of the pits):

in all probability mark locations where the Australian bodies were laid out prior to burial in the pits or alternatively they were dropped at these locations as bodies were being manoeuvred into the pits.

Overall GUARD believed their tests succeeded in:

locating the site of the pits within the modern landscape, with geophysical survey and ground-penetrating radar producing anomalies, albeit in some cases weak ones ... consistent with the pits shown on aerial photographs taken between 1916 and 1918. These subsurface traces also correspond to subtle changes in surface topography, with the pit surfaces generally sitting lower than the surrounding ground. Survey and analysis of rectified aerial photographs indicate pits around 3.0–3.5 m wide and 10 m long, with their depth beneath the present ground surface varying between 2 m and 2.5 m.

The report noted that the 'scatter' of material found by the metal detector, both from the time of the 1916 burial and also the later fighting over the site prior to the final German withdrawal in 1918, was consistent with his conclusion that

would suggest that burials are still present in the pits dug by the Germans in July 1916.

It expanded on the GUARD team's efforts to establish whether the allied dead buried after the battle in July 1916 are still in situ. It referred to the archival research carried out on Pollard's behalf in the UK, Germany, Switzerland and the Australian War Memorial that 'failed to locate any definitive evidence for the removal of the bodies in the immediate post-war era' and concluded that:

the location of the graves was certainly no secret, and by the end of the war was known to the Germans, the Australians and the British.

Technically, of course, this is true. We have previously seen, as GUARD pointed out, that Major Allen of the Graves Recovery Unit was asked to search for the graves in the years immediately after the war. But, while the Pheasant Wood reference popped up in various reports and papers it was certainly not publicly well known, then or now. Indeed, had Lambis and his team not methodically retraced the Diggers' steps during their quest, the graves of Pheasant Wood would remain hidden in the archives.

The GUARD Report also touched on a number of issues raised in relation to the Pheasant Wood site: the possibility that the mass graves could have been constructed as minenwerfer (trench mortar) positions or that they may contain Portuguese soldiers (both raised by John Williams' report to the Australian Army's Panel of Investigation); or further that the graves may have been destroyed by inadvertent shellfire.

On the first issue, the report concluded:

considering the Germans' supremely careful application of camouflage and concealment in this region, this interpretation of works so plainly obvious to aerial scrutiny is more than a curious one.

Interestingly, GUARD used Peter Chasseaud, one of the world's leading World War I trench map experts. ROAM had previously also used him to come to this conclusion. Neither John Williams nor the Expert Panel consulted him.

On the possibility of Portuguese remains, it said:

There is little chance of Portuguese soldiers being interred in Pheasant Wood. The German advance of April 1918 was so swift that it left the seriously under strength Portuguese reeling. A great many died, the casualties being buried in the dedicated Portuguese National Cemetery at Richebourg L'Avoue, just behind the original line of defence. Although Portuguese and British prisoners from this offensive action were marched back through Fromelles to captivity, given the speed and

urgency of the German advance it is more than unlikely that bodies
of enemy soldiers would have been carried between two and three
kilometres from the battlefield to be buried at Pheasant Wood.

On the possible destruction of the graves by shelling, the report
concluded it

can categorically be ruled out as the area was never heavily fought
over or bombarded.

Overall, the GUARD Report examined the archival material and
concluded that, in the absence of any document trail to the contrary,
the balance of the weight of evidence tipped in favour of the bodies
still being where they were buried in July 1916. Supporting this
argument, GUARD cited the results of its geophysical and metal
detector surveys, as well as the likelihood that the pits would have
been difficult to locate by 1919 or 1920. In this regard the report
unearthed a fascinating reference to Commonwealth War Graves
Commission 'tips' for recognising post-war graves:

Experience only teaches men where bodies will probably be found, in
graves which are not visible; but the following signs are characteristic:

1. *Rifles, or posts bearing helmets or equipment, placed at the head*
   of graves.
2. *Small stakes marked E (burnt into the wood) showing spots where*
   British soldiers have been buried by the Germans. In some cases
   these stakes bear a number instead of the letter E, but in the
   majority of such cases troops other than British have been buried
   there. Such bodies, however, should be exhumed, inasmuch as

every body, whether allied or enemy forces, must be concentrated [within a military cemetery].

3. *Remains or equipment upon the surface or protruding from the ground.*
4. *Rat holes. These sometimes will show small bones or pieces of equipment brought to the surface by the rats.*
5. *Discolouration of the grass, earth or water. Grass is often a vivid bluish-green colour where bodies are buried, while earth and water turn a greenish black or grey.*

GUARD reported to the Australian Army that, although the results were 'compelling',

we still lack absolute proof that remains buried here in 1916 and/or later, were NOT recovered after the war. The only way to verify or 'ground truth' this conclusion will be to carry out a secondary programme of limited trial trenching on the site (a process known as 'sondage' to the French).

This would establish without doubt whether the bodies are still there, as well as providing evidence on the numbers of remains and their condition. GUARD noted that only after this further test should any further thought be given to a subsequent excavation and exhumation, if that is the decision of the authorities.

The report also recommended a 'comprehensive and systematic' exploration of all the relevant archives to support the next stages of the investigation.

It has become clear during the course of this project that despite many years in gestation a comprehensive archive research programme has never been carried out.

Lambis Englezos and his team couldn't have agreed more. They had been calling for an extensive search through the archives for years. In their work to date they had, of course, been greatly limited by their numbers, by their available time and by geography. In fact, it had been remarkable that a group of enthusiastic amateurs had been able to achieve so much without the experience and the background knowledge possessed by the experts.

Finally, the GUARD Report pointed out how the discovery of the Pheasant Wood mass graves differed from the normal way that remains were found on battlefields. Usually, they were found by accident.

> At Fromelles, however, answers are being sought by design, and the treatment is naturally very different to the methodology applied to 'adventitious' finds. Pheasant Wood demands a different approach entirely, not least because of its political scale, the archaeological practicalities of the search, excavation and reporting process, and the financial implications for the various governments involved, plus of course the CWGC.

For Lambis, the GUARD Report was a powerful vindication of his work. He remembered how anxious he felt after Tony Pollard and his team had finished their examination at Pheasant Wood:

> On the last day, after they'd finished all their testing, we said our goodbyes and we packed up. I walked back to VC Corner, as I had done many times in the month I was there, and I confess I had a bit of a sob. I was a bit of a sook. I thought I was something of a hard bastard but I had my sob there ... probably for a lot of reasons ... but mainly relief. There's never been a point when I haven't thought about resolving it for the men who are there. This was another step along the way.

Lambis has been consistent in his view that those buried at Pheasant Wood are men from the 14th and 15th Brigades. His rationale centres on the fact that the 8th Brigade went out against Delangré Farm, the 14th went out against Rouges Bancs and the 15th went out against the Sugar Loaf.

We know from the German Red Cross records that only seven, I think, of the 15th Brigade were among the missing. We know that nobody could have taken the Sugar Loaf. They were massacred by the machine guns there so those who made it through the German lines were mainly the 8th and 14th Brigade. I've read all their individual files.

I believe the 8th Brigade's missing are buried at Marlaque Farm. They would have gone around the other side of Delangré Farm and died there. They would have been taken across field by the Germans and buried at Marlaque Farm. There was a rail line past the Marlaque site. The British historian Peter Barton had a range of photographs showing it.

Lambis was content with the progress of the investigation. He knew and accepted there was a long way to go to final resolution: the excavation of the mass graves, the exhumation of the remains of the missing Diggers and Tommies in them, hopefully, the identification of the remains and, finally, their re-interment at a specially created cemetery at Pheasant Wood.

That is my hope. I hope the authorities agree to recover and try to identify the missing. There are 316 missing Englishmen from that battle. Indeed, the Pheasant Wood site is mainly English, as the final German document made clear when it blew away all that bullshit and smoke. They were from that battle, from the 182nd and 183rd

Pheasant Wood, then and now. (COURTESY LAMBIS ENGLEZOS AND JOHN FIELDING)

Brigades of the British 61st Division, collected from in front of the German lines.

What was the objective: Aubers Ridge or Berlin? We knew there was a lattice of rail lines behind the German lines and that the mass grave at Fournes, which was recovered in 1923, had 50 bodies in it – 10 of them Australian and 40 English. That's the line that cuts through Pheasant Wood.

The Germans tell us in that document from the 21st July that we separated them by nationality and buried them before Pheasant Wood and in mass grave I.M.4.3 at Fournes. When they say nationality, they mean separated into English and Australian. There were Germans as well but the document reads that we took care of the Germans and we separated the others, from their kit and their badges and the like, into Australian and English. They knew the units facing them. They knew everything ... when it was going to happen and by whom. The whole sad, stupid business of the whole thing was had they not have attacked, they would have achieved their aim – to keep the Germans where they were – and not lost a single man. By assaulting, the Germans knew it was a feint, not a genuine threat, and they could leave.

The Germans suffered too but the simple fact is that the Australian 5th Division was wiped out and of no further use for many months. The Germans probably saw no point in counter-attacking.

The allies didn't take up the German offer of a truce the following day. What would have happened if they had agreed to a parlementaire would have been that they would have taken our wounded and dead and we would have taken their wounded and dead and then swapped them. There would have been no missing. None. The wounded would have been taken care of, the 23 Australians who were killed in the week afterwards, going out because they couldn't resist the call to go and save their mates, would not have been killed. So there would have been no missing. The dead would have been retrieved on both sides. McCay or Haking could have shown some compassion. There were precedents.

Lambis got some hints during the testing that the investigators were on the right track but he still remained on tenterhooks until he received the final report acknowledging that the weight of evidence pointed to the missing men still being in their resting places.

I was given signs on the last day. The nudge came that there would be every likelihood that I may have to come back. They said, in effect, to wait until the report comes in but the signs were good. I knew the technology appeared to do what you would expect, with *the sounds in all the right places. But ultimately it'll be the technology of the shovel that will tell.*

The investigation team were very thorough and very professional, and very inclusive of me – cheap convict labour! It was not very glamorous work, this archaeology. It was a fantastic time and they were very funny people. Whenever the top brass, like the French authorities or the Australian ambassador came down, I'd disappear, make myself scarce. I didn't pry or ask too many pointed questions about what they were finding because they were commissioned to do a job by the Australian Government. I think it's an excellent report.

After the GUARD team packed up they were joined by Monsieur Hubert Huchette, the Mayor of Fromelles, who toasted their work and wished them a safe journey home. Lambis added his thanks and best wishes.

They were headed off to Arras and then going home. I unloaded our shovel and a few other tools back at Martial's place and then I walked down to VC Corner and then the pent-up emotions of five-years' work, burst forth ... I'd left a note for Martial and he came down. He was emotional about it too. He is very emotional about the whole thing. I knew I needed to be there. I hope I'm there when they break the ground for real.

On 19 July for the previous fifteen years, Lambis Englezos had attended the commemoration for the Battle of Fromelles at Melbourne's Shrine of Remembrance. But he did so in 2007 with a renewed passion, secure in the belief that his quest was close to its resolution. He was delighted to hear that Roger Lee, the Head of the Australian Army History Unit, had conceded that he had established his case:

*In this case I have to admit it, Lambis was right and I was wrong.
It wasn't so much doubt these pits once existed, but the fact I could
not believe post-war recovery units could possibly have missed such
mass graves.*

It was a generous and heartfelt concession. Roger Lee had never
doubted Lambis' sincerity, nor had he doubted his passion. He had
often complimented Lambis and his team on their research and their
persistence, but his admission that Lambis was right in his assumptions
and his claims meant much to Lambis. It meant that all the hours at
the computer and on the phone were worth it; all the doubts, all the
anguish and all the criticisms, were washed away.

But both Lambis and Chris Bryett knew that their quest had long
hours and many roads still to travel. They had proven their argument.
They had prompted the authorities to act. But they knew that only
the shovel would finally decide whether the missing Diggers and
Tommies who fell at Fromelles were still in their mass graves at
Pheasant Wood.

They were aware that some doubts had arisen about the GUARD
Report's findings, which attracted considerable debate amongst the
tight-knit international forensic archaeological community. A number
of peer examinations of the report cast doubt on whether its conclusions
could be justified from its scientific findings. I have included the main
elements of the debate in Appendix VI. They centre on a series of
technical challenges made by a number of experts to GUARD's
methodology and equipment, and to the report's interpretation of its
findings.

The final question still remained unanswered: were the missing
Diggers of Fromelles, and their British mates, *still* lying in the shadow
of Pheasant Wood? We could now be certain that they were buried
there after the battle in 1916, as Lambis and his supporters had

maintained from the start. But, despite the conclusions of the GUARD Report, some element of doubt still lingered as to whether the remains were removed some time after the war and reburied elsewhere, with any record of reburial either destroyed during World War II or languishing unfound in the archives.

The next step in the saga would be a dig commissioned by the Australian Army, in cooperation with the British Army and the French authorities, in the summer of 2008. The delay was necessary because the wet conditions that prevail in the area until summertime would make digging deep narrow trenches unsafe.

If Lambis and his supporters were proven correct, Pheasant Wood would be the largest mass grave (outside genocide cases) found in Western Europe since World War I.

The likely numbers would greatly complicate the recovery and the identification of the remains. The general principle adopted by the Australian Army on the recovery of war has been that they are exhumed, then identified and finally re-interred in the nearest appropriate Commonwealth war cemetery. The likely numbers at Pheasant Wood would mean that recovery, and certainly the identification process, would be lengthy and very costly.

First, the recovery team would have to try to separate the remains according to their nationality. This could be problematic should the uniforms have deteriorated past the stage of recognition – a distinct possibility. Second, the team would be faced with the massive task of trying to identify individual remains. It is possible that some may have artefacts that could help, but this seems very unlikely as the German burial teams generally took the identification tags.

Relying on DNA for identification would be an uncertain option until the condition of the remains was known. The worst-case scenario would be is that the remains had been subjected to constant wetting and drying and the leeching would render DNA recovery a remote chance. This would be complicated by the substantial task of gathering DNA samples from descendants of the missing and cross-referencing them against any recovered from the remains.

Lambis Englezos and Chris Bryett and their teams had no doubt that the Australian and British Governments were morally obliged to make every effort to recover and identify every individual who lies in the graves at Pheasant Wood. They have often pointed out that the Australian Prime Minister at the time, William Morris Hughes, was on record guaranteeing on behalf of his nation that no expense would be spared to recover the Australians who gave their lives for their country. Lambis remained uncompromising on the subject:

> We should accept nothing less than a total dedication of our resources to identifying and finally laying to rest these heroes whose lives were squandered at Pheasant Wood. It is the very least we can do for these men and their families.

30

THROUGH GERMAN EYES

The battalions were told by their officers that this part of the front was quiet.

EXTRACT FROM GERMAN INTELLIGENCE REPORT ON
INTERROGATION OF AUSTRALIAN PRISONER CAPTURED BEFORE
THE BATTLE OF FROMELLES

On 6 February 2008, the Australian Minister for Defence Science and Personnel in the newly elected Rudd Labor Government, Warren Snowdon, made the announcement that Team Lambis had been waiting for: he confirmed that he had authorised a limited excavation of the Pheasant Wood site to be undertaken by GUARD, starting in April. He said:

GUARD was appointed by the Department of Defence following a recommendation from Nigel Steele, the Co-Secretary to the British All Party Parliamentary War Graves and Battlefield Heritage Group. [emphasis added]

> *The limited excavation work GUARD undertakes **will determine,*** ***beyond doubt, the presence or otherwise of remains at the*** ***site as well as provide information on the quantity and condition*** ***of any remains.*** *[emphasis added] The work is being planned under* *the auspices of the Commonwealth War Graves Commission with* *approval of French authorities and the local land owner, and assistance* *is being sought from the British Government.*

Snowdon praised Team Lambis' work and credited them as those 'who first located the possible burial site'. Lambis made immediate plans to travel to Fromelles for the dig.

In preparation for the dig, the Australian Army History Unit had commissioned British historian Peter Barton to conduct a detailed search of the Bavarian archives in Munich to provide the GUARD team with as much background as possible. He was asked in particular to discover whatever he could on the Germans' burial of Allied dead after the Battle of Fromelles, especially on their burial of Allied soldiers in the mass graves they dug at Pheasant Wood.

Barton's report of his findings, which was delivered in April 2008, is impressive. The result of three weeks' solid investigative work by two experienced researchers at Munich's Hauptstaatsarchiv Krieksarchiv in November and December of 2007, it runs to more than 300 pages, accompanied by an extensive array of additional appendices, maps and battlefield panoramas. The report confirms that the systems and record keeping of the German defenders at Fromelles were astonishing, even more so considering they were initiated and undertaken under battle conditions. Meanwhile the dig, which was originally scheduled for late April, had to be postponed until late May because of the wet conditions at the site.

The Munich archives are the only German military archives that form a relatively complete collection. Barton explains that this occurred because the Bavarian archives were the only German kingdoms' archives that had been checked and copied in Berlin and returned to Munich before the Allied bombing of Berlin began in 1944. (The archives of the other German kingdoms had either not been returned at all before the bombing or had been only partially returned and accordingly were variously and considerably damaged.) The Munich collection is a vast – indeed Barton calls it gargantuan – mix of

> *printed, typed, and mimeographed copies of directives, orders, guidelines, instructions, reports and forms, maps, plans, technical drawings, purchase orders, invoices, receipts, photographs and paintings/sketches, accompanied by much original handwritten material including diaries and correspondence.*

Barton approached this daunting treasure trove of World War I historical information, in general, to try to find additional information about Fromelles, through German eyes, and particularly to see whether any definitive list of those buried at Pheasant Wood existed. It was a monumental task and clearly required many more weeks than Barton had available. Nevertheless, he and his team did an admirable job and, as a result, they have shed extensive new light on the battle and its aftermath.

Barton decided on what he called a 'top-down' approach to his search: to follow the German command chain from the highest echelons downwards. He faced considerable difficulties in dealing with manuscripts in their original handwriting. As digital photography was forbidden in the archives, he was restricted to a laborious system of copying, using an external reprographic service.

One of the first things he noted was the archives' extensive photographic album collection. By the time of the battle of Fromelles, the Allied command had imposed strict censorship on photography by its troops. In contrast, the Germans allowed their troops carte blanche, even encouraging them to transform their more sensational shots into postcards for use in propaganda. Unfortunately, because of a bureaucratic hitch, Barton didn't get the access to the Munich photographic archives he desired. He was able to secure copies of some remarkable panoramic photos the Germans had taken of Fromelles but could not trawl through the archives as he would have liked. He pointed to them as being a 'potentially very valuable resource' that remained to be examined.

Barton quickly established that the normal German practice was to collect detailed information when they buried enemy dead. He found a list, dated 19 April 1916, referring to British prisoners who had died in German hands in 1915. The details included full names, service numbers, units, dates of admission, hospitals, dates of death and the nature of the deceaseds' wounds. This led him to hope for a similar list of details for Fromelles. He knew that if such a list existed it would be the smoking gun that would solve the mystery of the burials of Pheasant Wood.

Contemporary German photos showing their troops searching for identification and intelligence from enemy bodies, prior to burial.

He revisited the previously known (and previously discussed) crucial order of 21 July 1916 by Major-General von Braun to the 21st Bavarian Reserve Infantry Regiment for the burials after the battle of Fromelles.

Barton arranged for the order to be re-translated, in the light of the considerable experience his team had gained of the style and personnel involved in the German side of the battle since the document was originally translated for the first GUARD report. The new translation (shown in full in Appendix VII) revealed some subtle but important differences that led Barton to suspect that the management and execution of the British and Australian burials at Pheasant Wood may have been a relatively 'unsophisticated exercise', in contrast to the Germans' burial of their own dead nearby.

Barton's research also confirmed the extent of the German victory at Fromelles. It showed the Germans were able to recover quickly after the battle, to such an extent that they immediately instituted a strategy of capturing prisoners and retrieving papers and identity discs from Australian and British troops in no-man's land. Starting from the evening of 20 July, German patrols worked through the killing field, seeking prisoners and intelligence. Daylight patrols resumed the following day. It also became clear that the underlying rationale behind the German burial of Allied dead was battlefield hygiene – something the Germans had planned for from the start. Barton was able to conclude:

> Burial of enemy troops appears to have required no more than a brief order to be issued and an equally brief report added to regimental records. The longer the war went on, the less detail of this kind seems to have been gathered as a matter of course.

The archives revealed that the German casualties were considerably less than those claimed by the Allies after the battle, but serious losses nevertheless. The 6th Bavarian Reserve Division lost 17 officers killed, 26 wounded and 2 missing, along with 425 other ranks killed, 952 wounded and 204 missing for a total casualty list of 1626.

But despite his prodigious efforts, and probably because of his time constraints, Barton was unable to unearth any definitive list of the dead buried at Pheasant Wood. He suggests that bagging, tagging and despatch of the Allied dead's personal effects may have been the only records regarded as necessary by the Germans. But he leaves open the possibility that such a list was made and that perhaps the only copies were sent elsewhere: to the Red Cross (now in its Geneva archives); or that they may be found somewhere in the Australian War Memorial or the Australian National Archives in Canberra.

He quotes from a document in Bean's papers, found in March 2008 by Nigel Steel and Craig Tibbits of the Australian War Memorial. Dated 23 February 1925, it contains a list of 46, mostly unidentified, Australian soldiers 'found at Fromelles during the last three years'. They were variously buried at Cabaret Rouge, Rue Petillon, Y Farm and Pont du Hem cemeteries. Towards the end of the note (referring to the battlefield), it says:

About 3 years ago, when the ground at 36N 8,9,10,14,15 was still in a rough state there was many surface indications of a very heavy death toll and traces everywhere of bodies blown to pieces. A great number must still be in the ground and too deep to be located by ploughing and probing.

Barton points out that the document shows the care taken by the post-war recovery teams in recording detailed trench map references of the sites where they recovered remains. He also notes that it shows that the Germans had passed on some records of burials they had made because some of the Australians are noted as having been found by reference to German records.

The search of the archives also highlighted the remarkable German defences against which the Allied attackers were thrown. The Germans had built shellproof shelters, on average, every 25 metres along their front line and these havens, usually beneath a metre of steel-reinforced concrete, were to prove the difference during the battle. Indeed, they were constructed in such outstanding fashion that, as the records noted, nothing could destroy them except 'a direct hit at the required optimum depth by a heavy delayed-action high explosive projectile'.

> *The archives also confirm what the attackers learned too late and to their great cost: the German front lines were still being developed and the old positions which the attackers had been told were the second German line were in fact either abandoned and largely underwater, or uncompleted and difficult to defend. In addition, had the attackers made it through to the real German second line, they would have met an even more daunting barrier: a series of fortified civilian houses and cottages, covertly reinforced within their external walls by concealed concrete to create observation posts, defences and accommodation.*

Indeed, Barton believes that the Germans viewed their defensive line entirely differently to the Allies. By this stage of the war, the Germans regarded their defences as the foremost extension of their national border. They saw themselves as defending the frontier out to which their nation had grown. By contrast, the Allies naturally saw their defences as temporary and maintained an overall attacking mindset, with the underlying aim of recovering the lost territory.

Having held their positions around Fromelles for more than eighteen months by the time of the battle, the Germans had used that time wisely to minutely survey, detail and record every feature in the battlefield and no-man's land to help in their defensive quest. In addition, prior to the battle, the Germans had acquired a remarkably accurate reservoir of intelligence from captured Allied soldiers. For example, their records show that they knew that the Australian front lines were

> *only two lines of trenches, approx 75m apart. In the front line, in addition to small funk holes, there are 15–20 foot deep dugouts. Patrols are sent out frequently, usually made up of men from different companies.*

They knew the Australian reserves were located in and around Sailly, they had full details of the Australians' insignia, including unit colours, and they knew that some were Gallipoli veterans but that the division had not yet taken part in a battle.

Documents from the interrogation of British prisoners taken after the battle revealed that they believed that their attack had been poorly organised and that they had not been properly prepared or briefed. Many had not even known that Australians were on their left flank and did not see them until after they were captured. They did not know the terrain, nor the extent of the action. Many were fresh recruits who had never fought before.

Barton quotes from the first report on the battle by the 21st Bavarian Reserve Infantry Regiment:

> *Our positions suffered grievously under the relentless fire, but the damage, in particular to the breastwork, was continuously repaired as it arose …*
>
> *At around 7pm the enemy detonated a mine in front of sub-sector 'b', which blew a large crater. At the same time the enemy assaulted our trenches in dense columns. On the regiment's left flank the enemy was bloodily repelled and heavy losses were inflicted. In the centre and on the right flank, the depleted remnants of the 3rd Battalion defended their shattered trenches with lion-like courage in bloody*

fighting at close quarters, but more and more columns of attackers came across and eventually over-ran the remainder of the gallant defenders.

The enemy halted in an old, dilapidated and water-filled trench behind our forward positions and hurriedly dug in ...

The fighting was fiercest at the upper end of the so-called Kastenweg ... the whole trench was filled with mounds of dead Australians. Our hand grenades had done terrible execution in their packed ranks ...

Step by step, our valiant attacking force pressed forward, throwing hundreds of hand grenades, and in bloody close-quarters fighting drove back the stubborn and tenacious enemy, who was also hard-pressed by our machine-gun fire in his rear, traverse by traverse until the entire trench, which the Australians abandoned and fled from at daybreak, was once more in our hands. In addition to a large number of dead and wounded, the enemy left some 200 unwounded prisoners, eight machine guns and innumerable items of equipment in our hands.

In addition Barton discovered, and has illustrated his report with, many detailed maps and sketches of the battlefield, showing the Australian and British attacks, the extents of their breakthroughs, the fall of the Allied shellfire and even the location of bodies on the battlefield.

The report details the Germans' well-documented approach to dealing with dead bodies on the battlefield. It reveals a strict code of battlefield hygiene, designed to avoid outbreaks of dysentery caused by flies moving from decaying human remains to food sources in the front trenches and even behind the lines. At the same time, the Germans balanced this need with the desirability of securing as much intelligence as possible from the enemy dead. Where bodies could not be recovered (for example, from deep in no-man's land) the Germans sprayed them from their trenches with a solution of potassium permanganate, dyed

German trench map (discovered by Peter Barton in the Munich Archives) showing the location of enemy bodies found on the battlefield.

deep red so they would know which corpses had been treated. This reduced the stench but had no effect on decomposition.

The German orders required recovery teams to wear protective clothing, gloves and overalls, and banned any men with open wounds on their hands. Barton refers to one document relating to the continuing treatment and recovery of the dead that was dated 10 August 1916, almost three weeks after the battle. He could find no document ending the collection process and concludes that it was planned to continue into the foreseeable future.

The research uncovered many references to orders requiring German troops to remove all personal and military papers from the enemy dead and to send them to the Divisional Intelligence Officer, Captain Lubcke. Other 'non-military personal material, including identification', was to be removed before burial and sent through the military echelons to eventually reach the Red Cross in Berlin for return to the families.

This opened up a rich vein of intelligence for Barton – in the shape of diaries and personal papers that had been captured by the Germans and collated for examination for their military and propaganda value. Some of these threw up interesting insights into the Allied troops' beliefs and actions. For example, one German order mentioned that

According to the prisoners, during the night the English and Australians retrieve the identity tags from the dead lying in no-man's land …

[It] is best not to prevent such efforts by the enemy to remove identification from their dead; rather we should use them as an opportunity to take as many prisoners as possible on the entire divisional front.

Perhaps this retrieval of identity tags by the Allied troops contributed to their subsequent inability to identify remains of many of their dead when they were ultimately recovered at war's end.

Undoubtedly one of Barton's most valuable finds was a list of ten dead Australian soldiers who were found in the 21 BRIR lines, together with a map on which is marked by name the exact location where each body was found. The soldiers were: Private Cyril Donald Johnston, 54th Battalion; Private Alfred Thompson, 55th Battalion; Private Joseph James Curran, 31st Battalion; Private Leonard Broadhurst, 55th Battalion; Private Thomas William Francis, 29th Battalion; Private Howard James Randall, 32nd Battalion; Private Thomas Cliff Cartwright, 32nd Battalion; Private Arthur Leslie Turner, 8th Machine Gun Company; Private James Lowther Mason, 31st Battalion; and Private John Joseph Goulding, 31st Battalion. All except Turner have a German death note in their Red Cross file. All of these men, again except Turner, are already on Lambis' list of those believed buried at Pheasant Wood. It seems therefore very likely that Private Turner would be there amongst them.

Barton has found evidence that the Germans continued to retrieve British and Australian bodies for at least a month after the battle. We know from the aerial photography that five of the Pheasant Wood pits were closed over by 29 July (and that the other three remained empty until the end of the war). Therefore, Barton says, this points to possible other burial sites beside Pheasant Wood. He suggests three: the two Australian saps, or communication trenches, dug across no-man's land during the battle; and a defensive fire trench built on the Australians' left flank, 'to within twenty yards of the German trench' (according to Bean). We know that in the final stages of the battle many Australian wounded sheltered in these saps and that many died in them. Barton says the German documents suggest they buried these Australian dead where they lay. Further, based on Australian war diaries, he says the saps were 'four to six feet deep' – more than sufficient to escape being disturbed by post-war ploughing.

The report concludes that the collection of the dead by the Germans fell into two categories and two periods. The first period was a mass collection and clearance by 'large dedicated teams' immediately after the battle, and the second a longer period of collection and recovery by 'small specialist squads' in the subsequent days and weeks.

German contemporary photos showing their troops burying dead soldiers in mass grave pits similar to those found at Pheasant Wood.

A regimental order from the German regiment facing the British attack, the 17th Bavarian Reserve Infantry Regiment, dated 21 July 1916 dictates that all bodies lying in the front lines must be collected as soon as possible, then separated – German from English – and placed out of the sun. It also ordered that trenches be cleaned up immediately and that the effects and equipment of the dead and wounded be stored separately from the bodies and then sent to the regimental headquarters in Fournes. It adds:

> nobody, without exception has the right to remove from the dead any kind of souvenir whatever these may be. Equally, no one has the right to remove equipment from dead or wounded Germans.

At this stage British dead from the battle were being sent to Fournes Cemetery for burial but Barton found a brigade order from the 12th

Reserve Infantry Brigade (made up of troops from both 17 and 20 Reserve Infantry Regiment) dated 24 July which stated:

> *English dead still remaining in and behind the trenches are not to be taken to Fournes, but are to be buried in a suitable place between the support line … and the second line positions.*

The order's timing becomes important when we recall the June 1920 exhumation by the Commonwealth War Graves Commission of six graves found at Fournes Cemetery under a German cross which stated they were casualties of 19 and 20 July 1916. In July 1923 Commonwealth War Graves Commission teams exhumed another 176 remains buried at Fournes, including a plot marked 'large trench grave No I.M.4.3' (which had come to Team Lambis' attention during their research). A sign on the grave said it contained 51 British soldiers buried from 23 to 25 July 1916.

Barton therefore concluded that the burial of British dead at Fournes did cease after the order. He suggested that British remains may have been taken to Pheasant Wood after the Australians were transported there. Battlefield logic would tend to support this view because the Australian dead were much closer to Pheasant Wood than the British dead, who were probably as far as three kilometres away. He further postulates that this fact could assist in dividing the nationalities at Pheasant Wood because it would seem likely that the pits nearest to the light rail line would likely have been filled first with Australian dead before the British were buried with them.

21BRIR had provided 100 recruits from its nearby training depot to help to transport the dead away from the battlefield. The order committing them to the task forbade them being used in the front line area. On 23 July, the German 3rd Battalion reported between 800 and 1000 *English* dead lying in front of their lines. Four days later, the brigade HQ reported:

Of the dead in front of the wire, the majority of the Australians lying in front of 'd' have already been brought in and removed to the rear. When further Australian dead are brought in from in front of 'd', they are to be investigated in accordance with Division's instructions and findings reported.

It is 'possible, perhaps even likely', according to Barton, that this report refers to Australian dead being collected from no-man's land and buried in Pheasant Wood. He also believes that the Red Cross files of the missing may offer suggestions that could assist attempts at identification, according to when and where they fell.

Barton makes a number of concluding remarks:

The curiously precise number of 399 dead recorded immediately post-battle, and von Braun's order to dig pits to accommodate 400 sets of remains are still the only actual figures we have for any individual burial site.

It may now, however, be suggested that this figure relates to allied remains that were collected and moved for burial only up to 27th July, for through the evidence of allied aerial photographs it appears that five pits were closed by 29 July.

No fresh indications of the actual number of remains that were interred at Pheasant Wood, nor where bodies recovered after this date were buried has yet been found. Nor has any information come to light that the remains have been disturbed.

Peter Barton's excellent report gave GUARD considerable hitherto-unknown background material to bring with them to the dig but, as always, the only certain resolution would come with the spade.

31

BROTHERS IN ARMS

We few, we happy few, we band of brothers;
For he to-day that sheds his blood with me
Shall be my brother.

WILLIAM SHAKESPEARE, HENRY V

Stephen Brooks lives at Barooga, on the New South Wales side of the Murray River. His passion for military history goes back more than 20 years and he has a special fascination for Australia's involvement in World War I. He was first captivated by the AIF's contribution to the war, in both service and sacrifice, which he always perceived to be far out of proportion to its numbers.

When he sold the family grain trading business a few years back, Stephen began researching Australia's contribution to the Battle of Fromelles in earnest. As he delved into the records he was astonished by the number of families who lost two brothers in the battle. Until his research, we had thought that a dozen sets of brothers had perished at Fromelles and we had thought this a shocking figure. Now Stephen has discovered that twice as many sets of brothers lost their lives there. And of those 24 sets of brothers, no fewer than sixteen sets died vainly trying to capture the Sugar Loaf salient. Their names are given in Appendix VIII.

At least one set of brothers and two single brothers (of pairs killed at Fromelles) are among those recorded as being buried by the Germans at Pheasant Wood.

The **Wilson** boys, Sam, 29, and Eric, 20, were both labourers from Port Macquarie on the NSW North Coast when they joined up. Both served as privates with the 53rd Battalion and charged with their CO, Lieutenant Colonel Bert Norris, as part of the 14th Brigade's heroic attack at Fromelles.

Private Eric Wilson and his brother Sam both charged with the 53rd Battalion at Fromelles and both are among the missing Diggers of Pheasant Wood. Little is known about Eric's fate but his name appeared on the German Death List for Pheasant Wood.
(AWM PHOTO P05445.002)

387

Private Samuel Wilson was last seen in the German lines holding off a German raiding party with grenades. He lies with his brother Eric at Pheasant Wood.
(AWM PHOTO P05445.001)

Sam was tall with ginger-coloured hair and bad front teeth. He was a bomber in 7 Platoon in B Company of the 53rd Battalion. He was last seen by his comrades in the German lines, singlehandedly trying to hold off a German raiding party in a sap with grenades. One eyewitness report in his file said:

> He held the sap all alone and was himself killed by a bomb when the others had safely got away.

Sam's name appeared on the German death list dated 4 November 1916. His younger brother Eric was also a member of 7 Platoon in B Company of the 53rd Battalion. Little is known of Eric's fate at Fromelles but he charged with his brother and was reported as killed in action. His name later appeared on the German death list.

Private Jim **Balsdon** was a 27-year-old miner who was born in Blythe in England but enlisted in East Maitland near Newcastle, NSW, in September 1915, along with his brothers Russell and Joe. They had consecutive regimental numbers, all served in the 30th Battalion and all attacked with it at Fromelles.

Two of the Balsdon brothers died as a direct result of the battle, although as so often happens in the fog of war there are conflicting versions of their deaths. One suggests Jim died as a POW after the battle. Another has a report from an eyewitness who was returning to his lines after being wounded on the night of 19 July who claimed to have seen Jim Balsdon's dead body in no-man's land. Jim's identity disc and pay book were returned by the Germans in November 1916. He's likely to have been buried at Pheasant Wood.

Russell Balsdon was hit in the neck by a bullet during the attack. He was brought back to his lines and lingered for a week before dying in the 13th General Hospital at Boulogne. He was buried in the Boulogne Eastern Cemetery. The third brother, Joe, was also severely wounded in the arm at Fromelles but survived and returned to Australia in May 1917.

The **Bromley** brothers, Sid and Bert, came from Brewarrina in far western New South Wales. Sid, at 23 the elder, was a plumber and Bert, 19, was a clerk with the NSW Railways. They were both in A Company of the 53rd Battalion and both boys were good mates. It seems one brother was wounded and the other died trying to save him, as a note in Bert's Red Cross Wounded and Missing file attests:

> the soldier A.C. Bromley was killed by bullet wound at Fleurbaix [read Fromelles] on No Man's Land, he was quite close, and S. R. Bromley, the brother of the soldier, went to pick him up, and was also killed, both evidently by machine gun fire … The brothers were much alike, 5'10", fair complexion, light brown hair, and were much attached to each other.

Another witness, who knew both brothers well, states in Sid's file:

he was told by Sgt. Angus of A Coy that he had seen both these
brothers killed by the same shell at Fleurbaix on July 19th. They
were blown to pieces in No Man's Land.

Yet another witness was told by one of Bert's friends that he saw him
shot dead by a sniper in the German first lines. Such was the confusion
of the battle. Sid's body was recovered by the Graves Registration Unit
after the war, possibly as late as 1921, as his identity disc was sent to
his parents around this time. One of the few who fell in no-man's land
who was able to be identified, he is buried at Ration Farm Cemetery.
Bert is one of the Fromelles missing. His name is on the German death
list and therefore on Lambis Englezos' list of those likely to have been
buried at Pheasant Wood.

One of the saddest family tragedies at Fromelles centres on the
McLeans from Geelong, Victoria. Remarkably, Alexander McLean,
aged 47, served in the 60th Battalion, alongside his two sons Alexander
Jr, aged 22 and a shop assistant, and Victor, 19, a plasterer.

Both boys were killed in the battle and their dad, who was with
the 60th's Pioneers, was initially reported as missing but later found
his way back to his unit. His file reveals that on 30 August 1917 the
Acting Secretary of the Department of Defence forwarded this poignant
letter to the AIF Headquarters in London:

The following copy of a communication which has been received in
this Department is referred to you for consideration and favour of
report please: -

'Excuse the liberty I am taking in writing to you. I will state my
case and leave it for you to judge. It is now close on two years since
my husband and two sons enlisted. They sailed together and were
in the same Battalion up till the 19th July of last year, in which I
lost my sons, one missing and the other killed. My husband has never

been the same in health since that awful day and after being in the trenches last year. He has been before 4 or 5 boards and marked unfit, still they keep him there, although he has been put at H.D.Q. carrying letters etc. I think he has done his bit, and after losing two good sons as Captain Kerr says whom any mother can be proud of, I wish to ask you if you can do anything for me in returning him before another winter sets in now being unfit. His age was 47 last month. Late of the 60th Battalion, now No.3202 Private A. McLean with HDQ, 3rd Division AIF, abroad.'

The plea must have touched hearts in London because Private Alexander McLean was returned to Australia in December 1917 *for family reasons.* He was honourably discharged in February the following year.

The **Henderson** brothers, Ern and Les, came from Kensington, Victoria. Both attended the Boundary Road State School in North Melbourne. Ern was a 20-year-old labourer and Les, a year younger, was an apprentice boilermaker. Both boys were in the same section of 12 Platoon in C Company of the 60th Battalion and took part in its charge against the Sugar Loaf. Ern was seen to be hit in the neck and crawling back towards the Australian lines. Although he wasn't far from the Australian parapet when spotted, his body was never found. All that was known of Les was that he was killed in the charge. Both are remembered on the wall at VC Corner.

The list of brothers goes on.

Tim and John **Carey** were both farmers from Kinchela on the northern NSW coast. They were both in the 53rd Battalion. Tim, 25, died from a gunshot to the head in the attack. John, 32, was hit in the head during the bombardment of the support lines while waiting to attack. Tim is on the VC Corner wall, John was buried at Rue du Bois Cemetery.

Three **Choat** brothers fought at Fromelles in the 32nd Battalion. Archie and Ray were killed in action, Wes was taken prisoner. In an astonishing feat of courage and ingenuity, Wes escaped to Holland in late 1917, after learning German and disguising himself as a Belgian worker. His brother Archie was buried at Rue Petillon Cemetery and Ray is remembered on the VC Corner wall.

Charlie and Bert **Franklin** attended Melbourne Grammar. Charlie went on to Dookie Agricultural College and Bert studied at Bradshaw's Business College before they joined up and served with the 60th Battalion. The brothers were apparently killed by an exploding shell as they were crossing the River Laies. Charlie was reported killed by shell concussion. One report said his body remained in an upright position sitting in the creek (the Laies). The same witness saw Bert lying dead on the top of the bank of the creek. He tried to reach him but was driven back by relentless machine-gun fire. Both brothers are listed on the VC Corner wall.

Hec and Rod **McAulay** were born at Chatsworth Island, near Maclean in the Clarence River district of northern New South Wales. They were amongst 16 McAulays who joined up from the district. Hec and Rod served with the 54th Battalion under Lieutenant Colonel Walter Cass. Rod, 35, was a carpenter before enlisting and Hec, 29, worked with the Sydney department store Anthony Hordern and Sons. They were both Lewis gunners and they charged with Cass and the 54th Battalion. Little is known of their fate except that it seems they died during the 54th's heroic stand behind the German front lines during the night of 19 July. A curious note in Rod's file states that he was buried by Padre Kennedy, the Catholic Chaplain of the 53rd Battalion, at the military cemetery at Sailly-sur-la-Lys and that a cross with inscription marked the grave. But apparently his body was never recovered because both brothers are listed on the wall at VC Corner.

Private Hec McAulay and his brother Rod were Lewis gunners with the 54th Battalion. Both charged with Colonel Cass and both died during the 54th's heroic stand behind the German lines. (AWM PHOTO P02599.004)

Private Rod McAulay and his brother Sam were two of sixteen McAulays who joined up from the Clarence River district of northern New South Wales. Both brothers died in the fighting behind the German lines. (AWM PHOTO P06085.003)

George and Robert **Wills** came from Werribee, Victoria. Robert attended Werribee State School and George went to Maldon Grammar. George was a contractor and Robert a chaff-cutting contractor when they enlisted.

Both served with the 29th Battalion and charged together at Fromelles. George was 28 when he died on 20 July. No details of his death were recorded but his body was recovered and he was initially buried at Eaton Hall Military Cemetery and later re-interred at Rue Petillon. Robert, 24, suffered a gun-shot wound at Fromelles and was evacuated to England via Boulogne on 21 July but died of his wounds on 2 August at Edmonton Military Hospital and was buried at Tottenham and Wood Green Cemetery Middlesex.

Arthur and Harry **Turner** came from Petersham in Sydney's inner west. Arthur was 19 and an electrician and Harry was two years older and a sawyer. They both embarked with the 3rd Battalion as 11th Reinforcements but were posted to 13 Platoon, D Company of the 53rd Battalion. They attacked with Lieutenant Colonel Bert Norris' men at Fromelles and both were apparently killed about halfway across no-man's land. A comrade who reported that he saw Arthur described him as

a boy of about 19, about 5'8", fairly thickset. I think he came from Sydney … He fell forward and I went over and had a look at him. I am sure he was killed.

Both Turner brothers are listed on the wall at VC Corner.

George, John and Tom **Shephard**, from North Fitzroy, Melbourne, all joined up together, as their regimental numbers indicate. They all served in D company of 60th Battalion and they all died within a week of each other. George was a blacksmith, aged 26, who was born in Prahran and, like his two other brothers, attended George Street State School at Fitzroy. John, 24, and Tom, 22, had been born in Derby, Tasmania, and both worked as brush makers in Melbourne.

Tragedy struck the Shephard brothers one week before the Battle of Fromelles when the middle brother, John, died of illness on 12 July in Marseilles. His record says he died from rheumatism, albuminuria (an indication of damage to the kidneys) and pericarditis (an inflammation around the heart) and he was buried at Mazargues Cemetery Extension.

The surviving brothers, George and Tom, attacked with the 60th Battalion at Fromelles and, like so many of their comrades, fell in no-man's land in front of the Sugar Loaf. Private Stan Ronald had been a lifelong mate of George Shephard and found himself lying next to him in no-man's land:

> he was shot in the arm first, and then in the side and back as he lay alongside. Being a mate of his since birth pretty well, I have no hesitation in knowing that it was the senior brother I was with, as we were talking to each other whilst lying on the field, (No Man's Land). I asked him if he got a bad one, and he said my right arm is broken. I went unconscious at that moment and when I came to about 4 hours later, 2776 Pte. George Arnold Shephard was lying dead by my side. Being a personal friend of the family's I wrote to them telling them all I knew.

Apparently no one witnessed Tom Shephard's death. Like his brother George, he is remembered on the wall at VC Corner.

Bill and Bob **Miller** were yet another pair of brothers who charged to their deaths with the 60th Battalion against the Sugar Loaf. They were both born in Northcote, Melbourne. Their two other brothers also joined up, both surviving the war, although one, Richard, who served with the 13th Field Ambulance, returned home disabled.

Bill and Bob were in 9 Platoon of C Company of the 60th and went over the top in the first wave against the Sugar Loaf. A witness stated in Bill's Red Cross Wounded and Missing file:

> I saw W. Miller fall first, and his brother ran to speak to him, and he was hit by machine gun fire, I think. One of the same platoon, Alexander, who has lost an eye, and who is I fancy now home, told me that in coming back, he had seen the two brother's dead. They both came from North Fitzroy, Melbourne.

Both Miller brothers are on the wall at VC Corner.

Pat, Sam, Tom and Alf **McManus**, four brothers from South Melbourne, all fought on the Western Front. Pat, Sam and Tom were in the 60th Battalion and attacked at Fromelles. Alf served with the 22nd Battalion and was wounded at Pozières.

Pat and Sam both fell attacking the Sugar Loaf. Pat was apparently hit by a machine-gun bullet in the stomach soon after hopping the bags. Sam went over with the fourth wave and was hit in no-man's land. One of his mates reported:

> I knew McManus well. He was a friend of mine. He came from Melbourne. His name was 'Sam' and his number was 2819 [sic; actually 2719]. On the 19th July at Fleurbaix, we went over the parapet together in the 4th wave. I was wounded first, in the arm, and McManus was wounded through the lung by a machine gun bullet. We lay down together in a shell hole for 30 hours, when the S.B. came up and took charge of us. McManus died in the hospital.

There is no record of Sam McManus making it to a hospital, nor any record of his body being buried.

There is, however, a sad footnote to the story. Sam had a son, born 16 May 1916, two months before his father was killed at Fromelles, and christened Samuel James Anzac McManus. Sam Junior died as a prisoner of the Japanese on 27 March 1945. (VX32003 Lance Sergeant McManus, aged 28, the son of Samuel Paul and Violet May McManus, of Toorak, Victoria, was a member of the 4th Anti-Tank Regiment, Royal Australian Artillery. He was one of over 2000 Allied prisoners of war held in the Sandakan POW camp in north Borneo.)

David and Colin **Barr**, both came from Richmond, Melbourne, and attended Hawthorn West State School. Both were tanners and served with the 60th Battalion. David was 25 and Colin just 19, and both were Lewis gunners when they charged at Fromelles. A witness who saw David fall said:

> *just before crossing over, he and his brother shook hands, kissed one another and said 'Goodbye'. Directly he crossed a shell struck him, killing him instantly in the presence of his brother.*

Private David Barr and his brother Colin shook hands, kissed and farewelled each other before charging against the Sugar Loaf with the 60th Battalion. David was killed by a shell in no-man's land in front of his brother. (AWM PHOTO H05659)

Private Colin Barr charged with his brother David with the 60th Battalion. After David was killed, Colin was hit in the back and evacuated but died from septicaemia in England on 31 August 1916. (AWM PHOTO H05658)

Colin was hit in the back in the attack and eventually evacuated to England, where he died from septicaemia on 31 August in the Brook War Hospital. He was buried in London's Greenwich Cemetery. A copy of a bitterly sad letter he wrote to his family while in hospital sits in his file:

Dear Mother, father and all, I am in the hospital wounded and happy. I got hit in the back by shrapnel. I didn't know I was hit. I'm sorry to say that Dave got killed. I was lying down when he was speaking to me, he said he wanted father to forgive him for what he done some time back, he died a hero Mother. Visitors come here they are very kind. One girl said when I get better she will take me out for motor rides. The worst of it all mother I never fired a shot at them. We was in the trenches only for about 2 hours, then we done a charge. I was lying in No Man's Land for two days and two nights. How is Bob and Richmond getting on. All the Richmond boys done their best with the 60th. I don't know how G. Collins got on. The nurses are very nice and will do anything for you, your loving son, Colin, Ward 32, Brook War Hospital.

Geoff and Rolf **Jones** also charged against the Sugar Loaf, Geoff with the 60th Battalion and Rolf with the 59th. Geoff was a sergeant, who had taken command of 7 Platoon B Company. Formerly an engineer from Box Hill, Victoria, he was one of the original members of 8th Battalion and had survived Gallipoli after sustaining a gunshot wound to the scalp there. He was transferred to the 60th Battalion in Egypt and had been promoted to sergeant in February 1916. A witness saw him fall at Fromelles:

I saw him lying in a little ditch just outside our wire, as I came back out of the charge. He was shattered all below the thighs. I was

Sergeant Geoff Jones was a Gallipoli veteran who commanded 7 Platoon of B Company 60th Battalion at Fromelles. He led his men against the Sugar Loaf and died in no-man's land. His younger brother Rolf was grievously wounded as he attacked with the 59th Battalion alongside him. (AWM PHOTO H06658)

Private Rolf Jones was shot in the face during the assault against the Sugar Loaf. He made it back as far as England but died of his wounds in February 1917. (AWM PHOTO H06651)

alongside him for a bit. He was almost dead and could hardly talk. He must have died soon afterwards.

Geoff is remembered at VC Corner. His younger brother, Rolf, was 24, formerly a florist of Tunstall, Box Hill. He was grievously wounded in the attack – a gunshot wound to the face resulted in his nose being blown away. Infection set in after he was evacuated to England and he died at Aldershot on 15 February 1917 and was buried at Brookwood Military Cemetery in Surrey.

Alf and Ed **Phillips** were born in Carlton, Melbourne, but lived in Richmond. They were both farm hands before joining up. Alf was with the 59th Battalion and Ed the 60th Battalion at Fromelles. Alf was 32 and a Gallipoli veteran and Ed was 34 when they both died in no-man's land on 19 July 1916. Little is known of the circumstances of either brother's death. They are both on the wall at VC Corner.

Colin and Eric **Perkins** had both survived Gallipoli when they attacked at Fromelles with the 59th Battalion. They came from St Kilda in Melbourne. Col, 23, was an assistant at a chemical works and Eric, 25, an engineer. Both brothers were killed near the Sugar Loaf. No details of their deaths are recorded and they are remembered at VC Corner.

The **Mitchell** family from Gippsland, Victoria, is another to have tragedy visited on them three times. Trooper Bill Mitchell, a 28-year-old shearer, died in the famous charge by the 8th Light Horse at the Nek on Gallipoli on 7 August 1915. His younger brothers, Alf, 21, and Sid, 23, attacked with the 59th Battalion at Fromelles and both fell somewhere in no-man's land. No details of their fate were recorded and their names are on the wall at VC Corner.

Harry and Vivian **Clements** came from Healesville, Victoria. Harry was 26 and a teacher and Vivian was 23 and a linesman, both working in Bairnsdale. Both died in the attack by their 59th Battalion at Fromelles. Again, no details have emerged of their final moments. Harry is remembered at VC Corner and Vivian was buried at Rue Petillon.

Bill and Jim **Daly** were country boys from Ballarat, Victoria. Bill was 24 and Jim lied about his age to enlist. He said he was eighteen and half when he joined up but he had just turned sixteen. Both served with the 58th Battalion at Fromelles. Bill was hit in the arm and side

Private Bill Daly and his younger brother Jim attacked side by side with the 58th Battalion against the Sugar Loaf. Bill was badly wounded and died in a Canadian Casualty Clearing Station. (AWM PHOTO H05841)

Private Jim Daly was only sixteen when he lied about his age and joined up with his 24-year-old brother Bill. Jim was killed outright in no-man's land during the 58th Battalion's charge against the Sugar Loaf. (AWM PHOTO H05840)

during the attack. He made it back as far as the Canadian Casualty Clearing Station where he died of his wounds on 22 July. He was buried in the Bailleul Communal Cemetery. Jim was killed in the attack and was buried by Padre Williams on 20 July at Rue-du-Bois Cemetery.

Hector and Bill **McLeod**, from Rockdale, Sydney, served with the 55th and 53rd Battalions respectively at Fromelles. Hec was a 21-year-old plumber and Bill a 29-year-old labourer. Hec was killed outright by a shell burst in no-man's land and buried at Anzac Cemetery at Sailly-sur-la-Lys. Bill disappeared during the battle and is commemorated at VC Corner.

Rod and Alex **Fraser** came from St Kilda in Melbourne. Rod, 26, was a carpenter and Bill, a year younger, was a coachsmith. Rod attacked with the 60th Battalion and Bill with the 59th. Both were listed as missing after the battle and no information could be found as to their fate, other than they left the Australian parapet with their comrades. Their names are at VC Corner.

Gustave **Hosie** and his brother Russell came from Bairnsdale, where they worked as a butcher and a tanner respectively. Gus was with the 59th Battalion and Russell with the 60th at Fromelles. Gus disappeared during the battle and no details exist on his fate. Russell's file reveals the usual confusion after the battle, as different witnesses gave differing versions of his death:

> he was hit three times in the advance and I tried to rouse him but I couldn't.
>
> I was near this man during the big attack on Fromelles, and I saw him killed instantly by a shell. He was really blown to pieces. It was near Laventie Front. Hosie had just got over when a shell caught him. Ground was not held. It was not possible to bury him, fire was too heavy. Hosie was a brave man who would not remain in rear but pushed to the front.
>
> At VC Avenue, Armentieres Front, about the 22nd or 23rd of July, I was in the line after the attack which took place on the 19th July, and saw Pte. Hosie buried. I am sure it was Hosie, as he was well known to me, having served with me in the 8th Battalion.

The Hosie brothers are honoured on the wall at VC Corner.

The **Spooner** family of Brunswick, Melbourne, was particularly shattered by the Battle of Fromelles. It lost a father and a son. Ted Spooner, 45, had served with the 7th Battalion on Gallipoli before being transferred to the 60th Battalion in Egypt where he joined his 25-year-old son Jim.

Private Ted Spooner was 45 years old and a Gallipoli veteran when he joined his 25-year-old son Jim in the 60th Battalion. Jim was hit by a shell during the attack and died on the battlefield. Ted was wounded in both shoulders and made it back to England before succumbing on 31 July 1916. (AWM PHOTO H06136)

Private Jim Spooner served, and died, with his father Ted in the 60th Battalion. He was killed when hit by a shell in the open as he attacked the Sugar Loaf. His mates were forced to withdraw before they could retrieve him. His body was never found. (AWM PHOTO H06135)

Both father and son took part in the attack at Fromelles. Jim was killed while attacking the Sugar Loaf. A witness said:

I saw him fall, hit by a shell out in the open by Fleurbaix. He was badly wounded; nothing could be done for him. I took his pack off and made him a little more comfortable. We had orders to go back and did not hold the ground. He was about 5' 9", dark and came from Carlton, Victoria.

Ted suffered gunshot wounds to both shoulders and died of his wounds in Queen Mary's Royal Naval Hospital in Chatham England on 31 July 1916. He was buried at Southend-on-Sea Cemetery in Essex. His son Jim's body was never identified and he is remembered at VC Corner.

A number of families lost at least one son at Fromelles and another who was taken prisoner: Fred Parry of Brunswick, Melbourne, was killed with the 29th Battalion on 19 July. His brother Reuben was taken prisoner on the same night. Fred is on the German death list and was likely among those buried at Pheasant Wood. Reuben was released at war's end and returned home in March 1919.

The Wilken twins, Ernie and Harry, of Canterbury, Victoria, were also with the 29th at Fromelles. Ernie was killed and Harry taken prisoner. Ernie is among those at Pheasant Wood. Harry remained a POW for the duration of the war and returned home in March 1919.

Maurie and Ted Claxton of St Arnaud, Victoria, suffered a similar fate serving with the 32nd Battalion. Maurie was killed and Ted captured. No sign was ever found of Maurie. Ted was repatriated to Australia in early 1919.

Both the Antrobus brothers, Aub and Harry, were captured attacking with the 29th Battalion. They both returned home on the same ship in early 1919. Similarly, Dan and Bernard Neill, of the 32nd Battalion, ended as POWs after the battle. Dan lost a leg and was repatriated by the Germans in early 1918. Bernard was held for the duration but returned home safely in April 1919.

Both Reg and Syd Purdon and Horrie and Alf Bolder, all of the 55th Battalion, spent the war as POWs after being captured at Fromelles. All made it home safely in early 1919.

Today it seems almost incredible that so many brothers could have been sent into battle together. Surely there can be no greater illustration of the shattering impact of the Battle of Fromelles on Australian families than the loss of so many siblings, most in a single night.

32

COMPLETING PADRE MAXTED'S WORK

Listening only to my instincts,
I discovered superb things.

CLAUDE MONET

When Dr Tony Pollard and his GUARD team of battlefield archaeologists from Glasgow University arrived in Fromelles in the last week of May 2008, Lambis was waiting for them. He'd been there waiting for them for two months.

Although he'd always been confident that the missing Diggers and Tommies were still lying where the Germans had buried them alongside Pheasant Wood in July 1916, Lambis' anxiety levels had risen as the moment of truth drew near. While he waited for the investigators, he spent long hours walking the battlefields, sitting and musing at Pheasant Wood and visiting the neighbouring cemeteries. At Rue Petillon Military Cemetery, a few kilometres north-west of Fromelles, he sought inspiration from the spirit of the Reverend Spencer Maxted.

Lambis Englezos reflects at the grave of Padre Spencer Maxted at the Rue Petillon Cemetery, near Fromelles. (PATRICK LINDSAY PHOTO)

Padre Maxted was one of Lambis' special favourites. The much-loved chaplain of the 54th Battalion had been resting in the front lines, exhausted after days helping to recover the dead and wounded from no-man's land, when he was killed by a stray artillery shell while he slept. Lambis has always seen himself completing the work begun by Maxted and his mates.

In the final weeks before the dig, Lambis pitched in and helped as Martial Delebarre and his colleagues from the local division of the Commonwealth War Graves Commission prepared the Pheasant Wood site for GUARD's arrival, delivering fencing, tents, a demountable office and temporary toilets.

Lambis knew that GUARD's non-invasive investigation at Pheasant Wood in May 2007 had confirmed the existence of the mass graves there. In addition, they could find no evidence that the graves had been disturbed and the remains removed. But, although the evidence supported his contention, Lambis could not rest easy until they actually turned the soil over and opened the graves.

Tony Pollard and his team greeted Lambis warmly. They had met during the earlier investigation and, by the end of their stay, they regarded Lambis as part of the furniture. Like Lambis, Pollard was confident the pits were occupied but he was also nervous:

You arrive on site on the first day of a project and the tensions are high. You've brought your team together and you've got all your resourcing together, which has been a lot of preparatory work, and then the first day of any project is always a pain because you're not bedded in.

The GUARD team begins works on the archaeological dig at Pheasant Wood in May 2008. (TIM WHITFORD PHOTO)

And we were met on the first day with a barrage of the world's press, largely Australian granted, but one end of the compound was full of TV cameras and newspaper cameras.

At 9.30 am, on Monday 26 May, under the glare of this media contingent, GUARD's earthmoving machine expert Gary Andrews started his shiny yellow and orange digger and began to roll back the topsoil carefully. The man overseeing the dig on behalf of the Australian Army, retired Major-General Mike O'Brien, joined Pollard and the others and they watched, eyes peeled, searching for the outlines of the original burial pits below.

Outwardly, Tony Pollard was a picture of cool control as he moved about. Inwardly, he was in turmoil:

You just think, what if there's nothing there. That's not going to play well. I can put all the spin I want on it about checking that they're in there but, at the end of the day, it would have been major egg on the chin if they weren't there.

Make no bones about it, it's the most nerve-racking project I've ever done, by and large, due to its profile. There were two very uncomfortable hours on that first Monday morning, when we were taking off the topsoil and revealing the clay underneath and I was thinking, God I can't see anything! Where are the original pits?

As the GUARD team went about its work, Lambis was joined by Tim Whitford, great great nephew of Private Harry Willis, the likely owner of the Alberton medallion found by GUARD during its non-invasive investigation of the Pheasant Wood site in May 2007. Tim had come to Fromelles for the dig with his wife Liz and their eight-year-old daughter, Alexandra.

Tim Whitford as a young battle tank commander in the Australian Army, and overwhelmed by emotion as the dig progresses at Pheasant Wood. (TIM WHITFORD PHOTOS)

Tim and Lambis chatted quietly as they paced up and down the public area at the eastern end of the Pheasant Wood site. For Tim, seeing the first sods turned in the Pheasant Wood soil was a deeply emotional step in a journey that started in his childhood.

Like Lambis, Tim can almost touch the resolution that the GUARD dig may bring them. A burly, straight-talking realist with a gentle compassionate side, he often provided a dose of hard logic to counter Lambis' flights of faith and passion. He forced himself to look at Lambis' theories objectively.

Some of his theories had no basis in reality but every time I tried to discount the pits, I couldn't do it. Being a professional soldier, I'd look at those pits and I'd think, well the Army History Unit had put forward all this crap that they were defensive in nature. I thought that was absolute bollocks. Aerial reconnaissance was a reality in 1916 – hence the photos that showed the pits – and the Germans didn't give a toss if anyone saw these very symmetrically dug pits that were right beside a railway, just behind a wood. Everyone has forgotten all those earlier nonsense answers.

As they waited and watched the GUARD team slowly uncovering the pits, Tim and Lambis recalled the journey that brought them here: the long nights on the phone or the computer, poring over maps and records and books; speaking at RSLs and Rotary clubs; the frustrating knock-backs and the delays.

For Tim, the turning point was a phone call from Lambis telling him that the first GUARD investigation had uncovered a medallion ... and it was from Alberton Shire. Tim knew the only man from the 170 Missing Diggers who could have owned the medallion was his great great uncle.

*I couldn't believe it. You know when you go over a hill too fast and
your guts come up, it was like that. I just broke down on the phone.*

In the weeks leading up to the dig, Tim often found himself in tears
as he drove to work. He would imagine the possible results of the dig

One of the partially exposed pits, with the original pit dug by the Germans clearly
delineated by the colour change in the clay. (PATRICK LINDSAY PHOTO)

The GUARD dig at Pheasant Wood, taken from the steeple of the Fromelles
church and showing the extent of the work. (PATRICK LINDSAY PHOTO)

and rehearse in his mind how he would react to them. Now the dig and the emotions were real and he watched transfixed as the earthmover slowly peeled back the grass and topsoil.

Tony Pollard started the dig at Pit 6. He and his team knew there was more than a good chance that it did not contain remains: they knew the bodies were believed to have been buried in Pits 1–5 and Pit 6 was one of the three pits left uncovered at war's end. Nevertheless, Pollard had foreshadowed the possibility of some remains in Pit 6 because he believed the wartime aerials showed that one end was less defined than the other and could have been partially backfilled. But in the early hours of the dig, Pollard wasn't worried about that:

What I was worried about was what if I can't even see the cuts of the original pits? After a couple of hours, we settled in. We got our eye in and the edges of the pits started to pop up. You get a sort of blue-grey clay coming up, a greyer clay with a slightly browny-orange outer side.

By the end of the first day Pollard could take some solace from the fact they had delineated two original pits. They stood out clearly after the earthmover had scraped away the first half a metre of topsoil. It was a major relief. But then it wasn't rocket science. They always knew where the pits had been dug to within a few metres. And today if you compare the 1916 aerials of Pheasant Wood with a Google Earth satellite photo you'll see they are virtually identical – the wood is exactly the same size and the same distinctive shape. Mike O'Brien summarised day one:

The Army has undertaken a thorough and painstaking process to get to this point and we were confident that we would discover the outline of each burial pit in relatively good time.

GUARD team leader, Dr Tony Pollard, and the project commander, retired Major-General Mike O'Brien of the Australian Army, at Pheasant Wood. (PATRICK LINDSAY PHOTOS)

What continues to be uncertain is whether the remains of soldiers who were buried here are still present, or whether they have been disinterred since they were laid to rest by German forces almost 92 years ago.

Tony Pollard was already looking ahead confidently:

The next question was: were they intact? From the start the signs were good because the upper edges of those pits were straight. If they'd been messed about with, we would have expected jagged bits and smears around the edges but they seemed as straight as a die.

The GUARD team at work carefully sifting through the exposed topsoil in the pits as they gradually move deeper. (TIM WHITFORD PHOTOS)

Another great relief! By the second day, the team had uncovered three pits down to their original starting point.

Pollard had already decided that his team would not be able to uncover each pit completely and dig down into it to discover whether it held human remains. He chose instead to hand-dig a series of sondages (test pits), positioned differently in each pit to give the maximum chance of an accurate overall cross-section. Each sondage was the width of the original burial pit (a little less than two and a half metres) by a metre and a half. The idea was then to dig down through the pit to the bottom or until they discovered human remains. Each sondage took around four hours to dig.

I can still feel the relief when, at the bottom of the sondage through Pit 5, we exposed human bone. We found it about one metre twenty from the top of the pit, which is over 1.75 metres or so from the top of the present ground surface.

This first major breakthrough came late on the second day but initially the GUARD team made no public announcement.

Lambis was away from the site – at the Fromelles Museum above the town hall, being interviewed by a camera crew from the BBC. Tim Whitford was chatting to a group of Australian journalists when all of a sudden they picked up a clear change in the atmosphere in the dig area:

We saw huddled conversations, people on mobiles, a distinct buzz in the air. The journalists picked it up and said: they've found something. I knew they were right but the GUARD team said nothing as they finished for the day. What was most telling was that they couldn't hold eye contact with us as they left.

Lambis arrived back at the site as the GUARD team was packing up and he too immediately picked up the vibe. Everyone left for home that evening in high spirits.

Tim Whitford woke the next morning to a text message from one of his workmates in Australia: 'They've found human remains, congratulations'.

I wanted to hear it from the GUARD team. We just jumped in the car and went straight out to the site and the press conference was about to start and the word was the Minister in Australia had announced overnight that they'd found human remains.

I didn't give a toss about not being told. To me it's always been all about those lads. But I thought, Holy Hell, it's happened! They're there! I sat down sobbing, sobbing. I felt this immense sense of relief, followed about ten seconds later by a wave of sorrow. How could we leave them there for 92 years?

In Canberra, the Minister for Defence Science and Personnel, Warren Snowdon, had made the announcement that excavation of a small trial trench over one of the pits had uncovered human remains at around 5pm local time on Tuesday 27 May. He added:

Human remains have been uncovered during the limited excavation of a suspected World War I burial site which is being investigated by the Australian Army in France.

At this stage there is no indication of the number or condition of any remains which may be found at the site and the archaeology team still have a large task ahead to attempt to resolve these questions. While it is believed that the bodies are likely to be Australian and British soldiers, the nationalities have so far not been confirmed.

Snowdon said that the army suspected that the remains of up to 400 Australian and British soldiers who fell during the Battle of Fromelles lie at the Pheasant Wood site and that the original outline of two of the five suspected burial pits had been confirmed within five hours.

Lambis arrived on site to the news. Tony Pollard came across to Lambis and gave him a hug:

> *That was very special. It was beautiful. It might have been reported that we were annoyed, distressed, but we really knew on the Tuesday night.*

Tony Pollard and the team found themselves in a quandary that would repeat itself several times over the duration of the dig: how much information should be made public? Should they report on

Major-General Mike O'Brien briefs the media at Pheasant Wood as Dr Tony Pollard looks on. (PATRICK LINDSAY PHOTO)

progress as it was made, with the possibility of making premature announcements that would later have to be corrected? Or should they keep a tight hold on the detail of their findings until they were certain of the overall result?

Over the next couple of days Pollard's elation grew as each sondage in the first five pits revealed human remains. The team also quickly ascertained that the bones were 'articulated' (or formed part of a more complete skeleton).

> *You may have an articulated arm but if your pit is only 1.5 metres wide, you don't really know what's on the end of it. But all of the signs were good because the pit fill did not look disturbed and they were deep. It looked pretty promising and I didn't have much in the way of doubt, fairly quickly, at that stage.*

And that was just as well because Pollard had gathered some world class experts in dealing with mass human remains deposition. He remembered thinking, what if he'd brought them all to France and they hadn't found human remains?

> *We would have had to stand by the machine and watch as every pit was emptied, bucket by bucket, just to check that there was nothing left behind. And to have a crack team of fifteen people standing there doing that would again have not done much for my self-esteem or standing. So it was a major relief. It was good to know that everybody that had been picked for the job they did would have a job to do.*

At the end of day three of the dig, Warren Snowdon had confirmed that, in addition to the initial discovery of remains in Pit 5, the dig had also uncovered remains in Pits 1 and 2.

The skeletal find was at a similar depth to the first discovery of human remains, which lay in Pit 5. Also, closer to the surface in Pit 1, the team uncovered remnants of a Commonwealth pattern brass strap end and stud which may indicate Australian or British identity.

As the day progressed, the team continued to widen the excavation trench in Pit 5, and more human bones were discovered along with fragments of material which could indicate clothing.

These somewhat limited initial media releases led some observers back in Australia to suppose that GUARD had only found disarticulated remains, or unattached bones. They assumed that this opened the possibility that the bones GUARD had found may have been scattered remains left after the graves had been previously opened and the bulk of the remains buried elsewhere. Pollard understood the rationale behind the speculation:

That was partially the fault of the press releases because we were trying to be completely accurate. At one level it was about the management of expectation. The authorities didn't want people to be over-excited about the fact that we'd found human remains.

For his part, Tony Pollard had long decided that there was no point in engaging with his critics in this high-profile project. The decisions on when and what to release to the public were out of his hands so he decided to just get on with his job.

I don't look at the discussion boards, because there's just so much discussion from ill-informed points of view by people who sit in an armchair and think they know what's going on when they don't have a clue. So I disengaged from that and just focused on the work because otherwise I'd have had a nervous breakdown.

Pollard's aim was to excavate a 20 percent sample of each pit. They had determined that each pit was roughly ten metres long by just less than two and a half metres wide and about two metres deep, from the bottom of the topsoil. They first used the earthmoving machine to remove the half a metre or so of topsoil covering each pit, then took away the machine and dug the sondages by hand, initially spading down and then using trowels, palette knives (known to archaeologists as leaf trowels) and finally plastic tooth picks to uncover, clean, identify and catalogue each artefact or piece of bone. Working around the human remains, they then set about trying to determine the bottom of the pits. This proved difficult as they did not remove any remains and kept themselves within the confines of the sondages.

During his planning for the dig, Pollard had considered a range of options, including cutting down the sides of the pits to form a window of their profiles. The team even brought Perspex sheets with them to slot down into the soil to make literal windows. But they decided against using them because of the danger of breaking the integrity of the pit sides, thus disturbing water tables and drainage and exposing the graves to potential pollution.

In retrospect, I'm glad we did because it wouldn't have given us that much more information because the bodies aren't right up against the side, so if you cut down the edge you're not going to see that much more and it could have given us a very false impression.

What they did manage to do was, in some cases quite extensively, to reveal a primary layer of remains, a secondary layer and liming (finding

The GUARD team battles on after a massive storm had inundated the surrounds of the dig. They were able to secure and protect the pits by covering them and creating an effective drainage system. (PATRICK LINDSAY PHOTOS)

fist-sized lumps of lime, or calcium oxide, commonly used in World War I burials to help break up organic matter and to sanitise the remains).

The maximum we found was two layers but you would be horrified at how many bodies you can squeeze into a small space.

By the end of day six, the team had found remains in five of the eight pits, just as they had expected. Mike O'Brien reported:

It's anticipated that further non-invasive excavation of the five burial pits will reveal additional significant numbers of remains that would indicate that this site was used to bury a large number of soldiers.

O'Brien noted many additional discoveries, including

numerous buttons, believed to be from German groundsheets in which remains may have been wrapped, a bayonet scabbard of the type used by Australian and British soldiers, and live .303 ammunition.

He concluded that, despite these discoveries, the team could not confirm the presence of Diggers among the remains as none of the discoveries was distinctly Australian.

As the dig progressed, the pressures on the team grew as the emotional burden began to combine with the time constraints and, inevitably, the weather.

During the second week of the dig Fromelles was caught by a ferocious rain storm which lashed the site for two solid days and turned it into a quagmire. The GUARD team manned the pumps, huddled under the tents and worked on. Tony Pollard was amazed at the resilience of the ground and his team:

Any other dig in Scotland under those conditions we'd probably just say, right it's a write-off. If we'd been doing massive open-area excavation, it would've been. But because we were focused on localised small areas we could go on. We spent the day battling water outside but under the covers the job went on. We'd pre-planned with pumps and other gear so in fact we didn't lose much time.

Around this time, Lambis had a particularly emotional moment when he was visiting the cemetery at VC Corner. He received a phone call there from his 22-year-old son Anthony, telling him that he'd graduated from his basic training and was now a fully-fledged Digger. It was a wonderful case of coming full circle. The only son of a Greek-born immigrant had joined the Australian Army the week before Lambis left for France. Anthony did his initial training at Kapooka, marching out while Lambis was still away, and then was posted to Bonegilla, near Albury-Wodonga (curiously, this was the location of the migrant transition camp where one-year-old Lambis and his mum and dad had been sent when they first arrived in Australia in 1954).

Meanwhile, Tony Pollard battled with the vagaries of managing a project of Pheasant Wood's size and nature. His most tantalising doubt was whether he had budgeted enough time for his team to complete their task.

The GUARD team had been asked to answer three main questions: Were human remains in the graves? What condition were they in? And how many remains were there? Any investigation to answer these questions, working within the tight time frame available, necessarily involved some degree of guesswork. Pollard had gone some way to minimise the guesswork during his earlier non-invasive evaluation of the site. But he was still sailing into uncharted territory. And, as he pointed out, no World War I archaeological dig on this scale had ever been attempted:

Some places have an atmosphere. So did Pheasant Wood. All the evidence pointed to the soldiers being here but then you think how the hell could they miss them? How the hell could they miss them in the first place? It now looks to me as though they were looking in the wrong bloody place. I think they were probably looking in the wood.

The next morning Lambis found himself thinking back to where his research first threw his focus on to Pheasant Wood – in Jack Bowden's Red Cross Wounded and Missing file. He recalled reading the plaintive letters from members of Bowden's family as they tried to find out something – anything – about their loved one's fate. Despite all their efforts, they learned nothing. Indeed, on her death bed, Jack Bowden's sister told her kids: 'Find Jack!'

Now, looking on as the excavations continued, Lambis felt himself closer than ever to finding some answer for Jack Bowden's mum and the mothers and families of the hundreds of other soldiers, British and Australian, lying in the Flanders mud at his feet.

He was even more buoyed when the next big step forward came at the start of the final week of the dig. The GUARD team found a heavily corroded but unmistakable Australian Army 'Rising Sun' collar badge – confirmation, at long last, of the presence of Diggers amongst the remains. In the words of Mike O'Brien, the find immediately transformed the site into 'a place of national significance'.

This was the sign the GUARD team had sought since they began their dig two weeks earlier … definitive proof that Australian troops were among those resting in the five mass graves they had been examining. Later the same day, the team uncovered another 'Rising Sun' badge. Both were discovered in the chest cavities of skeletons, leading to suggestions that the soldiers may have placed the badges in their breast pockets prior to the battle.

The badly corroded but clearly recognisable 'Rising Sun' badge found by the GUARD team in the chest cavity of one of the skeletons. The find elevated the Pheasant Wood site into a 'place of national significance' for Australia, according to Major-General Mike O'Brien. (PATRICK LINDSAY PHOTO)

Those observing the dig, who at that stage had not read Peter Barton's report on the Munich archives, had been surprised at the lack of insignia or personal effects that the GUARD team had found on the remains at Pheasant Wood. Had we read Barton's report we would have possessed a compelling explanation for their scarcity.

In his detailed research at the Munich archives, Barton discovered a range of orders that called on the German troops to collect any items from Allied dead that could provide intelligence or allow a unit to be identified. These were to be removed from the dead and sent to battalion headquarters. A note accompanying one order goes even further:

Companies are to search every dead body that can be reached in front of their company sector. Effects recovered from the men are to be placed in a sandbag, labelled accordingly … and sent each day with the morning report …

The Regiment is offering rewards for diligent recovery of these items, which are of exceptional importance in the evaluation of the enemy attack (remember also that insignia are to be collected, where possible and where recognisable).

These rewards for recovery were underlined by another reference to handing-in of captured equipment:

Captured weapons, equipment and munitions are to be sent without delay to the Intelligence Officer, 6th Army, if they (1) Are of a previously unknown type (2) Enable an enemy unit to be identified (this applies in particular to 'English' cap badges and shoulder titles).

If any finder has a particular interest in an item, he should declare it when handing it in, and the item will be returned to him after evaluation.

Clearly, the German troops had been following these orders zealously and left very few identifying objects on the remains they buried in Pheasant Wood.

Nevertheless, the GUARD team soon also quietly turned up two British general service buttons which confirmed the presence of Tommies among the remains. Minister Snowdon welcomed their discovery on the last day of the dig:

The unearthing of two British general service buttons is an important find, similar to the discovery of the Rising Sun badges for Australia, and we join with the British Ministry of Defence in welcoming the news.

No doubt this discovery had prompted the visit to the site on 12 June by the British Minister for Veterans, Derek Twigg. He was obviously moved by his tour of the pits with Tony Pollard and Mike O'Brien. Later he said he was a keen student of World War I and that he felt a personal connection to the Western Front as his grandfather had fought there and won a Military Cross.

The previous day, former Australian Prime Minister John Howard and his wife Janette also made an emotional private visit to Pheasant Wood to pay their respects to the missing Diggers. Howard's father and his grandfather had both served on the Western Front. A visibly moved John Howard emerged from a tour of the exposed burial pits to chat to Lambis and Tim Whitford. He had read of Lambis' quest and said:

A Greek-born art teacher from Melbourne full of the Anzac spirit on a quest to find our lost Diggers … that's a great Australian story.

Interestingly, John Howard had known about the Missing Diggers of Fromelles since 2003. In September of that year, as Prime Minister, he had responded to a request from then NSW Premier Bob Carr that the Federal Government investigate the claims raised by Team Lambis in the original *Australian* newspaper report by saying that the reports were 'sketchy and would need to be substantiated' but then added:

I strongly agree, however, that if the reports can be substantiated and a mass grave containing the remains of Australian soldiers does exist, every effort must be made to identify and appropriately honour these soldiers.

Day fourteen of the dig was one of consolidation on the site, so Lambis and Tim Whitford took the chance to once again walk in the footsteps of the Diggers across the Fromelles battlefields.

Starting at the Australian Memorial, where the Cobbers statue stood out against a clear blue sky flanked by the Australian flag and the French *drapeau tricolore*, they walked along the old German front line heading towards the British sector. Most of the fields were covered in knee-high wild grass, but at the Sugar Loaf the ground had been recently ploughed and planted and the neat, budding rows of the new season's grain gave it a strange air of innocence.

What had once been a squat, impregnable concrete fortress, bristling with barbed wire and machine guns, was now a flat innocuous field, barely half a metre higher than the surrounding grassland. But Tim and Lambis looked through older eyes as they paced out the dimensions of this once lethal stronghold. They looked across the hundreds of metres of the football-field-flat no-man's land to the Australian and British front lines and they were again struck by the hopelessness of the task facing the troops attacking the Sugar Loaf.

The author speaks with a deeply emotional former Australian Prime Minister John Howard after he had toured the graves at Pheasant Wood.
(TIM WHITFORD PHOTO)

The German machine-gunners had complete control of the terrain, able to fire to the front and both sides down the attacking lines (enfilade fire). By keeping their aim low (known as grazing fire) they could cut down the attackers, first hitting them in the legs and then striking them two or three more times as they fell. Shooting down the lines they could even strike a number of their enemy with the same bullet. As a former soldier experienced in machine-gun fire, Tim was particularly struck by the image:

> It brings tears to your eyes looking across those fields. From the German position the machine guns would have been accurate for up to 2000 metres. It would've been so easy for the gunners to traverse their weapons sweeping a hail of bullets across the ground there. And there was nowhere to hide. Nowhere!

Tim and Lambis' sad reverie was aided by the constant reminders in the soil beneath their feet. The fields were so heavily sown with the deadly detritus of war that, with every step, they still revealed the extent of the horrors played out on them almost a century earlier. They walked through a continuous stream of shrapnel balls, shell casings, spent bullets, remnants of gas masks and water bottles and high explosive shell fragments, all churned up by the recent ploughing.

In front of the British positions, near the Wick Salient – a deadly protrusion in the German line similar to the Sugar Loaf – they even found a ten-metre segment of the German light-rail line used to transport ammunition and supplies to their front lines and, sadly, the Allied dead after the battle.

As they stood in the German lines facing the British attackers on the right of the Australians, they realised what a vast distance they were from Pheasant Wood – probably around four kilometres. It occurred to Tim (although Lambis steadfastly disagreed) that the logic

Some of the vast array of personal effects collected from the Fromelles battlefield over 30 years by Martial Delebarre and on exhibit at the town's wonderful museum. (PATRICK LINDSAY PHOTO)

Lambis Englezos and Tim Whitford with the segment of the original German light railway that they found near the Wick Salient, in front of the British position on the Australians' right flank at Fromelles. (PATRICK LINDSAY PHOTO)

431

of the battlefield would make it far less likely than he previously thought for the Germans to have transported the British dead over such a great distance to bury them at Pheasant Wood. It seemed much more likely that at least some of the British dead may have been buried behind this area of the battlefield, somewhere on the way to Aubers village on the high ground. Lambis relied on his instincts and held firm that British dead were buried alongside the Australians at Pheasant Wood.

Back at Pheasant Wood, spending each day face to face with the remains began to have a deep and increasing impact on Tony Pollard and the other members of his team.

> *Everybody is affected in their own way. I tend to find the lunch area claustrophobic. I've never really been a lunch person anyway so I tend to wander off. One day I wandered off and sat next to Pit 1 where there were two guys in a groundsheet. I just sat there next to them, like you would at a gravestone in a cemetery, and I realised then that this is what it was all about and that everybody was doing that in their own little way.*
>
> *But when you're on the job, when you're working with somebody in the same pit, you'll say, hey look at this, look how that bone's broken and there is some terrible trauma, a lot of bone shattering, dislocation – that's what is was like.*

When Lambis was eventually invited to view the skeletal remains in their partially excavated burial pits, he found himself strangely calm:

> *I'd read the letters from their parents and their loved ones. I was comfortable with them. I think I felt I knew them. I knew the*

Australians' names. I'd seen their photographs. I'd talked with the descendants. I felt like I wanted to see the boys.

I wasn't sure how it would go. It was grim but I wasn't really fazed by it. They had been names and photographs but now they were tangible. From the moment I saw them I had a very strong feeling of hope that they would now be able to be recovered and they would be given the dignity of individual reburial. Now it was quite clear that the ground would reveal something more substantial than just scattered war debris. There was something very tangible about it all.

They were soldiers killed doing their work. There were clearly skeletal remains, full skeletal remains and the remnants of battle gear and stuff. I felt I knew them. They were just names before but here they were. I really felt at last we were finishing the work of Simon Fraser and Reverend Maxted.

When Tim Whitford's turn came the experience was chillingly different. As a relative of one of the missing, he was first shown remains some days earlier than Lambis, during a guided walkthrough of the site.

They'd exposed the top end of a foot in one place and in Pit 5 you could see up against the wall of the pit, a man's arms. You couldn't see his head yet but it seemed he was leaning back against the wall, just as he'd landed there.

And that's what's changed things for me. If they were all laid out carefully, buried covered in groundsheets, it may have been different but some of those men have not had that privilege. Some have been laid there with the utmost care but others have been thrown in there like yesterday's fish and chips.

Towards the end of the dig, Tim Whitford was one of the last outside the GUARD team to again see the exposed remains before they were covered back over.

> In Pits 4 and 5 it is a scene of abject horror. Men have been thrown in on top of each other without any care or reverence. There are men lying in grotesque positions. One man has been thrown in and is lying unnaturally against the side of the pit wall. Another has been hoiked in. These men are not at rest. If we leave them like that it is a travesty. And if anyone believes anything different they should come here, get off their chesterfields and come here.

The scene is seared into Tim Whitford's memory. He vividly recalled one skeleton that had been thrown into the pit, landing in a half-sitting, slumped position with his arms raised above his head. Another had the telephone wire which the Germans used to drag him into the pit still wrapped around his limbs. A third wore the remnants of a cloth tourniquet on his severed limb, perhaps tied there by a mate vainly trying to save his life. A man in Pit 4 lay in a foetal position with another man dumped across his chest lying on his back in a most undignified position. Tim also saw a skeleton that the investigators estimated was around six foot six inches tall (almost two metres) – physical characteristics which could make him identifiable from available records.

The sight of these remains changed Tim's views on the next steps for the remains from a flexible preference for exhumation, identification and individual reburial to a position where he was absolutely convinced and deeply passionate that the men were not resting in peace and deserved nothing less than exhumation, identification and individual reburial.

Tony Pollard was similarly affected:

You cannot have the moral wherewithal to look for these guys, find them, then see what condition they're in and how they've been buried and then say, well that's adequate, we know where they are.

You would have to have the heart of most solid granite and I don't care whether you're religious or not – and I'm pretty a-religious – but I look into those pits and I think you boys deserve better than this!

Pollard was also deeply moved by the remains found in Pit 5:

The first skeleton we encountered is a guy slumped around the side of the trench on his front. You can see his charger clips, bullets protruding into his rib cage and he's curved around. Then lying next to him into the centre of the pit there is a guy, head thrown back, jaw agape – which is what happens with decay, it looks like a scream but it's not – his arms wide in the shape of a crucifix.

Then you dig down further into Pit 5 and there are two guys with their heads toward the opposite side of the pit, lying side by side, on the floor of the pit with soil thrown over them.

So, obviously in some cases there has been some care in the initial deposition of the bodies, then, as the task has got more laborious, time has changed things. That to me is my abiding image of Fromelles.

Lambis had great admiration for the way Tony Pollard and his team showed respect for the remains they found. He also found admiration for the Germans who had buried their enemy's dead with care, kept such detailed information on them and tried to pass it on to their families through the International Red Cross.

They documented the burials, removed all the personal items and sent them back to Australia, which is a terrific process. The majority of our guys who died of wounds are buried in marked graves because the Germans did a similar thing for them. Post-war they were discovered and sent to a receiving cemetery.

For Tim Whitford, and many other passionate supporters of the quest to find and honour the missing soldiers of Fromelles, the most important thing now is to finish the job. ROAM's Chris Bryett, sees this final stage as the 'Third Battle of Fromelles':

The first was fought in July 1916, the second was the fight to find the missing men and the third is the struggle to exhume them, identify them and bury them with the dignity they deserve in individual graves.

Tim Whitford agrees and is determined to fight on so that, having now been found, his great uncle Harry Willis is not consigned once again to an anonymous grave through what he fears as 'a lack of imagination and uninformed sentiment':

Harry has been there ever since the Germans tossed in his body and covered it with clay after he was killed in battle in July 1916. His mother never knew that, nor did his brothers or sisters, nor his nephews or nieces down through the generations. But he has never been forgotten.

As to those who have called for the Fromelles missing to be left in peace with their mates (including some senior members of the RSL), Tim responds:

All I can say to those who are calling for anything less than a complete exhumation, processing and reburial on-site is that, if they had seen what I saw during the dig, I know they would change their minds.

In Pits 4 and 5 there are no neat rows, no order, and no dignity in death for the diggers. They are a sight of abject horror and it would be nothing less than a travesty to leave these fine men like that.

Tim Whitford, who is a member of the RSL, refers today's leaders to one of the organisation's founders, Lieutenant Colonel Frederick Toll, one of the heroes of Fromelles.

These were his men. Harry Willis was one of his Diggers. Toll would be rolling in his grave at the attitude of the RSL in suggesting that they be left as they lie. He would have paternal ownership of those men. They should have been found when he was still alive.

Having seen the remains uncovered by the GUARD team, Tim knows that the remains are in excellent condition:

Each man is readily discernible having been locked in place by the glutinous and oxygen-free blue Flanders clay. Each set of remains is frozen in the final pose in which the man was thrown into the pit and tells its own very moving story.

Like Lambis, Tim has respect for the German troops who buried the missing at Pheasant Wood.

They may have thrown many of our lads in holes like rotting silage but they had the decency to tell us they had done it, where they did it and to whom they did it. I don't blame them. They had an abhorrent job to do. Many of the Diggers had been in the sun for days and were well on the way to putrefaction. I was a soldier once and couldn't think of a more unpleasant job, especially considering that they also had to care for their own dead and wounded.

For Tim Whitford, simply covering the men at Pheasant Wood where they lie and placing a memorial on the site would deny them any chance of regaining their identity and individuality.

> *We may not be able to give all of them their names back but we can bloody well try. I agree wholeheartedly that they should remain at Pheasant Wood in the long term. It's a beautiful location, inexorably linked to them, and they will be in the care of a village that knows their sacrifice and loves them.*

Tim believes the men at Pheasant Wood should finish their journey with their mates who fought and died with them, but they should be granted the basic right of an attempt at individual identification, a soldier's funeral, and an individual grave.

> *Every other Australian soldier found since the end of World War I has been afforded these basics, why change now? Is it because more years have elapsed? Is it the money? I'd hate to think our war dead were inconvenient.*
>
> *The last person to handle the Fromelles Diggers shouldn't be a German if we have the ability for it to be an Australian.*

The final act of the dig at Pheasant Wood took place on the morning of Friday 13 June. The GUARD team had filled in their sondages. They had inserted protective materials to ensure the remains they had uncovered would not suffer any deterioration and they had placed metal sheaths in place over the pits under the topsoil to prevent the abhorrent practice of grave robbing. (This was a genuine threat. French and Belgian authorities face it regularly as robbers seek artefacts that they then sell on the black market and even on eBay. The people of Fromelles, and especially the town's schoolchildren, have undertaken

Mme Marie-Paule Demassiet, the owner of the Pheasant Wood site, at the closing
ceremony after the GUARD dig. She would later donate the land 'pour les soldats'.
(PATRICK LINDSAY PHOTO)

to watch over the site, supplementing the official security cover that
will be provided by private contractors and the Gendarmerie.) Finally,
the GUARD team had covered over the pits and smoothed over the
drying Flanders mud.

Mike O'Brien arranged for a brief but solemn closing ceremony on
the site. The local equivalent of the RSL provided a wonderfully
colourful guard of honour in their dress uniforms and carrying their
regimental colours. The Mayor of Fromelles, Monsieur Hubert Huchette,
led a large group of local townspeople. The gendarmerie and the
French, Australian and British Armies sent representatives. The
GUARD team, led by Tony Pollard, stood proudly in the crowd. The
guest of honour, Mme Marie-Paule Demassiet, the owner of the land
on which the graves stood, took her seat in front.

A scratchy recording of the Australian national anthem opened proceedings. The only other sound was the wind gently rustling the leaves of the trees along the edge of the wood. The mood deepened when 'La Marseillaise' began playing. From the first line, 'Allons enfants de la Patrie' (Arise children of our country), the townspeople of Fromelles began singing, softly at first, but building to a heartfelt chorus. Few present could doubt the sentiment. It was filled with passion and respect for the land and for those who had fought and died for its liberty.

Mike O'Brien thanked the townspeople for their unstinting support for the project and for their friendship to the team. He thanked Mme Demassiet for her permission to carry out the dig on her land. He thanked the mayor and the local authorities and the veterans who provided the honour guard. He thanked GUARD for their diligence and professionalism.

The dignitaries then laid wreaths around a temporary memorial stone beneath the French, British and Australian flags. The stone read:

In memory of the Australian and British soldiers who lie here and who gave their lives at Fromelles in July 1916. Lest we forget.

Tim, Liz and Alexandra Whitford laid a wreath for Tim's great uncle Harry and Lambis laid one on behalf of the Friends of the 15th Brigade.

Fromelles mayor, Hubert Huchette, responded that the people of Fromelles remembered and honoured the sacrifices of the Australian and British troops who fought to save their liberty. He promised that the memory would be passed on to future generations and never forgotten.

It was after the ceremony had concluded that the most emotional moment of the day occurred. While most people were mingling, and

Mme Marie-Paule Demassiet, great friend of Australia. With her late husband Pierre, she owned the Pheasant Wood grave site and donated it to the Commonwealth War Graves Commission. (PATRICK LINDSAY PHOTO)

Lambis and Tim were being interviewed by the TV crews present, Mme Demassiet quietly approached Mike O'Brien. Without any fanfare she said she felt she no longer owned the land and that it now belonged to the soldiers who lay in it.

Earlier in the week, Mme Demassiet had told us that she had been asked to sell the land many times over the past twenty years. Prospective purchasers had wanted to use it for hunting, to turn it into a fishing pond and to extend the wood over it. But she told us:

Something always stopped me selling it. I could never understand why I needed to keep it because it would never grow anything worthwhile. But now I understand. The soldiers were making me keep it.

Now she told Mike O'Brien the land belonged to 'les soldats' (the soldiers who lay in it). Having lost two of her uncles in the Great

War – one of whom was never found – Marie-Paule Demassiet has always understood the feelings of the families of those who lie in Pheasant Wood. Her beautiful gesture was born of these feelings, as wonderfully expressed by her grandson, Guillaume, in a letter to Lambis, addressed 'To our Australian brothers who died in the Battle of Fromelles in 1916':

The 19th and 20th of July are days which will forever link the history of our two countries. During that hard period of the Great War, you came from the other side of the world, voluntarily and filled with courage, to fight at our sides to preserve our freedom.

Your spirit will never be lost from our land and our hearts. We have been brothers until death, you have had your blood spilled for us and there is no bond stronger than that.

From the bottom of our hearts, we express our eternal gratitude for your sacrifice. You will never leave our hearts.

Guillaume Mooreel, Grandson of Marie-Paule Demassiet

Mme Demassiet's gift lends strength to the logic of exhuming the remains in the graves at Pheasant Wood and reburying them in a new cemetery on the site.

Sitting in the Fromelles Cafe after the ceremony, Lambis sipped his new favourite beverage, a *panache* (pronounced *pan-nah-shay*, a French version of the shandy, beer and lemonade) and looked around the room, now packed with a fascinating amalgam of locals and visitors, all impassioned by the emotions of a remarkable morning. He couldn't help thinking how Padre Maxted would have viewed the scene. He decided he would have joined in and toasted the work of those present, offered a prayer for his newly discovered comrades and encouraged all involved to make sure the job was completed, just as he had intended 92 years earlier.

Saturday 19 July 2008 is a fine but overcast day in Melbourne. A chilling wind whistles down from the imposing stone pile that makes up the city's beautiful Shrine of Remembrance and it tugs at the heavy blue cloth shrouding the large statue set on a pile of concrete. Four members of the Shrine Guard (ex-soldiers from the Victoria Police, in World War I uniforms) form a catafalque guard, arms reversed, around the statue as the crowd grows silent.

This is another moment that Lambis had been anticipating for years. For almost fifteen years, he and his fellow members of the Friends of the 15th Brigade have been trying to get some recognition for the men of Fromelles in Australia. As we've already seen, the name Fromelles does not appear on any of our major war memorials, a legacy of the cover-up that began almost immediately after the battle. Today, that will change.

The sculptor, Peter Corlett, has made a second casting of his evocative bronze work, Cobbers, that has graced the Australian Memorial Park outside Fromelles since July 1998. Today, on the 92nd anniversary of the Battle of Fromelles, the replica is to be jointly unveiled on the corner of St Kilda Road and Domain Road by the Premier of Victoria, John Brumby, and the Mayor of Fromelles, Hubert Huchette.

At last, the descendants of the men who fought and died at Fromelles will have a place in Melbourne commemorating them. The deeds of the heroic Sergeant Simon Fraser, who inspired the statue, and his mates will be permanently honoured and remembered. The name Fromelles will be there for all to see. The crowd is filled with descendants of the men of Fromelles, including a group of Fraser's family and another large group of Harry Willis' extended family. There is a pervading feeling of relief, a sense of accomplishment, of justice finally done.

Lambis Englezos and his family, wife Suzanne, son Anthony and daughter Sophia, at the unveiling of the Cobbers statue in the grounds of Melbourne's Shrine of Remembrance on 19 July 2008. (PATRICK LINDSAY PHOTO)

Lambis, as always, stands to the side, away from the official party, surrounded by his wife Suzanne, daughter Sophia and his strapping son, Craftsman Anthony Englezos, proudly wearing the uniform and slouch hat of the Royal Australian Electrical and Mechanical Engineers. Tim Whitford, Liz and Alexandra are there with Young Harry and the rest of Harry Willis' mob. Martial Delebarre watches quietly at his mayor's side.

With Lambis, Tim and the posse of descendants willing them on, the Premier and the Mayor pull down the shroud and reveal the magnificent bronze snapshot of Simon Fraser, frozen in time, carrying a mate on his shoulders. The statue is positioned so that Fraser is carrying his precious load up the grassy knoll to the Shrine, symbolically taking him home. A stirring rendition of 'La Marseillaise' and an equally passionate response of the Australian national anthem seal the occasion.

You couldn't knock the smile off Lambis Englezos' face as he shakes hands with his son.

POSTSCRIPT

I consider it no sacrifice to die for my country. In my mind we came here to thank God that men like these have lived rather than to regret that they have died.

GENERAL GEORGE S. PATTON, SPEAKING AT AN ALLIED CEMETERY IN ITALY, NOVEMBER 1943

The irrefutable confirmation in June 2008 that the missing soldiers of Fromelles were lying at Pheasant Wood had a profound impact on many people around the world.

For Lambis Englezos and his team, especially those who have been at his side throughout the long six years of his quest, it brought a sense of fulfilment, tinged with vindication. Lambis is now focused on doing all in his power to ensure that the fallen are honoured properly.

For Tim Whitford and the many other descendants of the missing, both in Australia and in Britain, it brought some long-awaited closure. After almost a century of uncertainty and impotence, they now know the fate of their loved ones. At last, they have somewhere to visit to pay their respects. They can look forward to the creation of a new cemetery, with individual headstones, devoted to preserving the memory of their kinsmen.

For Martial Delebarre, Fromelles Mayor Hubert Huchette and the townsfolk, the final resolution added a new dimension to their unswerving dedication to honouring the memory of those who came from Britain and from halfway across the world to fight for their liberty.

Nobody knows more about Pheasant Wood and the men who lie in it than Martial Delebarre. His family have lived in the region for more than 700 years. They have survived countless ancient conflicts, the French Revolution and two world wars. The Great War battlefields of Fromelles were Martial's playground as a child and he has spent his working life tending to the cemeteries that decorate the region. The skeletal remains unearthed by the GUARD Team touched a deep well of emotion in Martial, feelings magnified by his visceral connection with the land.

When I saw the skeletons I knew we had to do something to give them a new resting place. These men were thrown into the pits, some without regard to any sense of dignity – understandable in the cauldron of war, inexcusable in the cold light of today. These men are not at rest.

In Australia, the man with the ultimate responsibility for honouring the Missing Fromelles Diggers is the Minister for Defence Science and Personnel, Warren Snowdon. Born and raised in Canberra, he first moved to the Northern Territory in 1976. He worked there as a history teacher and as an advisor to the Central Land Council before entering Federal Parliament in 1987. He is the member for Lingiari, Australia's second-largest electorate – 1.3 million square kilometres of the Northern Territory and including the Christmas and Cocos Islands.

Warren Snowdon was imbued with the Anzac spirit by his father, who served in New Guinea with the 2/2nd Independent Company, commandos who saw fierce hand-to-hand fighting there.

I grew up with my father not talking very much about his experiences. Sadly, for me, I left home in my early twenties, when I should have been spending time with him, so I got to know about his war service through his mates.

My father brought us all up as Catholics and made sure we went to mass every Sunday, and usually much more often, but he never went to church, except once a year ... on Anzac Day. As I grew up I realised what impact the war must have had on him. My father went to war aged eighteen and spent the best years of his life fighting a terrible war. The youngest of the missing we've found at Fromelles is probably only fifteen. I've got a son aged eighteen. How could you do this to them?

Now 58, Snowdon was appointed to the ministry when the Rudd Labor Government swept to power in December 2007. He regards his ministerial responsibility as a great privilege. He is working with his British ministerial counterpart, Derek Twigg, and the French authorities to ensure the Fromelles missing are properly honoured.

In essence, to me this means that we exhume each set of remains, identify those that we can and then re-inter them with full military honours, each with an individual headstone.

The plan is to start the exhumation process in the French summer of 2009. Snowdon recognises that while the Pheasant Wood gravesite, donated by Mme Demassiet, is the logical site for the new cemetery for the missing, it has considerable logistic challenges. The land itself

Mme Marie-Paule Demassiet tells an emotional Lambis Englezos that she has donated the Pheasant Wood site to the memory of the men who lie there. (PATRICK LINDSAY PHOTO)

has major drainage problems. In addition, it may be too small to house all the reburied remains, it has poor vehicle and pedestrian access, and the increased visitors it will attract will require substantial parking and traffic changes.

Snowdon is also conscious of the preferences of the Fromelles community. While they are totally supportive of the reburial of the missing soldiers, they have expressed some concerns: that the new cemetery should fit in with their overall plans for an extended museum; and that the town's infrastructure needs to be strengthened to handle the expected growth in visitors.

One possibility is that the new site for the cemetery for the missing be created alongside the existing VC Corner Cemetery, in the open ground between it and the Cobbers statue. This has the benefit of allowing preparation of the new cemetery to begin concurrently with the exhumation of the Pheasant Wood graves. On the other hand, if the Pheasant Wood site were chosen as the new cemetery site, its preparation would have to wait until the next summer after the exhumation was completed – possibly dragging out the reburial for three years.

Not surprisingly, Lambis has a strong emotional connection to the Pheasant Wood site. He believes it has become the missing soldiers' spiritual home and should be the number one choice for their final reburial. Others can see merit in the VC Corner site as it would have been the likely burial site for the missing Diggers had they been found, as they should have been, in 1916 and they would finally rest alongside their comrades.

The response of the Australian descendants of the missing Fromelles Diggers to the news of the discovery of their relatives has been remarkable. Already more than 450 individuals have contacted the Army, offering to be DNA tested to try to identify their loved ones.

Snowdon and the other authorities are at great pains not to raise unrealistic expectations about the chances of identifying the missing soldiers. Because we know the names of the vast majority of the Australian missing, we are in a relatively better position than the British, who lost key records during the Blitz in World War II. Nevertheless, identification will be a case-by-case proposition and will depend on the condition of the individual remains.

Warren Snowdon believes the best way to proceed with identification is to take DNA samples, where possible, as the remains are exhumed. The remains would be then re-interred in the new cemetery under individual 'unknown soldier' headstones. Later, as and when they can be identified, their headstones would be changed to reflect their identities.

Postscript

It is extremely unlikely that all of the soldiers lying at Pheasant Wood will be identified. We have waited almost a century to find them. The least we can do is to make every effort to identify as many as is humanly possible. Their mates would expect nothing less from us.

Appendix I

THE ORDER OF BATTLE, FROMELLES

COMMANDER IN CHIEF
General Sir Douglas Haig

GOC* FIRST BRITISH ARMY
General Sir Charles Monro

GOC XI CORPS
General Sir Richard Haking

GOC I ANZAC CORPS
(1st and 2nd Australian Division and NZ Divisions)
General Sir William Birdwood

GOC II ANZAC CORPS
(4th and 5th Australian Divisions)
General Sir Alexander Godley

---

* General Officer Commanding

BRITISH 61ST DIVISION

GOC
Major General Colin McKenzie

182ND BRIGADE
Brigadier General Alister Gordon
2/5th Royal Warwickshire Regiment
2/6th Royal Warwickshire Regiment
2/7th Royal Warwickshire Regiment
2/8th Royal Warwickshire Regiment

183RD BRIGADE
Brigadier General Gordon Stewart
2/4th Gloucestershire Regiment
2/6th Gloucestershire Regiment
2/7th Worcestershire Regiment
2/8th Worcestershire Regiment

184TH BRIGADE
Brigadier General Charles Carter
2/4th Oxfordshire and Buckinghamshire Regiment
2/1st Royal Berkshire Regiment
2/4th Royal Berkshire Regiment
2/5th Gloucestershire Regiment
2/1st Buckinghamshire Regiment

5TH AUSTRALIAN DIVISION

GOC
Major General James McCay

8TH BRIGADE
Brigadier General Edwin Tivey

29th Battalion	Lieutenant Colonel A.W. Bennett
30th Battalion	Lieutenant Colonel J.W. Clark
31st Battalion	Lieutenant Colonel F.W. Toll
32nd Battalion	Lieutenant Colonel D.M.R. Coghill

14TH BRIGADE
Brigadier General Harold Pope

53rd Battalion	Lieutenant Colonel I.B. Norris
54th Battalion	Lieutenant Colonel W.E.H. Cass
55th Battalion	Lieutenant Colonel D.M. McConaghy
56th Battalion	Lieutenant Colonel A.H. Scott

15TH BRIGADE
Brigadier General Harold Elliott

57th Battalion	Lieutenant Colonel J.C. Stewart
58th Battalion	Lieutenant Colonel C.A. Denehy
59th Battalion	Lieutenant Colonel E.A. Harris
60th Battalion	Major G.G. McCrae

Appendix II

THE MISSING DIGGERS OF FROMELLES

8TH BRIGADE

29th Battalion (19)
Pte Henry Bell #191
Pte Justin Breguet #1983
Pte J.A. Cozens #210
Pte S. Farlow #80
Pte T. Francis #2584
Pte J. Gordon #1130
Pte H. Haslam #1390
Pte A. Johnson #2203
Pte F. Livingston #1168
Pte S. O'Donnell #314
Pte E. Oliver #316
Pte W. O'Donnell #319
Pte F. Parry #320
Pte H. Pollard #324
Cpl J. Ross #1216
Pte G. Smith #1245
Cpl A. Tuck #1252
Pte A.J. Weir #358
Pte E. Wilkin #1314

30th Battalion (22)
Pte J. Balsdon #2274
Pte H. Bourke #1682
Pte D. Caswell #397
Sgt C. Church #635
Pte H. Crocker #2010
Pte R. Fenwick #882
Pte H. Gardner #889
L/Cpl Fred Glenn #1291
Pte C. Hawcroft #188
Pte W. Higgins #196
Pte A. James #689
Pte G. H. Lucre #467
Lt A. Mitchell
Cpl C. Murray #1590
Pte H. Nelson #728
2nd Lt J Parker
Pte D.B. Ryan #743
Pte M. Spence #4614
Pte J. Turner #767
Pte L.S. Vincent #777
Pte A. Wood #781
Pte J.C. Wynn #2485

8TH BRIGADE

8th Brigade Field Co. Engineers
L/Cpl H.T. Smith #4474

31st Battalion (16)
Pte T.H. Bills #605
Pte S. Broom #1522
Pte J.J. Curran #494
Pte L.C. Dunn #641
Pte J.J. Goulding #555 POW
Pte W.A. Grace #1537
Pte N.A. Hale #702
Pte T. Hunt #1054
Pte S.J. Hyams #2028
Pte J.L. Mason #470 POW
Pte J. Morley #258
Pte J. Nevill #269
Pte J.R. Smith #3983
Pte L.G. Walsh #311
Pte P. Weakley #318
Pte H.V. Willis #983

32nd Battalion (45)
Pte W. Barber #346
Sgt O. Baumann #10
Pte A. Batt #352
L/Cpl A. Bennett #1602
Pte J.H. Boswell. #891
Pte W.E Boyce #1218
Pte E.N. Burney # 1226
Pte T.C. Cartwright #1235
Lt E.H. Chinner
Pte M. Coriglians #2011
Pte J.E. Crocker #79
L/Cpl S.W. Dennis #1252

Pte E.C. Gray #20
Cpl R.C. Green #1274
Pte Bertie Greenfield #1275
Pte P.J. Greenwood #3115a
Pte G.A. Griffiths #1276
Cpl L.W. Hart #865
Pte C.R.S. Hoffman #2050
Pte A. Holmes #955
Pte G. Honey #1291
Pte T. Hunt #347
Pte A.W.J. Irving #1528
Pte J. Joyce #1624
Pte A.T. Knable #1603
Pte D.M. Lawlor #126
Pte F.O. Loader #2064
Pte R.H. Magor #3209
Pte R.T. Maudsley #137
Pte A.M. McKenzie #1797a
Pte J.G. McKenzie #151
Pte H. McLean #293
Pte A.V. Momplhait #3282
Pte E.W. Parham #2092
Pte A.M. Perry #2095
Pte H.C. Pitt #595
Pte Walter H. Pretty #1556
Pte. H.J. Randall #1558
Pte M.L. Reid #3256
Pte S.T.J. Ridler #1036
Pte M. Ross #1040
Pte R.G.M. Scott #1046
Pte A.G. Smith #1640
Pte J.R. Stead #187
Pte W.C. Tucker #1581

14ᴛʜ BRIGADE

53rd Battalion (14)
Pte A.C. Bromley #4744
Pte A.S. Clingan #3168
2nd Lt Clarence Timbwell Collier
Sgt C.S. Hill #842
Pte George William Hungerford #3327
L/Sgt E. Jentsch #3331
Pte G.H. Johnston #3096
Lt Harry Lowry Moffitt
Lt Col Ignatius Bertram Norris
Pte P. Shannon #3433
Pte A. Verpillot #4885
Pte F.J. Williams #3605
Pte E.R. Wilson #4887
Pte Samuel Charles Wilson # 3534

54th Battalion (30)
Pte Michael Balkin #4254
Sgt Jack Campbell #495
Pte Roy Allison Clark #4155
Pte W. Connolly #3585a
L/Cpl William Andrew Craigie #4420
Pte Henry Alfred Cressy #4179a
Pte William Joseph Cuckson #3032
Pte E.H. Dibben #4183a
Pte Willie Hilton Doust #3557
Pte B.J.A. Dunston #4483
Pte F.A. Dyson #3560
Pte G.R. Gray #2927
Pte Laurence Harriott #4509
Pte C.D. Holliday #4801
Pte J.L. Holmes #4305
Pte E.J. Hope #4188
Pte C.D. Johnston #4315a
Pte P.L. Myers #4850
Pte A. Needham #4946

L/Cpl G. Pagan #2966
Pte W. Pheasant #3462
Sgt H. Richardson #4581
Pte B. Richardson #4581
Pte A. Russell #4299
Pte J. Scott #4873
Cpl J. Toole #690
Pte J. P. Wailes [Wallis] #4617
Sgt W. Wass #239
Pte R. R. Wildman #1888
Pte A. Williamson #4249

55th Battalion (15)
Pte V. Baker #3007
Pte V. E. Baker #3247
Pte R.A. Barrett #3031
Pte R.C. Bishop #3761
Cpl H.T. Bolt #3009
Pte L. Broadhurst #3013
Pte R.A. Dewar #3047
Pte P.W. Fahey #3060
Cpl F. Fletcher #3310
Pte J.J. Harris #3819
Pte L. Leister #4840
Pte R.J. McGuarr #3873
Lt B.L. Mendelsohn
Pte H. N. St Smith #3924
Pte A. Thompson #2825

56th Battalion (1)
Pte D. Dodd #4770

14th Machine Gun Company
Pte N.T. Lee #2779
Cpl G.F. Stalgis #2898
Lt R.D. Burns

15ᴛʜ BRIGADE (7)

57th Battalion
None

58th Battalion
None

59th Battalion
Lt J.C. Bowden
Cpl R.W. Johnson #3367

60th Battalion
Sgt. V.M. Grogan #3114
Pte F.G. Holst #2925
Sgt D.C. McCaul #1980
Pte J.L. Nitchie #146
C.Q. Sgt J. Ralston #1501 (1382?)

The soldiers who are on the wall at VC Corner as missing / unidentified plus the additional soldiers who are on the memorial wall at Villers-Bretonneux. They all have files in the Red Cross records showing they were gathered at Fromelles and buried by the Germans.

Appendix III

5TH DIVISION AIF DEATHS, FROMELLES

| | | VC Corner | |
	Total	Unknown	Known
8th Brigade			
32 Infantry Battalion	197	163	34
31 Battalion	143	53	90
30 Battalion	105	79	26
29 Battalion	51	37	14
8 Brigade Machine Gun Company	15	5	10
8 Brigade Engineers	8	1	7
8 Brigade Trench Motor Battery	0	0	0
Total Brigade deaths	**519**	**338**	**181**
14th Brigade			
53 Battalion	222	189	33
54 Battalion	155	98	57
55 Battalion	66	44	22
56 Battalion	29	7	22
14 Brigade Machine Gun Company	17	6	11
14 Brigade Engineers	5	3	2
14 Brigade Trench Mortar Battery	1	0	1
Total Brigade deaths	**495**	**347**	**148**

	Total	VC Corner Unknown	Known
15th Brigade			
60 Battalion	358	312	46
59 Battalion	301	239	62
58 Battalion	77	52	25
57 Battalion	17	2	15
15 Brigade Machine Gun Company	8	0	8
15 Brigade Engineers	5	2	3
15 Brigade Trench Mortar Battery	0	0	0
Total Brigade deaths	**766**	**607**	**159**
Total 5th Division deaths, 19–20 July 1916	**1780**	**1292**	**488**
Official figures	1917	1299	618
Plus Villers-Bretonneux add-ons		9	
		1308	

Appendix IV

CASUALTIES OF WORLD WAR I

Countries	Total mobilised	Killed and died	Wounded	Prisoners and missing	Total casualties	Casualties % of mobilised
Allied Powers						
Russia	12,000,000	1,700,000	4,950,000	2,500,000	9,150,000	76.3
France	8,410,000	1,357,800	4,266,000	537,000	6,160,800	76.3
British Empire	8,904,467	908,371	2,090,212	191,652	3,190,235	35.8
Italy	5,615,000	650,000	947,000	600,000	2,197,000	39.1
United States	4,355,000	126,000	234,300	4,500	364,800	8.2
Japan	800,000	300	907	3	1,210	0.2
Romania	750,000	335,706	120,000	80,000	535,706	71.4
Serbia	707,343	45,000	133,148	152,958	331,106	46.8
Belgium	267,000	13,716	44,686	34,659	93,061	34.9
Greece	230,000	5,000	21,000	1,000	17,000	11.7
Portugal	100,000	7,222	13,751	12,318	33,291	33.3
Montenegro	50,000	3,000	10,000	7,000	20,000	40.0
Total	42,188,810	5,152,115	12,831,004	4,121,090	22,104,209	52.3
Central Powers						
Germany	11,000,000	1,773,7000	4,216,058	1,152,800	7,142,558	64.9
Austria-Hungary	7,800,000	1,200,000	3,620,000	2,200,000	7,020,000	90.0
Turkey	2,850,000	325,000	400,000	250,000	975,000	34.2
Bulgaria	1,200,000	87,500	152,390	27,029	266,919	22.2
Total	22,850,000	3,386,200	8,388,448	3,629,829	15,404,477	67.4
Grand Total	65,038,810	8,538,315	21,219,452	7,750,919	37,508,686	57.6

Source: http://www.greatwar.nl/index.html

Appendix V

FIRST GUARD REPORT, EXECUTIVE SUMMARY

The Centre for Battlefield Archaeology at the University of Glasgow, a sub division of GUARD, was commissioned by the Australian Army to carry out a non-invasive archaeological survey/evaluation of an area of land adjacent to Pheasant Wood, which stand to the north of the village of Fromelles in northern France. The first aim of the project was to establish whether or not the site had been used as a mass grave or graves for the burial of Australian and British troops by the Germans after the battle of Fromelles, fought 19–20 July 1916. Written orders for the digging of burial pits behind Pheasant Wood were issued on 21 July 1916 by Major General von Braun of the Imperial Bavarian Reserve Infantry Regiment No. 21. Evidence that these orders were carried out is provided by a series of aerial photographs taken by the Allies from 29 July 1916 onwards, which show that eight rectangular pits were dug adjacent to the wood in the days following the battle. By 29 July 1916 five of these pits had been backfilled, probably as mass graves. The remaining three pits remained open until at least 1918 and may have been used during and after the war to dispose of military debris.

Following research by Lambis Englezos and others in Australia it had been suggested that between 60 and 160–70 of more than 1,300 Australian troops listed as missing after the battle may have been buried in these pits, along with a number of British dead. The German set of orders relating to the burials states that grave pits were to be dug to accommodate 400 'English' dead, which suggested that up to 230 British troops may be buried alongside the Australians (these figures, however, were estimated before the present research).

The second major aim of the project, should the presence of burials be verified, was to establish the likelihood of the bodies still being in the pits today. Numerous grave pits and battlefield cemeteries were cleared both during and after the war by exhumation parties, the recovered remains then being re-interred in the permanent military cemeteries widespread in this part of northern France. Prior to the project reported here no documentary evidence for the exhumation and reburial of bodies from these pits was known – though evidence that the bodies were still there was also lacking.

In order to accomplish the project aims a multi-faceted programme of survey and investigation was implemented; the techniques enlisted included geophysical survey (resistivity and gradiometry), ground-penetrating radar (GPR) topography survey, metal detector survey and archive research. The fieldwork was carried out by a team of six between 16–28 May 2007 with archive research taking place both before and after this period. During the metal detector survey, the discovery of two copper alloy medallions bearing ANZAC and AIF insignia clearly indicated that Australians had been present on the site, probably as bodies brought from the front line by the German light railway which ran alongside the pits (as detailed in the German orders). The metal detector survey also recovered a number of buttons, some of which may have become detached from clothes and accoutrements worn by the dead. In addition, bullets, both fired and unfired and various elements from shells, including shrapnel balls, shell fragments, pusher plates and shell casings were recovered from across the site.

The apparently intact nature of the metal artefact scatter, which includes material dating to the final Allied advance in Autumn 1918, along with the relatively undisturbed nature of the pit fills suggested by the geophysical surveys, in addition to the lack of any documentary evidence for exhumation, pushes the weight of evidence in favour of the bodies still being *in situ* in the pits. However, a trial trenching evaluation would be required to establish beyond doubt whether or not this was the case – any such exercise should also be supported by an exhaustive programme of archival research to establish the full character of the documentary record, as relating to the identification of individuals and the activities of German burial and allied exhumation parties.

Appendix VI

THE FIRST GUARD REPORT DEBATE

As experts began to examine and evaluate the first GUARD Report, some serious concerns arose.

Paul Cheetham, a forensic archaeologist from Britain's Bournemouth University who specialised in the geophysics of mass graves, publicly stated that he believed the report's conclusions were not supported by the evidence it showed. Cheetham was quoted in *The Australian* newspaper on 24 August 2007:

> *I could see no evidence supporting their conclusion that the pits exist, the graves contain human remains or that they are undisturbed.*

Another forensic archaeologist from Bournemouth, Ian Hanson, agreed:

> *The historical evidence is cherry-picked to fit in with what they're finding [in test results]. It's not uncommon in [conventional] archaeology.*

Both academics were quoted as saying they were not criticising Pollard's work as a battlefield archaeologist but they queried why someone with the relevant mass-grave experience wasn't commissioned and why the project was not put out to tender before being awarded to GUARD.

Pollard was quoted by the *Australian* as conceding his lack of mass-grave experience but standing by the conclusions of the report:

Any of the techniques individually would not come up with the goods, but all combined together, they came up with the goods.

Professor Richard Wright, from ROAM's team, told *The Australian* he was very disappointed because 'we already knew the location of the pits from the aerial photographs' and the report added 'little to what was already known about the site' beyond finding the medals, buttons and bullets.

Ian Hanson subsequently raised further concerns about the expectations raised by the GUARD Report and Tony Pollard's public statements. He believed the report should have been peer reviewed to test its conclusions and methodology:

My reading of the report's 'positive outcome' from a negative is that because a consistent spread of artefacts was present this inferred the graves had not been redug, and that because there was not a stronger response from some geophysics, this also meant the graves had not been disturbed, therefore the graves are intact.

This presumes the graves are there (not demonstrated in report), discounts other explanations for the artefact spread (there are several not discussed in report) and presumes the geophysics survey has been done effectively (not demonstrated in report). Overall, I can't find a justification for the positive comments having read the report.

467

Amplifying his concerns about the report 'raising expectations', Hanson referred to the 2001 discovery of 24 British soldiers in a mass grave near Arras. The grave was found accidentally by developers excavating to build a new BMW factory. The skeletal remains were found placed in line in a common grave. Media reports immediately latched on to the appearance of the remains, saying variously that they were 'lying arm in arm' or 'arms linked, a testimony to that special camaraderie that binds men in battle'. Alain Jacques was quoted in the *Independent* newspaper:

In the common grave, the skeletons are arranged in a line, arms joined, probably to show that they came from the same battalion.

In *The Times*, Jacques said:

Can you imagine the friendship and dedication of those who went about laying down the remains in this way? To go and get a leg and position it in the line – what a remarkable act. They must have died within hours of each other.

As an example of the extremes to which an emotional viewing of the facts can bring, Hanson referred to a military history chatline that extrapolated the facts even further:

While the majority of the burials are close together – Alain Jacques felt they were actually arm in arm – the one on the right is slightly apart from the others with his arms by his side. This distance, although slight, might perhaps be intentional. Could it indicate that this soldier was something apart from the others – perhaps an officer? If so, and if this is the Lincolns, he must be Lieutenant Cocks.

This highly charged interpretation of facts is what Hanson warned about. He believed there was a rational and dispassionate explanation for the position of the bodies:

It was clear to me from an examination of the photographs that the bodies were not placed arm in arm at all, but were carried by people holding the feet and armpits which caused the elbows to cross the next body. Any anthropologist would have been able to determine this by looking at the arrangement of arm bones. But none was consulted at the grave.

More than 300 families contacted the British Ministry of Defence after a report speculating that most of the men from the Arras mass grave may have come from the same regiment.

But it was the methodology of the GUARD Report that most concerned Professor Richard Wright:

I had assumed that GUARD would be trying to model the contents of the pits. But they couldn't even locate them by geophysics.

I think the report's diagrams of resistivity and magnetometry/ gradiometry are wishful thinking, so far as its claims to have found the pits go.

Wright was also puzzled by the report's claims that the magnetometry and gradiometry anomalies would have been stronger had the post-war recovery teams exhumed the bodies, leaving the pits empty:

Quite frankly this is a nonsense. It indicates no understanding of the method and theory of magnetometry.

Magnetometry, Wright observes, measures the polarity of soil particles. Over thousands of years, soil particles left undisturbed will take on a north–south magnetic polarity. When a pit or grave is dug it randomises the particles of the disturbed soil. The operator of a magnetometer is looking for the anomaly evident between the polarity in the undisturbed soil and the lack of polarity in the disturbed area of the pits.

Digging out the pit two or three years after it was originally dug merely randomises the already randomised particles. The anomaly will be neither lesser nor greater.

Wright also expressed serious concerns about the equipment GUARD used for its ground-penetrating radar (GPR) survey:

I had not heard of the Future I-160 equipment so I asked two GPR practitioners about it. They unhesitatingly told me that it is cheap equipment sold to treasure hunters. It is not for professional work, and would not have a hope in hell of modelling bodies within the graves. So the equipment itself was not fit for purpose.

When Wright consulted the manufacturers of the Future I-160, German-based OKM Ortungstechnik GmbH, they advised him that their products were not pure standard radar systems 'like you may know it'. The machine uses 'combined technology' consisting of gradiometry, radar components and metal detectors and is not comparable with ordinary radar systems:

Because of the combination of technology parts the working principle is quite different and can not be applied to standard systems. The radar component's frequency is based on 9 GHz with a band width of 2–750 Hz which is used to get a perfect combined result of each measurement. More details can not be given to protect this unique measuring system which was developed and optimised from our company.

In the light of this, Wright said that the I-160 was not a GPR instrument.

I must therefore conclude that a GPR survey was not done at Pheasant Wood. The 'radar component' was operating at a frequency that has no relevant penetration.

In Wight's view GPR is radar. He has pointed out that there are dozens of machines on the market designed to do radar, and that the relationship between frequency and penetration is well understood.

The I-160 has a radar component of 9 GHz. This could not penetrate more than about 0.250 mm in wet soil – that's a basic property of electromagnetic waves of that frequency. To achieve a GPR, with penetration to up to 2 m, the machine would have to operate with longer wave lengths, at a frequency of around 400 MHz.

Curiously the manufacturer, in what is admittedly a confused web page devoted to treasure hunting, eschews conventional GPR and redefines the acronym to mean 'Geophysical Phase Reader'. Is it possible that Glasgow did not read these words in the specifications and misunderstood what the words GPR stood for in the catalogue.

To clarify things I have asked the manufacturer about the penetration I could expect from the radar component of their equipment. Nobody I have spoken to can see how one can enhance

radar waves of 9 GHz to penetrate as though they were 400 MHz
– though Dr Who might be able to, one of the experts said to me.

Perhaps the best summation of the situation comes from Dr Paul
Cheetham:

The geophysical work done at Fromelles so far has contributed to
our knowledge of the site and so can be used to inform how the
project may proceed, but the results are not at all clear, and so any
interpretations will remain highly speculative until confirmed by ground
truthing. However, the techniques employed by GUARD were very
basic and very limited in their capabilities in terms of providing results
that would allow the aims of the work to be met.

Health and safety issues aside, the metal detecting survey is
excellent but unfortunately incomplete so it is difficult to assess the
true distribution and relative frequency and the significance of the
material found.

Earth resistivity was an appropriate technique but the equipment
and methodology employed severely limited its effectiveness in meeting
the survey's aim and in my opinion a much more sophisticated variant,
electrical imaging, which provides deeper penetration and depth
discrimination should have been employed.

Magnetometry was an appropriate technique but the equipment
employed limited its effectiveness in meeting the survey's aims and
in my opinion a total field sensor gradiometry system should have
been employed, again to allow detection at a greater depth and provide
depth discrimination.

The documented ground-penetrating radar (GPR) survey is not
a conventional GPR survey and so really this needs to be redone
using an appropriate conventional instrument, employing appropriate
survey and data processing methodologies.

A slingram EM should have also have been considered as a further possible survey technique to confirm and complement the results of the other techniques.

While the First GUARD Report concluded that the totality of its findings 'pushes the weight of evidence in favour of the bodies still being *in situ* in the pits', it was far from definitive. It confirmed what Team Lambis had always claimed: that the Missing Diggers and Tommies of Fromelles were buried at Pheasant Wood after the battle in 1916. But many experts believed it left the final question still very much open: were they still lying in the shadow of Pheasant Wood?

Appendix VII

MAJOR-GENERAL VON BRAUN ORDER NO. 5220

No. 5220   21.7.16

Bayer. Res. Inf. Rgt. No. 21

(21st Bavarian Reserve Infantry Regiment)

Subject: Bringing up of materials and recovery of bodies

1. The following are assigned to the Regiment to undertake recovery of the wounded and dead:
    a. 1 NCO and 24 men of the Medical Company. These will be billeted at Desprez (Eck Farm) and draw rations with the 21st Infantry Pioneer Company. They will be employed as directed by the Regimental Medical Officer.
    b. Three motor lorries. These will be loaded at Brulle with screw pickets, rolls of wire and long stakes, which will be unloaded beside the light railway line, E of Fromelles, on the Mittlere

Hochstrasse. The unloading will be carried out by a working party from the h-Company. The lorries will then be loaded in the vicinity of the Regimental Command Post with German dead, which are to be deposited in the SE quadrant of the cemetery at Beaucamps. The Regimental Band will detail men to carry out this work as ordered by the Regimental Medical Officer, who will also arrange for the necessary supervision by a Medical Officer and other personnel, as required.

Sergeant-majors are to be in attendance during the laying-out of the bodies and will collect papers and identity disks in such a way that the personal effects and identity disk are removed from each body individually and are immediately placed in a sandbag, tied off and tagged with a cardboard or stiff paper label (pendant address label), on which the number and company appearing on the identity disk are recorded.

Each body thus registered is to be laid immediately in one of the mass graves excavated in accordance with 3. below. The Medical Officer in attendance, who will direct the operation, is to ensure that each layer of bodies is immediately covered with a layer of earth mixed with chloride of lime, and that, when full, the grave is immediately covered over in a suitable manner. The grave sites will be allocated by the Ortskommandant (Town Major) of Beaucamps. Consecration of the bodies and the graves will take place later.

Tent squares [Zeltbahnen] may be used to move the bodies, but must not be used as burial shrouds. Detached body parts are to be wrapped in cloth and buried.

The other vehicles used to transport the pioneer materials are likewise to bring back German bodies; the light railway is also to be used for this purpose as far as the halt at Beaucamps, from where the bodies will be transported on stretchers. The unloading points are to be sited to one side, fenced off at a suitable distance with barbed wire and guarded in watches by sentries posted by the Regimental Band.

The civilian population is to be prevented from loitering and staring at the bodies.

The entire recovery operation at Beaucamps will be carried out in four-hour shifts until specific arrival times are known. The sergeant-majors of the IIIrd Bn will begin at 8.00pm today, followed by those of the 1st, then those of the IInd Bn, etc.

The 'English' bodies will be buried in mass graves immediately to the south of Pheasant Wood. The removal of effects and identity disks, in the same way as for the German bodies, is to be carried out by the h-Company, supported by one medical NCO and 4 men of the regiment, under the orders of the Regimental Medical Officer.

In order to expedite the rapid removal of the bodies, the dead are to be separated by nationality and laid out at depots close to the light railway, Grashof and Christuskreuz.

The misappropriation of even the most insignificant item of property from a body (German or 'English') constitutes robbery of the dead and will be severely punished. The collection of effects, as ordered above, may only be carried out by the sergeant-majors at Beaucamps or in the presence of a senior NCO of the h-Company at Pheasant Wood.

The IIIrd Bn is to provide one section, in rotation, to assist at Beaucamps. The assistance of stretcher bearer sections from RIR 20 is requested.

2. From today, three motor lorries are assigned to undertake double trips during the night to take forward the pioneer materials. See 1. above.

The h-Company will provide a squad from 10pm to carry out the unloading at Fromelles (tonight, the occupying Company for the first trip, then the relieving Company for the second trip).

The IIIrd Bn will provide two squads each day to load the other vehicles at Desprez when requested by the commander of the Infantry Pioneer Company. The e-Company will provide two sections to unload the materials at Christuskreuz. Times to be decided by Leutnant Marx.

3. The Ortskommandatur (Town Major's Office) at Beaucamps is to have mass graves dug for approximately 300 bodies, separated by unit, but alongside one another. The officers are to be laid out separately in the centre. For the burial of the 'English' dead, the h-Company is to excavate mass graves for approximately 400 bodies. Until that time it is only to be employed on remedial works within the [*] position.

Signed: von Braun

Copies to:

Regiments:	2
Battalions:	3
Companies:	14
Reg. Med. Off.:	1
IInd & IIIrd Bn. Med. Offs:	2
Ortskommandatur:	<u>1</u>
	23

[*] Translator's note: there is a gap in the text here: "… in der Stellung verwendet." It appears that a space has been left for later insertion of another word. In the context, the missing word is probably '2' or 'zweiten' and the sentence would then read: "Until that time it is only to be employed on remedial works in the second line position." The second line position or 2 Stellung is the major defensive German line running along the ridge crest — see maps.

Appendix VIII

BROTHERS WHO DIED AT THE BATTLE OF FROMELLES

(List researched by Stephen Brooks)

8TH BRIGADE

1 **Wills**

Pte George Charles	#652	29th Bn	kia 20 July 1916
Pte Robert Joseph	#651	29th Bn	dow 2 August 1916

2 **Balsdon**

Pte James	#2274	30th Bn	kia 19/20 July 1916
Pte Russell Henry	#2276	30th Bn	dow 28 July 1916
Pte Joseph Tucker	#2275	30th Bn	wounded 20 July 1916

3 **Choat**

Pte Archibald Percy	#66	32nd Bn	kia 20 July 1916
Pte Raymond Hadden	#68	32nd Bn	kia 20 July 1916
Pte Wesley Paul MM	#67	32nd Bn	POW 20 July 1916

14TH BRIGADE

1 **Bromley**
   Pte Sidney Reginald   #4903   53rd Bn   kia 19 July 1916
   Pte Albert Clive   #4744   53rd Bn   kia 19 July 1916

2 **Carey**
   Pte Timothy Joseph   #3480A 53rd Bn   kia 19 July 1916
   Pte John Stephen   #3481A 53rd Bn   kia 19 July 1916

3 **McLeod**
   Pte Hector John   #3273   55th Bn   kia 20 July 1916
   Cpl William Edward   #3121   53rd Bn   kia 19 July 1916

4 **Wilson**
   Pte Eric Robert   #4887   53rd Bn   kia 19 July 1916
   Pte Samuel Charles   #3534   53rd Bn   kia 19 July 1916

5 **Turner**
   Pte Arthur   #3462A 53rd Bn   kia 19 July 1916
   Pte Harry   #3455   53rd Bn   kia 19 July 1916

6 **McAulay**
   Pte Hector   #3491   54th Bn   kia 19/20 July 1916
   Pte Roderick   #4270A 54th Bn   kia 19/20 July 1916

15TH BRIGADE

1 **Daly**
   Pte William Warren   #4474   58th Bn   dow 22 July 1916
   Pte James Fitzgibbon   #4643   58th Bn   kia 19 July 1916

2 **Clements**
   Cpl Harold George   #4076   59th Bn   kia 19 July 1916
   L/Cpl Vivian John   #3055   59th Bn   kia 19 July 1916

3 **Fraser**
   Pte Roderick John   #3282   59th Bn   kia 19 July 1916
   Pte Alexander Gregory   #1703   60th Bn   kia 19 July 1916

4 Hosie

L/Cpl Gustave George	#2844	59th Bn	kia 19 July 1916
Pte Russell William	#1948	60th Bn	kia 19 July 1916

5 Jones

Sgt Geoffrey Ernest	#798	60th Bn	kia 19 July 1916
Pte Rolf Stanley	#3523	59th Bn	dow 15 February 1917

6 Mitchell

Pte Alfred Charles	#2746	59th Bn	kia 19 July 1916
Pte Sidney James	#2714	59th Bn	kia 19 July 1916
Tpr William	#414	8th Lt Horse	kia 7 August 1915

7 Barr

Pte David	#3474A	60th Bn	kia 19 July 1916
Pte Colin Campbell	#3479	60th Bn	dow 31 August 1916

8 Franklin

Pte Charles Wyndham	#3105	60th Bn	kia 19 July 1916
Pte Herbert Leyshon	#3104	60th Bn	kia 19 July 1916

9 Henderson

Pte Ernest Albert	#3798	60th Bn	kia 19 July 1916
Pte Leslie Donald	#2603	60th Bn	kia 19 July 1916

10 McLean

Pte Alexander Leslie	#3200	60th Bn	kia 19 July 1916
Pte Victor Henry	#3209	60th Bn	kia 19 July 1916
Pte Alexander	#3202	60th Bn	served Fromelles (father)

11 McManus

Pte Patrick	#3831	60th Bn	kia 19 July 1916
Pte Samuel	#2719	60th Bn	kia 19 July 1916

12 Miller

Pte William Henry	#2735	60th Bn	kia 19 July 1916
Pte Robert Charles	#2736	60th Bn	kia 19 July 1916

13 Perkins

Pte Colin Ernest	#2014	59th Bn	kia 19 July 1916
Pte Eric	#2421	59th Bn	kia 19 July 1916

14 Phillips

Pte Alfred Ernest	#1804	59th Bn	kia 19 July 1916
Pte Edwin John	#1743	60th Bn	kia 19 July 1916

15 Shephard

Pte George Arnold	#2776	60th Bn	kia 19 July 1916
Pte John Ernest	#2777	60th Bn	died of illness 12 July 1916
Pte Thomas Henry Phillip	#2778	60th Bn	kia 19 July 1916

Father and Son
Spooner

Pte Edward Mason	#2663	60th Bn	dow 31 July 1916 (aged 45)
Pte James Edward	#3941	60th Bn	kia 19 July 1916 (aged 25)

kia: killed in action
dow: died of wounds

Appendix IX

FROMELLES MUNICH RESEARCH REPORT

(by Peter Barton)

CONCLUSIONS AND RECOMMENDATIONS

The period under study can be said to be a part of the peak era of 'data collection' by the Bavarians. Soon they were moved to the Somme battlefield, and the information flow would alter from the closely confined intimacy of the Fromelles/Aubers sector where their knowledge of the terrain and the enemy was considerable, to one in which the 6 BRD became a small cog in a great defensive wheel. In these papers we can see a move from personal, almost 'familial', divisional records towards a more tactical and even strategic information database. In 1918, and with Germany in the grip of the allied blockade with all the shortages that entailed at the front and in the homeland, record keeping had dissolved further; along with every other commodity, the paper upon which actions and orders were recorded was at a premium.

Reports are found to be much briefer and more focused, with maps printed on the back of redundant examples from earlier in the war. In short, there is no better era in which to find the resources for the information that we seek.

The records in Canberra, Munich and London clearly show that at Fromelles by far the greatest number of allied casualties either died or sustained their injuries in no man's land whilst in attack, support, forging communication and supply, or withdrawal. At present it is still not possible to offer a number of those who died 'within the area in which recovery by the Germans was undertaken', i.e. within the German lines and in those parts of no man's land where it was possible to recover bodies relatively safely.

The curiously precise number of 399 dead recorded immediately post-battle, and von Braun's order to dig pits to accommodate 400 sets of remains are still the only actual figures we have for any individual burial site. It may, however, now be suggested that this figure relates to allied remains that were collected and moved for burial only up to 27th July, for through the evidence of allied aerial photographs it appears that five pits were closed by 29th July. No fresh indications of the *actual* number of remains that were interred at Pheasant Wood, nor where bodies after this date were buried has yet been found. Nor has any information come to light that the remains have been disturbed.

It has become clear that recovery was by far the most satisfactory method of achieving the German aims of avoiding sickness, decreasing the aroma, and collecting personal items from bodies. Apart from the saps and the order to find suitable locations in the *hintergelende*, no further evidence has yet been uncovered for sites of mass (more than four sets of human remains) graves other than the pits at Pheasant Wood. However, we now know that retrieval of bodies continued for several more weeks after the Pheasant Wood site was closed, therefore these 'late-recovery' remains are likely to be buried in other locations. If so, this has serious implications. The suggestion that a secondary site existed at Depot (Marlacque) Farm has been investigated. The suspect features are clearly marked upon German maps as short trenches organised for defensive fire. Their exposed position makes them poor candidates for grave sites. *Depotwald* (Depot Wood), being adjacent to the *forderbahn (Depot Linie)*, further to the rear and completely hidden, would be a better candidate with similar attributes to Pheasant Wood.

Because it is known that the Germans removed the personal belongings of all or most of the dead who were buried at Pheasant Wood (and elsewhere), post-excavation establishment of individual identities is unlikely to be possible. Should remains be present, the eventual appearance of a German list would therefore assist matters only a little; in this case the use of DNA testing may become necessary. The author is advised that such a route would be costly and indeed potentially unforthcoming. Such a list, however, might assist the CWGC if it is decided that a memorial be erected on the site of the graves. It must be remembered, however, that all the men concerned are already memorialized at VC Corner, Villers Bretonneux and upon monuments elsewhere.

It appears evident that no concerted effort to properly historically research this subject has been undertaken until the author was commissioned to produce this report and the earlier GUARD document. The work of Nigel Steel and Craig Tibbits suggests that further investigations must include research in Australian archives, resources which for some reason appear to have been under-investigated.

Should human remains be uncovered at Pheasant Wood during Phase Two of the project in May 2008, and given that there is likely to be some considerable need for time in the planning of Phase Three, the author's recommendations are as follows:

1. Research of 6 BRD and AOK 6 papers in Munich should be fully completed, and any subsequent leads in other German archives followed.
2. The whereabouts of post–Pheasant Wood era burials should be investigated.
3. A mechanism to gain access to Munich's photographic collection should be engineered from the highest level.
4. Comprehensive research at the Red Cross Archives in Geneva should be undertaken.
5. Appropriate research be instigated at the Australian War Memorial and in the National Archives in Canberra.
6. Subject to the results of A1 above, geophysical investigations might be undertaken in the area of the saps in 6 BRD sector II.
7. The historical account of the battle from the German viewpoint be completed in full.

ACKNOWLEDGMENTS

My thanks to Lambis Englezos, for his friendship, foresight, passion and determination. Without Lambis, the missing Diggers of Fromelles would still be languishing in their unmarked and lonely graves at Pheasant Wood.

Martial Delebarre, for his friendship, knowledge and unquenchable passion for Fromelles, and the men who fought for her liberty.

John Fielding and Ward Selby, for their devotion to the cause well beyond the call of duty.

Chris Bryett, for his friendship and his untrammelled determination and energy in pursuing the story of the fate of the missing Diggers of Fromelles.

Peter Reece for his wise counsel and his enduring advocacy on behalf of the Digger.

Tim, Liz and Alexandra Whitford for their friendship and their deep emotional connection to the men of Fromelles and their determination to keep the story alive.

Richard Wright for his knowledge and experience so freely given.

Acknowledgments

Roger Lee, for his help and devotion to the Digger.

Sarah Lindsay for her love and support and her hard work in Fromelles.

Robin Corfield and Neville Kidd for their wonderful scholarship and devotion to the Diggers.

Stephen Brooks for his diligent sleuthing into the casualties of Fromelles.

Bruce Billson and Cameron Hooke for their openness and concern for the men of Fromelles and their descendants.

Mike Kelly, George Jones and Martin Brown for their support and efforts to keep the story alive.

Mme Carole Laignel, M. Hubert Huchette, the late M. Pierre Demassiet, Mme Marie-Paule Demassiet and the people of Fromelles for their hospitality and generosity of spirit in remembering the men who fought for their freedom so long ago.

My admiration and special gratitude to Mme Marie-Paule Demassiet for her selfless donation of her land at Pheasant Wood 'pour les soldats'.

Jenny Ingham, Judy Fitzhenry, Jill Potter and the many other families of the missing for keeping the faith. May their prayers be answered.

Kevin O'Brien for his support.

The Hon. Warren Snowdon, Minister for Defence, Science and Personnel, for his candour and passionate support of the Digger.

Sandy Grant, Keiran Rogers, Pam Brewster, Fran Berry, Julie Pinkham, Jenny Macmillan, Rod Morrison, and the team at Hardie Grant for all their skill and support.

My special thanks to Carl Harrison-Ford for his wonderful work editing this manuscript.

BIBLIOGRAPHY

BOOKS

Adam-Smith, Patsy, *The Anzacs*, Nelson, Melbourne, 1978

Bean, C.E.W., *Anzac to Amiens*, Australian War Memorial, Canberra, 1948

Bean, C.E.W., *Official History of Australia in the War, 1914–1918*, Vol. III, Australian War Memorial, Canberra, 1929

Bourne, John, *The Great World War, 1914–1945*, HarperCollins, London, 2000

Carlyon, Les, *Gallipoli*, Pan Macmillan, Sydney, 2001

Carlyon, Les, *The Great War*, Pan Macmillan, Sydney, 2006

Carthew, Noel, *Voices From the Trenches: Letters to Home*, New Holland, Sydney, 2002

Cobb, Paul, *Fromelles 1916*, Tempus Publishing, London, 2007

Corfield, Robin S., *Don't Forget Me, Cobber!*, Corfield & Co., Melbourne, 2000

Corfield, Robin S., *Hold Hard, Cobbers*, Vol. I, Corfield & Co, Melbourne, 1992

Coulthard-Clark, Chris, *The Encyclopaedia of Australia's Battles*, Allen & Unwin, Sydney, 1998

Dixon, Norman, *On the Psychology of Military Incompetence*, Jonathan Cape, London, 1988

Gilbert, Martin, *The First World War*, Holt, London, 1996

Gilbert, Martin, *The Somme*, Henry Holt, New York, 2006

Grey, Jeffrey, *A Military History of Australia*, Cambridge University Press, Cambridge, 1999

Hanson, Neil, *The Unknown Soldier*, Doubleday, London, 2005

James, Lawrence, *Warrior Race: A History of the British at War*, Abacus, London, 2002

Keegan, John, *The First World War*, Pimlico, London, 2002

Kidd, Neville, *An Impression Which Will Never Fade*, self-published, Sydney, 1999

Knyvett, Captain R. Hugh, *Over There With the Australians*, Charles Scribner's Sons, New York, 1918

Kyle, Roy, *An Anzac's Story*, Penguin, Melbourne, 2003

Lindsay, Patrick, *The Spirit of the Digger*, Pan Macmillan, Sydney, 2004

MacDonald, Lyn, *Somme*, Michael Joseph, London, 1983

McMullin, Ross, *Pompey Elliott*, Scribe Publications, Melbourne, 2002

Miller, William Ian, *The Mystery of Courage*, Harvard University Press, Cambridge, Mass., 2000

Odgers, George, *100 Years of Australians at War*, Lansdowne Press, Sydney, 1999

Pedersen, Peter, *Fromelles*, Leo Cooper, South Yorkshire, 2004

Pedersen, Peter, *The Anzacs: Gallipoli to the Western Front*, Penguin Viking, Sydney, 2007

Pelvin, Richard, *ANZAC: An Illustrated History, 1914–1918*, Hardie Grant Books, Melbourne, 2004

Stevenson, David, *1914–1918: The History of the First World War*, Allen Lane, London, 2004

Travers, Tim, *The Killing Ground: The British Army, The Western Front and the Emergence of Modern War, 1900–1918*, Pen & Sword, London, 2003.

Williams, John F., *Anzacs, the Media and the Great War*, UNSW Press, Sydney, 1999

Williams, John F., *Corporal Hitler and the Great War, 1914-1918: The List Regiment*, Cass Military Studies, London, 2005

Wray, Christopher, *Sir James Whiteside McCay*, Oxford University Press, Melbourne, 2002

INDEX